# Resource Security and Governance

China's phenomenal economic growth in the past 30 years has witnessed the rise of its global natural resources companies. At the same time, the emerging of a middle class in China and their desire to improve living standards, including better dwelling conditions, better health and nutrition, has driven strong demand in mineral resources, energy and quality food. The so-called socialist market economy in China has seen this growing demand being met partially by companies with 'national significance'. In the resources sector, companies listed on stock exchanges in China as well as globally, such as in New York and London, represent these companies; at the same time, the Chinese government also controls most of these companies.

China's resources companies have expanded overseas in search of new acquisition targets whilst seeking to extend their global reach with a focus on resource-rich countries. The expansion of these companies internationally, and the unique ownership structure of these companies, has posed challenges for regulators, trading partners of these companies, investors and other interested parties seeking to understand how these companies are governed and the implications of government ownership for resource security globally.

*Resource Security and Governance: Globalisation and China's Natural Resources Companies* contains case studies of the global expansion efforts of Chinese global natural resources companies; it reviews the governance structures of these companies and analyses how these have affected the inter-relationship between these companies and their trading partners, governments, regulators in targeted countries and investors globally. In addition, this book examines how the unique structure of these companies may affect resource security globally and touches on other related matters such as climate change and air and water security in China.

**Xinting Jia** is an Environmental, Social and Governance (ESG) Specialist at CareSuper, Australia.

**Roman Tomasic** is a Professor of Law, School of Law, University of South Australia and Visiting Professor of Company Law, Durham University, UK.

# Routledge Studies in Corporate Governance

1 **Corporate Governance Around the World**
*Ahmed Naciri*

2 **Behaviour and Rationality in Corporate Governance**
*Oliver Marnet*

3 **The Value Creating Board**
Corporate Governance and Organizational Behaviour
*Edited by Morten Huse*

4 **Corporate Governance and Resource Security in China**
The Transformation of China's Global Resources Companies
*Xinting Jia and Roman Tomasic*

5 **Internal and External Aspects of Corporate Governance**
*Ahmed Naciri*

6 **Green Business, Green Values, and Sustainability**
*Edited by Christos N. Pitelis, Jack Keenan and Vicky Pryce*

7 **Credit Rating Governance**
Global Credit Gatekeepers
*Ahmed Naciri*

8 **Mergers and Acquisitions and Executive Compensation**
*Virginia Bodolica and Martin Spraggon*

9 **Governance and Governmentality for Projects**
Enablers, Practices, and Consequences
*Edited by Ralf Müller*

10 **The Making of Shareholder Welfare Society**
A Study in Corporate Governance
*Alexander Styhre*

11 **Resource Security and Governance**
Globalisation and China's Natural Resources Companies
*Edited by Xinting Jia and Roman Tomasic*

# Resource Security and Governance

## Globalisation and China's Natural Resources Companies

Edited by Xinting Jia
and Roman Tomasic

Routledge
Taylor & Francis Group

LONDON AND NEW YORK

First published 2018 by Routledge

2 Park Square, Milton Park, Abingdon, Oxfordshire OX14 4RN
52 Vanderbilt Avenue, New York, NY 10017

*Routledge is an imprint of the Taylor & Francis Group, an informa business*

First issued in paperback 2019

*Library of Congress Cataloging-in-Publication Data*
Names: Jia, Xinting, editor. | Tomasic, Roman, editor.
Title: Resource security and governance: the globalisation of China's
    natural resources companies / edited by Xinting Jia and
    Roman Tomasic.
Description: New York: Routledge, [2017] | Includes bibliographical
    references and index.
Identifiers: LCCN 2017038458
Subjects: LCSH: Mineral industries—China. | International business
    enterprises—China. | Natural resources—Management—China.
Classification: LCC HD9506.C62 R47 2017 | DDC 338.8/
    87220951—dc23
LC record available at https://lccn.loc.gov/2017038458

ISBN: 978-1-138-68055-5 (hbk)
ISBN: 978-0-367-87762-0 (pbk)

Typeset in Sabon
by Apex CoVantage, LLC

# Contents

*List of Figures, Charts, Tables, Boxes and Appendixes*    vii

*About the Contributors*    ix

*Introduction*    xiii

1   Economic Development, Resource Governance and
Globalisation: The Growth of China's Resources Companies    1
XINTING JIA AND ROMAN TOMASIC

2   Resource Security and Corporate Social Responsibility
Norms in the Governance of Globally Active Chinese
State-Owned Enterprises    27
ROMAN TOMASIC AND PING XIONG

3   Extractive Governance, Environmental Management
and Community Engagement: China Versus Global    57
XINTING JIA

4   CSR-Related Risk Management in the Overseas Investments
of Chinese Companies: Context, Dimensions
and Effectiveness    83
ZHIRONG DUAN AND PEIYUAN GUO

5   Challenging Issues in China's Mining Industry:
Human Resources and Others    105
YING ZHU

6   China's Rising Online Food Trading: Its Implications
for the Rest of the World    123
PINGHUI XIAO

7   Enforcement of Food Standards in China—Impact of the
    State- Led Stakeholder Model of Corporate Governance          143
    JENNY FU AND GEOFFREY NICOLL

8   Water Security, Governance and Sustainable Development
    Goals in China—Radical Laws, Institutions and Courts          165
    JENNIFER McKAY AND JIN ZHENG

    *Index*                                                       189

# Figures, Charts, Tables, Boxes and Appendixes

## Figures

1.1 Ownership Structure and Regulatory Environment
for Listed SOEs in China's Strategic Industries 8
4.1 Distribution of Chinese Construction Projects in Sample
(2010–2015) 93
4.2 Geographical Distribution of Overall Contracting Value
(2010–2015) 94
5.1 The Diagram of Workers as Victims Under the Process
of Social and Economic Transformation in China 119
8.1 Diagram of Water Institutions in China 172

## Charts

5.1 Food Safety Chain 127
5.2 Categorizing Chinese Online Food Trading 127

## Tables

1.1 Levels of Control and Foreign Listings of Selected Chinese
'National Champions' 5
2.1 Key Policies and Regulations Regarding Sustainable
Overseas Development by Chinese Companies 46
4.1 Selected Indicators for Assessment of (Host) Country 90
4.2 Factor Structure of Risk Indicators 91
4.3 Reliability Test of Composite Factors 92
4.4 Results of Logistic Regression on Responsibility Risk
Incidence 95

# Boxes

8.1 The Sustainable Development Goals Are 17 Steps to a
Better World (UN 2015) 166
8.2 Implementation Plan for Comprehensive Water Law
System 2017 By Ministry Water Resources 173

# Appendixes

Chinese SOEs Under the Direct Control of SASAC 15
Country Responsibility Risk Index 2017 for
Chinese Overseas Investment 100

# Contributors

**Zhirong Duan** is assistant professor at the School of Economics and Management, Tsinghua University, China. She obtained a PhD in management from Tsinghua University and a PhD in marketing from the University of New South Wales. Her major research areas include marketing systems, corporate social responsibility, international business and entrepreneurship.

**Jenny Fu** is an assistant professor in the School of Law and Justice at the University of Canberra, Australia. She holds a PhD in law from the Australian National University, a master of legal studies and an LLB from the University of Canberra, as well as a bachelor's from the Beijing Foreign Studies University. She teaches corporations law and conducts research in the area of corporate governance, particularly corporate governance in China. Prior to her academic career in Australia, Jenny worked as a legal researcher in the Legislative Affairs Commission of the National People's Congress of China.

**Peiyuan Guo** holds a PhD in management from Tsinghua University, China, and is the general manager of SynTao. Peiyuan focuses his research on corporate social responsibility (CSR) and responsible investment, and provides advice to companies, governments and non-governmental organisations. He also teaches at Tsinghua University and Beijing Normal University.

**Xinting Jia** has worked closely with institutional investors across the investment supply chain to integrate environmental, social and corporate governance (ESG) into the investment process. Her research interests include governance of listed companies, social factors such as community engagement and supply chain issues, as well as environmental issues such as climate change and how these factors may affect long-term performance of investments. Xinting co-authored the book *Corporate Governance and Resource Security in China: The Transformation of China's Global Resources Companies* (Routledge 2010, 2015) with Professor Roman Tomasic. Xinting was former Head of Asia, Responsible Investment at

Mercer and is currently managing ESG and responsible investing at Care-Super—a major superannuation fund in Australia. Xinting holds a PhD in corporate governance from Victoria University and an MBA in finance from Melbourne Business School.

**Jennifer McKay** is a Professor of Law at the University of South Australia. She holds a bachelor of arts hons and PhD from the University of Melbourne, a bachelor of laws from the University of Adelaide and a graduate diploma in human rights law and humanitarian law from American University, Washington DC, USA. She has published on sustainable development law, corporate governance, CSR and conducted empirical research on water law and governance in Australia, India, the United States and the Middle East. She recently co-edited a book titled *Natural Resources and Environmental Justice—Australian Perspectives*. She has made law reform suggestions and has written over 159 publications. She held a Senior Fulbright scholarship to Boalt School of Law at the University of California in 2009.

**Geoffrey Nicoll** (BA, LL.B (ANU), M Corp Law Hons (UC), PhD (Syd)) is a senior lecturer at the University of Canberra, Australia, researching corporate law and governance. Within the China-Australia investment relationship, he maintains research interests in the governance and regulation of China's state-owned enterprises, the evolution of the capital market in China and policy issues associated with China's investments in Australia.

**Roman Tomasic** obtained his LLB and masters degree from the University of Sydney, Australia, a PhD from the University of New South Wales and an SJD from the University of Wisconsin-Madison, USA. Since 2012, he has been professor of law in the School of Law at the University of South Australia, having previously served as chair in company law at Durham Law School in the United Kingdom. He is an emeritus professor at the University of Canberra and former chair of the Australasian Law Teachers Association, and member and fellow of the Australian Academy of Law. He has been internationally active as a legal scholar and commercial law researcher and has worked in Australia, Hong Kong, the United Kingdom and the United States. Dr Tomasic has research interests in China and in comparative corporate governance as well as in the use of empirical methods in legal research. He has published widely and recently edited *Handbook of Corporate Law* (Routledge, 2016) and *Research Handbook on Transnational Corporations* (with A. de Jonge; Edward Elgar, 2017).

**Pinghui Xiao** is a research fellow at the Center for Coordination and Innovation of Food Safety Governance at Renmin University, China. Pinghui is also a lecturer at the School of Law, Guangzhou University, China. After obtaining a PhD in law from the University of South Australia in 2013, he worked in the China Food and Drug Administration to conduct post-doctoral research on food safety regulation and has since been involved in proposing and drafting rules relating to online food trading.

**Ping Xiong** is senior lecturer at the School of Law of the University of South Australia. She holds a PhD in law from Victoria University Wellington, an LLM from the China University of Politics and Law in Beijing and received a BA from the Beijing Foreign Studies University. Dr Xiong maintains a research interest in comparative law analysis concerning the Chinese legal system and the application of laws in China in relation to the requirements of international law. Dr Xiong also researches and publishes in the area of international trade law with a focus on international intellectual property protection. She teaches various subjects including Chinese commercial law and corporations law.

**Jin Zheng** has been a lecturer in the School of Law at the South China Normal University in Guangzhou, China, since 2003. She obtained her PhD from Wuhan University where she studied in the School of Law and the Research Institute of International Law (2006–2011). She completed her LLM degree in international business law from the Vrije Universiteit Amsterdam Faculty of Law in the Netherlands (2001–2002). She is a member of the China Law Society and holds a certificate in Chinese lawyer's qualification and is a committee member of China's EU Law Association.

**Ying Zhu** is the director of the Australian Centre for Asian Business at the University of South Australia and is a distinguished scholar contributing to the vital nexus between the West and the East, including China, Vietnam, Japan, Taiwan and other Asian countries and regions. He has developed several large projects that shaped the research covering a wide range of topics such as employment relations, human resource management, labour law and regulations, cross-cultural management and business development. Professor Zhu's excellence in research and capability in the successful management of research projects can be demonstrated by his volume of publications related to China, with the most recent ones being *Law and Fair Work in China* (Cooney S, Biddulph S and Zhu Y, New York: Routledge, 2013), *Workforce Development and Skill Formation in Asia* (eds. Benson J, Gospel H and Zhu Y, London and New York: Routledge, 2012), *The Dynamics of Asian Labour Markets: Balancing Control and Flexibility* (eds. Benson J and Zhu Y, London and New York: Routledge, 2011), *Everyday Impact of Economic Reform in China: Management Change, Enterprise Performance and Daily Life* (Zhu Y, Webber M and Benson J, London and New York: Routledge, 2010) and *Trade Unions in Asia: An Economic and Sociological Analysis* (eds. Benson J and Zhu Y, London and New York: Routledge, 2008).

# Introduction

China's massive economic growth over the past 30 years has seen the rise of its resources companies. At the same time, the emergence of a middle class in China and the desire of its members to improve their living standards, including better dwelling conditions and better health and nutrition, has driven a strong demand for mineral resources, energy, clean air and water and quality food. China's so-called socialist market economy has seen this growing demand being met partially by companies with 'national significance' (its 'national champions'). In the resources sector, these companies are represented by companies listed on China's stock exchanges, as well as globally, such as in New York and London; at the same time, most of these companies are also controlled by the Chinese government.

In order to meet its growing domestic demand and to carry out the Chinese government's five-year strategic plans, China's resources companies have expanded overseas in search of new acquisition targets whilst seeking to extend their global reach with a focus on resource rich countries. The expansion of these companies internationally, and their unique ownership structures, has posed challenges for regulators, trading partners of these companies, investors and other interested parties seeking to understand how these companies are governed and the implications that government ownership has for resource security globally.

This book builds upon the themes in our earlier book, *Corporate Governance and Resource Security In China: The Transformation of China's Global Resources Companies* (Jia and Tomasic, 2010), and extends the debate by looking beyond the mineral resources sector to include other contemporary issues, such as corporate social responsibility (CSR) of resources companies, human resources management and food safety and water security.

In contrast to our first book, this volume has brought together other researchers and specialists to allow us to discuss a broader range of issues in this field. Given its wider coverage, this book will be of interest to academics, senior managers of companies, investment analysts, legal professionals and policy makers interested in China's global impact.

Specifically, Chapter 1 explores the governance of China's global resources companies, their expansion abroad and the efforts they have made to facilitate resource security. The globalisation and growth of large Chinese-listed state-owned enterprises (SOEs), with their distinctive governance structures, has highlighted the importance of understanding these companies when dealing with them. In the first chapter, Jia and Tomasic provide an overview of key features of China's large SOEs with a view to providing a basis for further analysis.

In Chapter 2, Tomasic and Xiong focus on Chinese outward-bound investment and the roles SOEs played in the investment process. Chinese SOEs have been the vehicles for the Chinese government to obtain resources from the international market, to participate in international market competition, and to expand Chinese national soft power. Investing abroad allows Chinese SOEs to gain controlling interests in foreign companies, which opens doors for other Chinese enterprises to sell goods and services abroad; this is a pattern that is well established from prior eras of foreign investment in countries such as Australia. However, these SOEs are also facing global challenges, especially those SOEs investing in the natural resources sector abroad. In order to meet the challenges of modern corporate governance, Chinese SOEs have sought to enhance their corporate governance practices whilst the Chinese government has also sought to reform its inefficient SOEs. In response to the challenges facing modern globally active companies, China has adopted CSR ideas to better regulate its enterprises. This has often been supported by legal mechanisms, such as through legislation. With increasing outward-bound investment by Chinese SOEs, many SOEs have also developed their own CSR codes. Chapter 2 explores some CSR norms developed by Chinese government agencies and China's SOEs and examines how Chinese SOEs have implemented CSR norms to protect non-economic interests in natural resources rich countries.

In Chapter 3, Jia looks at Chinese resources companies and community governance. Resources companies often face more challenges than companies operating in other sectors, especially when seeking to balance economic interest with the environmental and social risks embedded in their operations. This chapter compares the governance and CSR practices of China's resources companies with their global peers, focusing on environmental and community governance. Specifically, this chapter looks closely at the CSR practices of PetroChina and Minerals and Metals Group (MMG) and compares these with the practices of global resources companies such as BHP and Anglo American.

In Chapter 4, Duan and Guo further explore CSR and Chinese companies that are investing abroad. In recent years, CSR in the host country has become an unavoidable topic when discussing outbound direct investments by Chinese companies. In particular, risk in association with CSR considerations is seen to be increasing. Identifying those factors and understanding their dynamics would help companies prepare for unforeseen events and enhance decision making through risk-management tools. A corresponding evaluation system is thus developed incorporating available indicators and indices from not only traditional risk areas but also environmental, social and governance (ESG) related areas. Based on basic research and a large index pool constructed by the collaborative team from Tsinghua University School of Economics and Management and SynTao Ltd., the Country Responsibility Risk Index for Chinese Overseas Investment shows the latent structure of the index space where ESG dimensions stand out. Preliminary empirical evidence from this wider study has supported the effectiveness of the index. The index aims to keep track of ESG dimensions as well as the general operating environment of countries that attract Chinese investment. It shows the trend in CSR considerations in those countries and provides a benchmark for risk analysis.

In Chapter 5, Ying Zhu focuses on the Chinese mining industry and human resources management issues. China has one of the world's largest mining industries, producing coal, gold and most rare earth minerals. In addition, China is also one of the world's leading consumers of most mining products. However, in recent years, due to the slowdown in overall national economic development, as well as concern over serious air pollution in China, the central government has targeted the mining sector in general, and coal mines in particular, to reduce their capacity by closing certain poorly performing mines. So far, the key focus of the mining industry in China has been upon its production capacity, but key challenges regarding human resource issues in the mining sector, including employment entitlements and working conditions, migrant workers and their treatment, safety issues and injury and other related tensions, need to be discussed further. Therefore, this chapter seeks to address these issues by using recent statistical data and the author's previous fieldwork research in China.

The key themes for Chapters 6 and 7 are on food safety and security. In Chapter 6, Pinghui Xiao examines food safety and online trading in China. China has made strides since entering the Internet age; since then, a variety of modes of online food trading have become available; their business models have varied due to innovation arising from the Internet. China has been a first mover in introducing provisions to regulate online food trading through revisions to its Food Safety Law. The China Food and Drug Administration (CFDA), China's principal food regulatory agency, has created a number of measures on the basis of the aforementioned provisions. China's online food trading continues to evolve internationally facilitating cross-border food e-commerce, providing huge opportunities to other economies. However, this also poses challenges for existing international food trade regimes. Foods entering China's domestic market through cross-border e-commerce make compliance with China's food safety standards and labelling rules an issue, which may in turn cause a capacity deficit in government regulation.

However, government regulation has been compensated by co-regulatory mechanisms. Online third-party platforms are mandated to regulate those food operators selling foods via their platforms. Any violations of law by the food business operators may lead to the platform operators also being punished. This issue is also quite controversial even in western countries. In the United States and European Union (EU), for instance, some online platforms that have been part of the sharing economy, like Uber, Airbnb and EatWith, merely consider themselves as matchmakers and little more than this. As a result, these platforms often believe that they should be immune from punishment for any wrongdoings by businesses operating on their platforms. Nevertheless, since online platforms tend to be heavily involved in food businesses, public and private co-regulation gains increasing recognition. We find that growing food small and medium enterprises (SME) operate food businesses within these platforms so that the platforms' administrators in turn have the momentum to operate as co-regulators of food safety.

In Chapter 7, Fu and Nicoll explore an important issue of food safety in baby milk. This chapter uses the 2008 tainted milk scandal as a case study and examines the impact of this governance model on the enforcement of food safety standards in China. It argues that while the utility of this model in facilitating economic development and maintaining social stability is evident, it is likely to contribute to the lack of substantive improvement in the enforcement of food standards. Thus, examining the power and autocracy of the Chinese state, evident in its utilitarian approach to resolving competing objectives in the milk scandal, suggests some important limitations in the state-led stakeholder model of corporate governance and points to flaws in the wider regulatory framework in China. Continuing to address these limitations will be most important in maintaining China's credibility internationally as a global food supplier.

In Chapter 8, McKay and Zheng focus on water safety and security in China. As the *Peoples' Daily* proclaimed in 2002, in China, there were three freshwater issues that were matters of concern: inadequacy of total volume, unreasonable distribution of water and serious water pollution. These problems all affect current water security, especially in the context of the legacy issues of pollution. China is dealing with these issues some 50 years after some western economies began to regulate pollution and hence there may be lessons that can be transferred to China. Each of these three issues requires different legal and institutional approaches. Balancing economic development and protecting valuable water resources is of vital importance to the long-term health and well-being of the general public in China. To meet these demands, China has radically changed its laws, institutions and courts and devised some unique institutions and financing measures to approach all three issues. This has occurred in the last 20 years. For example, in 2016, China adopted the United Nation's Sustainable Development Goals, and this bold new initiative, with 17 goals, will force further changes on China; in this way, China has begun to adopt a more modern paradigm of water regulation. This chapter examines issues caused by water scarcity and safety and explores three new policy and law measures to tackle these issues.

In summary, the state control of major resources companies in China has given rise to the 'unique' characteristics of Chinese companies; this is not only reflected in their governance structure but also has affected the way business is carried out by these companies, including their methods of dealing with communities and fulfilling their corporate (social) responsibilities. The growing global reach of these companies has also added to the complexity of policy design and regulation in China's main trading partners. By exploring a broader range of issues, such as corporate governance, CSR, resource security, human resources management, food and water safety, this book seeks to build a better picture of the governance of China's resources companies and supports businesses, regulators and scholars to further advance their understanding of these companies and to enhance the level of sophistication in dealing with these companies in the future.

Xinting Jia and Roman Tomasic

# 1 Economic Development, Resource Governance and Globalisation

## The Growth of China's Resources Companies

*Xinting Jia and Roman Tomasic*

## 1. Introduction

China has experienced massive economic growth since the introduction of the 'open door' policy in 1978. Over the past 50 years, China's gross domestic product (GDP) has grown on average at around 10% per annum (World Bank, 2016) and by the end of 2014, China for the first time overtook the USA as the world largest economy (International Monetary Fund, 2014, Foxnews.com, 2014).

These impressive economic growth figures demonstrate that China's economic development has followed a distinctive growth path that calls for closer examination. In the past decade, not only has China grown in terms of its own economic power, it has also expanded its reach overseas through the acquisition of resource generating assets via companies of 'national significance' or its so-called national champions that are controlled by the government through the State-Owned Assets Supervision and Administration Commission of the State Council (SASAC). The global expansion strategy of Chinese companies has been based on the belief that it would help China to secure valuable resources to not only support its further growth but also to provide 'security' to the ever growing needs of its large population for natural mineral resources, energy and food.

China's participation in the global mergers and acquisitions market has brought fresh capital and competition which has contributed to the rise in value of desirable assets; at the same time, the nature of those acquisitions (in most cases with the Chinese government as their controlling shareholder) has added more complexity beyond pure market practices. Friction may sometimes arise from cultural misunderstandings in host countries that have received Chinese investment (Tomasic and Xiong, 2016); also, the distinctive governance structure of Chinese companies poses challenges to all market participants including target companies and regulators in host countries.

To help gain a better understanding of these unique government-controlled listed companies, this chapter will review the economic and enterprise growth of state-owned enterprises (SOEs) and 'national champions' in China, followed by a discussion of the emergence of China's global resources companies and their implications for corporate governance and resource security globally. This chapter thus provides an overview of the historical development of China's large companies and sets the scene for detailed discussions of the implications for corporate governance and natural resource security, food safety and security, water safety and related issues covered in later chapters.

## 2. Economic Development in China and the Emergence of China's Global Natural Resources Companies

For political reasons, China has taken its own distinctive economic development pathway. Since the adoption of the 'open door' policy in 1978, China has gradually transformed from being a 'socialist' economy into a 'socialist market' economy or into a system of 'state capitalism' (Lin and Milhaupt, 2013); others have described it as a system of 'authoritarian capitalism' (Witt and Redding, 2014).

As the backbone of the economy, SOEs have also been transformed gradually since the establishment of the Shanghai and Shenzhen Stock Exchanges in 1990 and 1991 respectively. Despite being listed on the two domestic stock exchanges and with some companies also listed in Hong Kong and on other overseas stock exchanges, a majority of China's large SOEs have not gone through complete privatisation. In fact, when these companies were first listed, they were only partially listed on stock exchanges, as the government only wanted to 'sell' part of these companies to the market in order to raise capital and bring more competition to revitalise large SOEs.

The partial privatisation of SOEs aligns with China's 'gradualist' approach to its social and enterprise reforms, as China has adopted a 'trial and error' method rather than the 'big bang' approach that was adopted by most former socialist countries in Eastern Europe in the 1990s (Liu and Garino, 2001). This also aligns with China's domestic strategy of 'grasping the big, letting go of the small' (*zhua da fang xiao*) and of nurturing companies in strategic industries without abandoning ownership control. This strategy seems to have facilitated the growth of large SOEs. As is evident from the sheer size of China's three largest SOEs—Sinopec, China National Petroleum and State Grid—between 2011 and 2013, these three largest SOEs had earned more revenue than the combined revenues of the largest 500 private domestic firms in China (Lee, 2013).

Overall, China's economic and enterprise reform has gone through what can be seen as four phases: Phase One (from 1978 to 1984), Phase Two (from 1984 to 1993), Phase Three (from 1993 to 2005) and Phase Four (from 2005 to the present) (Hemphill and White III, 2013: 195). The transformation of large SOEs has always been an important part of the Chinese government's reform agenda, ranging from 'small-scale privatisation' (i.e. partial listings on the Shanghai and Shenzhen Stock Exchanges) during Phase Two in the 1990s, to the promotion of 'national champions' in strategic industries during Phases Three and Four (Hemphill and White III, 2013: 195). In November 2000, for the first time, the 'go global' strategy was explicitly put forward at the Fifth Plenary Session of the Fifteenth National Congress of the Communist Party of China (CPC) (Wang and Lu, 2016: 27).

Since 2005, China began to promote its 'national champions' and leverage the ownership structure (as listed government controlled companies) of its 'national champions' to pursue its 'go global' strategy (Hemphill and White III, 2013). In essence, China has expanded overseas through the growth of its 'national champions', in the form of large listed SOEs, with the aim of raising the international competitiveness of its strategic industries (Lee, 2013) and to secure natural resources globally. This has subsequently seen a wave of overseas acquisitions by large Chinese companies, often raising national security concerns for the target country. At the same time, China has undertaken another measure to further reform its stock market listed SOEs; this has seen the conversion of shares from non-tradable into tradable shares.

When large SOEs were first listed in the early 1990s, use was made of the so-called split-share structure, whereby A-shares[1] listed in the domestic market were separated into tradable shares (held by the general public) and non-tradable shares (held by the government) with both types of shares having the same cash flow and voting rights (Firth et al., 2010: 685–686). The split-share structure has posed enormous corporate governance challenges to regulators, such as ensuring equal treatment of large and small shareholders (Jia and Tomasic, 2010) and aligning executive remuneration with company performance (Hou et al., 2012); as a result, the Chinese government has been determined to undertake further reforms so as to eliminate structural flaws in China's stock market (Jia and Tomasic, 2010: 7).

On 31 January 2004, China's State Council issued an official document entitled 'State Council's opinions on further reforming and maintaining the stability of the stock market', expressing the concern that 'the split ownership structure problem' needed to be dealt with properly (Jia and Tomasic, 2010). After trialling this reform in four companies, the China Securities Regulatory Commission (CSRC) issued an official policy document entitled "Guidance on Split-Share Structure Reform in Listed Companies" and clearly stipulated that the reform plan (i.e. converting non-tradable shares into tradable shares) for each listed company had to be approved by at least two-thirds of voting shareholders (Jia and Tomasic, 2010: 7). Despite the controversy surrounding this reform regarding corporate governance issues, such as the dilution of share ownership for existing tradable shareholders and the protection of minority shareholders' rights, the government nevertheless managed to push through its reforms and reduce its major shareholding in some listed companies in subsequent years.

This has been perceived as the government wanting to attract capital and to improve the efficiency of these large government controlled companies

(Liao et al., 2014) rather than to let go of its controlling rights. After the introduction of the split-share structure reforms, the government still owned more than 50% of shares in large SOEs or 'national champions' through CSOEs (centrally controlled state-owned enterprises) which are under the direct control of the State-Owned Assets Supervision and Administration Commission (SASAC). Table 1.1 shows the controlling shares held by the government through CSOEs in some selected 'national champions' that have been active in the global corporate acquisition market. A list of all CSOEs and their ranking in the Fortune Global 500 companies in 2015 can be found in the appendix.

As shown in Table 1.1, apart from the fact that government ownership in Chalco was 41.33%, in most cases, the Chinese government, as the 'dominant' shareholder, owned more than 50% of shares in the listed entity through a controlling state-owned enterprise.

Among these transactions, the most notable was ChemChina's US$43 billion takeover bid for Syngenta, one of the largest acquisitions by a Chinese company and by a Chinese government controlled company (Burger, 2016). The ChemChina/Syngenta takeover raised concerns regarding 'Chinese Nationalism' (Ellyatt and Chatterley, 2016), and the potential for conflict that could arise from the interaction of different governance, cultural and management styles and the effect of different policy preferences in the future. On the one hand, the acquisition would help China improve its long-term food security (Burger, 2016); on the other hand, some environmental activists have also expressed the concern that the acquisition may lead to the proliferation of 'genetically modified' seeds and pesticides for global agricultural development, which could have adverse environmental consequences (Greenpeace, 2016). Nevertheless, the deal was eventually approved by Syngenta's shareholders in May 2017 (Spegele and Wu, 2017).

Overall, the expansion of government controlled companies overseas has often been seen as raising concerns in other countries on national security grounds and as having created challenges for global politics (Umar, 2016).

## 3. Governance of Large Listed Chinese SOEs/National Champions

*The role of the CPC and the Chinese government in SOE management:* To help us gauge the root causes of national security concerns, we need to better understand how Chinese companies are governed as this can differ from the governance of their global counterparts. It is worthwhile to first gain an understanding of the relationship between the CPC and the Chinese government, and how China's political regime spills over into the management of major listed SOEs. The controlling role of the CPC blurs the line between the party and the government in China. Party meetings and decisions become central not only to the political regime but also

Table 1.1 Levels of Control and Foreign Listings of Selected Chinese 'National Champions'

| CSOEs | Name of listed arm | Percentage of shares controlled by the government through the parent company | Place of listing |
|---|---|---|---|
| China National Petroleum Corporation (CNPC) | PetroChina | 86.51% as at 30 June 2015 | New York Stock Exchange (2000), Hong Kong Stock Exchange (2000) and Shanghai Stock Exchange (2007) |
| China Petrochemical Corporation | Sinopec Limited | 70.86% as at 31 December 2015 | Hong Kong Stock Exchange (2000), New York Stock Exchange (2000), London Stock Exchange (2000) and Shanghai Stock Exchange (2001) |
| China National Offshore Oil Corporation | China National Offshore Oil Corporation (CNOOC) Limited | 64.44% | New York Stock Exchange (2001), Hong Kong Stock Exchange (2001) and Toronto Stock Exchange (2013) |
| Shenhua Group Corporation Limited | China Shenhua Energy Company Limited | 73.06% | Hong Kong Stock Exchange (2005) and Shanghai Stock Exchange (2007) |
| ChemChina | Controlling shareholder for nine listed companies including Syngenta | 100% of Syngenta if successful with the implementation of the takeover bid | Syngenta is listed in SIX Swiss Exchange (2000) and New York Stock Exchange (2009) |
| Aluminium Corporation of China (Chinalco) | Aluminium Corporation of China Limited (Chalco) | 41.33% at 31 December 2014 | New York Stock Exchange (2001), Hong Kong Stock Exchange (2001) and Shanghai Stock Exchange (2007) |
| China Minmetals Corporation | Controlling shareholder for seven listed companies including MMG | 74% as at 31 December 2014 | MMG is listed in Hong Kong Stock Exchange (2010) and Australian Securities Exchange (2015) |

Source: Data sourced from various websites, company websites and annual reports, accessed 2 May 2016; complied by Xinting Jia.

to the economic management of the country, including the management of large SOEs.

Central to China's governance are the Plenary Sessions of the CPC Central Committee. The history of CPC meetings can be traced back to the establishment of the CPC in 1921. Since the founding of the People's Republic of China in 1949, the Plenary Sessions of the CPC Central Committee have become one of the most important indicators in determining the direction that China will take in its further development. For example, the Third Plenary Session of the Eleventh CPC Central Committee in 1978 was a major landmark as it saw China announce that it would adopt the 'open door' policy under the leadership of Deng Xiaoping (people.com.cn, 2007).

In parallel, the Chinese government has developed five-year plans since 1953, following the model of the former Soviet Union (Central Intelligence Agency, 1959: 19). The decisions made at the Plenary Sessions of the CPC Central Committee have subsequently been reflected in China's five-year plans, demonstrating the tight control of the government and of government planning by the CPC. For example, 'the Five Ideas for Development' issued at the Fifth Plenary Session of the Eighteenth CPC Central Committee is considered as expressing guiding principles for the development of the thirteenth five-year plan (Guo, 2016). The plan would then be subsequently implemented via regional and local level meetings, as described by Brandt and Rawski (2008: 16):

> Functionaries at all levels must study and discuss the speeches and writing of top leaders, which lay out the desired course of public policy and explain what lower levels of officialdom should do and should not do. These guidelines become encapsulated in catchy slogans that gain wide currency in official circles and also among the Chinese public. These slogans, and the policy guidelines that inform them, direct the flow of policy implementation at all levels.

Given the fact that listed SOEs are not independent from the party and the government, it is appropriate to note that the question of how to better manage SOEs and carry out reforms also dominates government plans and policies. For example, in the 'Decision of the CPC Central Committee on Some Important Questions Concerning Comprehensively Deepening Reform' (*Zhonggong zhongyang guanyu quanmian shenhua gaige ruogan zhongda wenti de jueding*) (hereinafter 'the Decision') issued after the Third Plenum of the Eighteenth CPC Central Committee, the program of SOE reform was articulated as follows (China.org.cn, 2014: 6) which stated,

> We will improve the state-owned assets management system, . . . support qualified SOEs to reorganize themselves into state-owned capital investment companies. State-owned capital investment operations must serve the strategic goals of the state, invest more in key industries and

areas that are vital to national security and are the lifeblood of the economy, focusing on offering public services, developing important and forward-looking strategic industries, protecting the ecological environment, supporting scientific and technological progress, and guaranteeing national security.

It clearly shows that state/government control is very important in key industries and that national security is also of major concern for the Chinese government. In addition, 'the Decision' continued to set out the roles of SOEs in natural monopoly industries (China.org.cn, 2014: 6–7) as follows:

> Owned by the whole people, SOEs are an important force for advancing national modernization and protecting the common interests of the people. Although SOEs generally have assimilated themselves into the market economy, they must adapt to new trends of marketization and internationalization, and further deepen their reform by aiming the focus at regular decision making over operation, maintaining and appreciating the value of state assets, participation in competition on an equal footing, raising production efficiency, strengthening enterprise vitality, and bearing due social obligations.
>
> . . . In natural monopoly industries in which state-owned capital continues to be the controlling shareholder, we will carry out reform focusing on separation of government administration from enterprise management, separation of government administration from state assets management, franchise operation, and government oversight, separate networks from operations and decontrol competitive businesses based on the characteristics of different industries, and make public resource allocation more market-oriented. We will continue to break up all forms of administrative monopoly.

While the Chinese government is keen to push SOE reform and break the monopolies of SOEs in certain sectors, the focus will only be on SOEs with an 'administrative monopoly'. SOEs in natural monopoly industries such as oil, electricity and water are of vital importance to China's national interest and security, and are therefore less likely to be subject to the full opening up of the market and less state support (Brødsgaard and Grünberg, 2014). This also suggests that China is continuing with its 'gradualist' approach towards economic and enterprise reform so that any new plans to transform large listed SOEs will be incremental.

'The Decision' then went on to discuss corporate governance in SOEs (China.org.cn, 2014: 7) in the following terms:

> We will improve the corporate governance structure with coordinated operations and effective checks and balances. We will establish a system of professional managers, and give better play to the role of

entrepreneurs. We will deepen reform of systems concerning the promotion and demotion of management personnel, hiring and firing of employees, and salary increase and decrease. We will establish a long-term incentive and restraint mechanism, and strengthen investigations into the accountability of SOE operations and investment. We will explore ways to publicize important information, including SOE financial budgets. SOEs should appropriately increase the proportion of market-oriented recruitment, and rationally determine and strictly regulate the salary standards, position benefits, position-related expenses and business spending of SOE management personnel.

Despite the emphasis placed upon good corporate governance in the areas of proper remuneration structure and better disclosure, the way corporate governance is promulgated in 'the Decision' shows that it is the party and the government, rather than the market, are the key actors when governing large listed SOEs.

*Ownership control and the regulatory environment for listed SOEs/ national champions in strategic industries:* To illustrate the relationship between the government and large listed SOEs, it is worthwhile looking at ownership structures and regulatory forces surrounding China's SOEs. Figure 1.1 depicts the environment in which large listed SOEs operate.

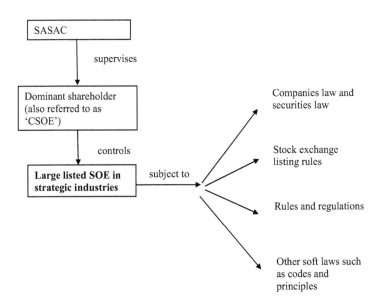

*Figure 1.1* Ownership Structure and Regulatory Environment for Listed SOEs in China's Strategic Industries

Source: Adapted from (Jia and Tomasic, 2010: 17)

As shown in Figure 1.1 and in Table 1.1, large listed SOEs usually have a dominant shareholder which is under the direct supervision of SASAC, an agency of the State Council. The dominant shareholder, often referred to as CSOE, is an enterprise wholly owned and centrally controlled by the Chinese government. This unique structure is the product of China's SOE reforms which can be divided into two stages: pre-2003 and post-2003 (Li and Brødsgaard, 2013). After 2003, the government decided to concentrate the management of CSOEs through a central agency—namely, SASAC (Li and Brødsgaard, 2013). When SASAC was established in 1999, its main role was to manage high profile initial public offerings (IPOs) for SOEs located in strategic industries (Wang et al., 2011).

In 2006, SASAC announced that, for national security reasons, seven industries should be under 'absolute (state) control' (Zhao, 2006); these are armaments, power generation and distribution, oil and petrochemicals, telecommunications, coal, aviation and shipping industries. In addition, other key industries such as machinery, automobiles, information technology, construction, iron and steel and non-ferrous metals were also to be kept under the tight control of the central government (Zhao, 2006). In 2015, 106 CSOEs were under the direct control of SASAC (SASAC, 2015); these are listed in the appendix.

As depicted in Figure 1.1, apart from the direct control by the central government via CSOEs, large listed SOEs also need to comply with PRC laws such as the Company Law, the Securities Law and other rules and regulations, as well as other soft laws or principles such as the Code of Corporate Governance for Listed Companies in China issued by the CSRC in 2002. Most large SOEs are also listed on overseas stock exchanges, which means that they need to comply with regulations and rules of those markets.

*Corporate governance model in China:* Apart from the dominant share ownership structure, China's corporate governance also has other distinctive features which include a two-tier board, the existence of corporate groups, as well as a large number of minority shareholders. It is often believed that China's corporate governance model is a hybrid which combines the 'insider-based' model and the 'outsider-based' model (Tam, 1999).

The 'insider-based' model refers to the corporate governance models found in Germany and Japan, under which 'insiders' are closely involved in corporate governance. In Germany's case, corporate governance is characterised with a 'two-tier' board (a supervisory board and a management board) reflecting Germany's 'co-determination' system, while a certain proportion of the supervisory board's members must be elected by employees, depending upon the size of the company (Wei, 2003). In Japan's case, the corporate governance system has been represented by a 'main-bank' system. The 'main' bank, the largest lender and perhaps the largest shareholder (Wei, 2003), supplies representatives to the board as well as providing finance to other companies that belong to the same corporate group or *keiretsu* (Nottage et al., 2008).

The so-called 'outsider-based' model is often illustrated by corporate governance in the United States and United Kingdom where there is a fluid and dispersed share ownership. The existence of a large number of widely dispersed small shareholders helped to make company management the 'de-facto' controllers of companies, giving rise to 'agency' problems (Berle and Means, 1932). In practice, it is also very difficult for small shareholders to engage with company management and collaborate with each other, therefore, most would choose to 'vote with their feet' rather than engaging with company management if the company was not responsive to shareholder concerns. Historically, institutional shareholders have also been very passive in engaging with their investee companies for various reasons. This has continued to be a problem, leading some to suggest that institutional shareholders need to be more engaged in the corporate governance process. After the global financial crisis, the United Kingdom has introduced a new Stewardship Code which sought to encourage UK institutional shareholders to take a more active role in corporate governance. However, this code has had a mixed reception and concerns about short termism in the management of listed companies continue to be aired (Kay, 2012).

China's experimental and gradualist approach to its enterprise reforms has resulted in a 'hybrid' corporate governance model. Listed companies not only have a 'two-tier' board, with a supervisory tier (following the German model) and a board of directors, it also has a dispersed body of shareholders (except in the case of the controlling shares held by the government), which is part of the characteristics of the corporate governance model in the United States and the United Kingdom. In China's case, the main role of the supervisory board is to monitor managers, review reports and oversee firm assets (Yang et al., 2011). In addition, the supervisory board's role should be independent from the board of directors (Yang et al., 2011). The supervisory board needs to have at least three directors, with one elected by employees and one by shareholders (Yang et al., 2011: 19). In reality, since the supervisory board and the board of directors are both appointed by the controlling shareholder—the government—it is difficult to see how it can be independent from the influence and control of government.

The complicated ownership and corporate governance structure found in China also gives rise to 'multiagency' problems. In China's case, these 'agents' include the supervisory board, the board of directors, senior management team, 'mother' companies (CSOEs) and SASAC, the government department that oversees CSOEs. Apart from the 'complex chains of agents' (OECD, 2015: 12) or the 'network hierarchy' (Lin and Milhaupt, 2013), listed SOEs also have a large number of minority shareholders. However, the protection of minority shareholders' rights in listed companies is problematic, with the prevalence of related party transactions which involve the transfer of corporate assets to related entities to the disadvantage of minority shareholders.

In addition, with recent economic growth in China and a rising demand for shares in Chinese listed companies, Chinese large listed SOEs have become an attractive investment target for major institutional investors globally, such as from superannuation funds, fund managers and sovereign wealth funds, who are seeking new investment opportunities and diversification. The involvement of overseas' institutional investors has also gradually changed corporate governance practices in these companies, albeit involuntarily in some situations. For example, in Hong Kong, institutional shareholders voted down China Merchant Bank's plan of granting discounted shares to its chairman and non-executive directors, and in another case, Hong Kong investors voted against CITIC Securities' issuance of US$1.5 billion worth of shares to China's own sovereign wealth fund: the National Social Security Fund (NSSF) (Larsen, 2015). In contrast, despite NSSF's substantial shareholding in some listed companies in China, it cannot vote its shares or engage with its investee companies as required by the government due to its 'conflict of interest'.[2] The complicated governance structure in China poses enormous challenges for China's counterparts when dealing with Chinese listed SOEs on a commercial basis.

## 4. The Expansion of Large Chinese SOEs Overseas and Resource Security Issues

The close connection between the Chinese government and China's large listed SOEs has raised national security concerns in western countries and in many cases a potential acquisition has been described as suspicious and alarming (Du, 2014). This is related to the important roles that these SOEs play in China's domestic economic development as well as the growing roles that they have been playing in China's 'go global' strategy.

China's outbound foreign direct investment (OFDI) has grown rapidly since the launch of its 'go global' strategy in 2000. In 2014, China's OFDI outflow totalled US$116 billion; compared with around US$20 billion for 2005–2007 (United Nations Conference on Trade and Development, 2015). In fact, both the inflow of foreign direct investment and the outflow of OFDI have grown rapidly and are expected to grow considerably in coming years (EY, 2015). For the first two months of 2016, OFDI outflow had already reached US$25.9 billion, representing a large increase over the same in the previous year (Ministry of Commerce PRC, 2016).

About 80% of all China's OFDI has been funded by SOEs, with the majority of these investments carried out by 'national champions', the listed arms of CSOEs (*The Economist*, 2012, Gallagher and Irwin, 2014). It has been argued that investments made overseas through these 'national champions' will help China 'acquire primary resources', 'gain access to advanced technology', 'enter foreign markets' and 'diversify foreign reserve holdings' (Gallagher and Irwin, 2014: 2).

Despite successful expansion overseas by Chinese companies, as represented by the growing OFDI, some foreign acquisitions were rejected on the basis of national security concerns. It is worth noting that national security issues are neither new nor confined to China. If we take the USA as a host country for example, there have been previous cases where such national security concerns have been voiced, including the national security concern over German investments in the USA during World War I and over Japanese investments in the USA in the 1980s (Graham and Marchick, 2006). In China's case, high-profile transactions that have raised national security concerns included the failed takeover bid of the US company Unocal by CNOOC in 2005, as well as the acquisition of shares in the UK-listed company Rio Tinto by Chinalco in 2009.

Failed acquisitions that have raised 'national security' concerns were not limited to natural resources acquisitions. In 2012, a report suggested that two Chinese telecommunications providers, China's Huawei and ZTE should be shut out of the USA market due to the Chinese government's influence on these two companies, raising concerns that these companies would give China access to sensitive technologies and therefore pose national security concerns for the USA (Arthur, 2012, Jongbloed et al., 2012)

Apart from these failed takeover bids, other challenging deals have included the failed acquisition of the iconic Australian cattle company, S Kidman & Co by Shanghai Pengxin (a private company), which had offered to pay AU$300 million for 80% of S. Kidman (Bloomberg, 2016). The deal was blocked twice by Australia's Foreign Investment Review Board (FIRB) citing national security concerns (Bloomberg, 2016).[3] S. Kidman & Co was eventually acquired by Australian mining magnate Gina Rinehart and Shanghai CRED, with the Chinese partner taking a one-third minority stake (Schwartz et al., 2016). The deal will not include the defence-sensitive Anna Creek Station or The Peake (Schwartz et al., 2016).

In addition, China's State Grid's bid for Ausgrid in Australia in 2016 also sparked another round of the national security concerns, leading to it being eventually blocked on national security grounds (Williams, 2016).

These failed bids have illustrated that foreign acquisitions by Chinese listed SOEs face additional layers of scrutiny due to the government controlled nature of these entities. The foreign commercial activities of these Chinese listed SOEs also pose challenges to the host country seeking to balance the need to attract foreign capital and the need to protect the national interest. For example, after the successful acquisition of Canada's Nexen Inc. by CNOOC in December 2012, the Canadian government immediately issued a stringent set of rules for the approval of foreign acquisitions in Canada (Du, 2014). This suggests that due to the nature of Chinese SOEs (with the Chinese government as the major shareholder), it is unlikely that they will be put in the same category as other commercial buyers as concern over 'national security' remain a priority for host country governments.

## 5. Resource Governance and Other Related Issues

China's active pursuit of natural resources through government controlled listed SOEs going abroad, reflects its desire to achieve energy diversity and security. China's energy security is generally understood "as a guarantee to ensure a reliable and adequate supply of energy for internal Chinese market demand to support economic growth and industrialization" (Gao, 2013: 3). Developed nations such as the USA and the EU have taken a similar approach; thus we have seen the USA pursuing a policy of energy diversification after the 1993–1994 oil shock, and the EU doing likewise after the end of Cold War as well as after the 9/11 crisis and the 2006 Russian–Ukraine Gas War (Gao, 2013: 4). To protect national security and national interest, China has also introduced its own regulations aimed at reviewing foreign acquisitions that have raised national security concerns (Bath, 2013).

Apart from the energy and mineral resource security, food security is also high on the agenda of the Chinese government. The cases of ChemChina's acquisition of Syngenta and Shanghai Penxin's bid for S. Kidman & Co. were closely related to China's desire to achieve long-term food security in order to feed its growing population. Over the next 30 years, food and water security will continue to be one of the significant challenges for China (Boulter, 2013). Historically, China's severe food shortages during the Great Famine from 1959–1961 (Xin et al., 2015) also caused high mortality rates in rural areas (Xin et al., 2015) as well as social unrest. The overseas expansion of global Chinese listed SOEs is aimed at helping China achieve continued economic growth through securing natural resources such as energy and minerals, as well as agricultural resources with a view to achieving greater food security.

In order to increase food supply, China has increased its purchases in the global market, thereby increasing global food prices (Patel, 2014). In addition, China has also started to obtain agriculture land in other countries, such as Shanghai Zhongfu's investments in the Ord River region in northern Australia (Carey, 2012), as well as the acquisition of companies like Syngenta to help improve crop yield.

In addition to food security, food safety is also of major concern to the general public in China. As China has evolved from food shortages to food sufficiency, food affordability and safety have become highly important issues (Connolly et al., 2016). A notable case of food safety scandal was the incidence of melamine-contaminated baby milk powder in 2008, which affected the well-being of Chinese babies and even led to some deaths (Fu and Nicoll, 2011, Connolly et al., 2016). It is also not surprising that a McKinsey research suggested that food safety is now highly placed on the list of Chinese consumer concerns, ahead of health care, unemployment and even crime (Woetzel and Towson, 2014, Connolly et al., 2016: 131).

As a number of other developed countries have found during the early stages of their development, China's economic growth has also not been without some difficulty. China needs to deal with the undesirable by-products of its rapid economic growth and industrialisation, especially the polluting of the environment through poor air quality and water contamination, as well as other climate change related issues. These issues can be interconnected—for example, water pollution has been so severe in China that 40% of rivers have been found to be heavily polluted and contaminated water resources, thereby adversely affecting the supply of irrigation for agriculture (Boulter, 2013). Food security can also be affected by pollution and contamination of land through industrial processes, especially through the use of chemicals and wide spread reliance on coal-fired power stations (Patel, 2014). All these issues have presented major challenges for the Chinese government and need to be dealt with in a timely and effective manner.

## 6. Conclusion

The complicated governance structures of large Chinese listed SOEs and the implications that these have for 'national security' requires closer study and examination. The globalisation of large Chinese listed SOEs and their unique governance structures has highlighted the importance of understanding these companies when dealing with them so as to avoid unnecessary misunderstandings.

It is important to bridge the gaps between the western world and China's global listed SOEs. In addition to natural resource security, other important issues involve Chinese food security and safety, water scarcity and climate change issues. This chapter provides an overview of the development of China's large SOEs, setting the foundation and paving the way for more detailed analysis.

## Acronyms

| | |
|---|---|
| AIIB | Asian Infrastructure Investment Bank |
| CPC | Communist Party of China |
| CSOE(s) | State-owned enterprise(s) under the direct control of the central government |
| CSRC | China Securities Regulatory Commission |
| FIRB | Foreign Investment Review Board |
| IPOs | Initial Public Offerings |
| NSSF | National Social Security Fund |
| OECD | Organisation for Economic Co-operation and Development |
| OFDI | Outbound Foreign Direct Investment |
| QFII | Qualified Foreign Institutional Investor |
| SASAC | State-Owned Assets Supervision and Administration Commission of the State Council |
| SOE(s) | State-owned enterprise(s) |

# Appendix
Chinese SOEs Under the Direct
Control of SASAC

| No. | Name of Chinese SOE | Industry | Revenue (USD million) for 2014 | Fortune Global 500 2015 ranking | Founding year |
|---|---|---|---|---|---|
| 1 | China National Nuclear Corporation | Power generation | NA | NA | 1955 |
| 2 | China Nuclear E&C Group Corporation | Power generation | NA | NA | 1999 |
| 3 | China Aerospace Science and Technology Corporation | Aviation | 27,190 | 437 | 1999 |
| 4 | China Aerospace Science and Industry Corporation | Aviation | NA | NA | 1999 |
| 5 | Aviation Industry Corporation of China | Aviation | 62,287 | 159 | 1951 |
| 6 | China State Shipbuilding Corporation | Shipping | NA | NA | 1999 |
| 7 | China Shipbuilding Industry Corporation | Shipping | 32,732 | 371 | 1999 |
| 8 | China North Industries Group Corporation | Armaments | 65,615 | 144 | 1980 |
| 9 | China South Industries Group Corporation | Armaments | NA | NA | 1999 |
| 10 | China Electronics Technology Group Corporation | Armaments | NA | NA | 2002 |
| 11 | China National Petroleum Corporation | Oil and Petrochemicals | 428,620 | 4 | 1998 |
| 12 | China Petrochemical Corporation (Sinopec) | Oil and Petrochemicals | 446,811 | 2 | 1998 |
| 13 | CNOOC | Oil and Petrochemicals | 99,262 | 72 | 1982 |
| 14 | State Grid Corporation of China | Power distribution | 339,426 | 7 | 2002 |
| 15 | China Southern Power Grid Company | Power distribution | 76,662 | 113 | 2002 |
| 16 | China Huaneng Group | Power generation | 47,401 | 224 | 1985 |
| 17 | China Datang Corporation | Power generation | 30,206 | 392 | 2002 |
| 18 | China Huadian Corporation | Power generation | 29,341 (Fortune 2013) | NA | 2002 |
| 19 | China Guodian Corporation | Power generation | 34,627 | 343 | 2002 |
| 20 | State Power Investment Corporation (China Power Investment) | Power generation | 29,584 | 403 | 2015 |
| 21 | China Three Gorges Corporation | Power generation | 4,370 (source: www.hoovers.com) | NA | 1993 |
| 22 | Shenhua Group | Mining | 52,731 | 196 | 1995 |
| 23 | China Telecommunications Corporation (China Telecom) | Telecommunications | 62,147 | 160 | 2002 |

| # | Company | Industry | | | Year |
|---|---------|----------|---|---|------|
| 24 | China United Network Communications Limited (China Unicom) | Telecommunications | 46,834 | 227 | 2001 |
| 25 | China Mobile Limited (China Mobile) | Telecommunications | 107,529 | 55 | 1997 |
| 26 | China Electronics Corporation | Power equipment | 33,084 | 366 | 1989 |
| 27 | FAW Group Corporation | Automobiles | 80,194 | 107 | 1953 |
| 28 | Dongfeng Motor | Automobiles | 78,978 | 109 | 1969 |
| 29 | China First Heavy Industries | Machinery | NA | NA | 1954 |
| 30 | China National Machinery Industry Corporation (Sinomach) | Machinery | 39,722 | 288 | 1997 |
| 31 | Harbin Electric Corporation | Power equipment | 3,209 (for year 2015) Source: www.reuters.com, US$1= HK$7.76 | NA | 1994 |
| 32 | Dongfang Electric Corporation | Power equipment | 5,665 (for year 2015) Source: markets.ft.com, US$1= CNY 6.64 | NA | 1984 |
| 33 | Angang Iron and Steel Group (Ansteel) | Iron and steel | 26,212 | 451 | 1958 |
| 34 | Baoshan Iron and Steel Group (Baosteel) | Iron and steel | 48,323 | 218 | 1978 |
| 35 | Wuhan Iron and Steel (Group) Corporation | Iron and steel | 23,720 | 500 | 1955 |
| 36 | Aluminum Corporation of China | Non-ferrous metals | 45,445 | 240 | 2001 |
| 37 | China COSCO Shipping Corporation Limited | Shipping | 27,483 | 432 | 1961 |
| 38 | China National Aviation Corporation (Group) Limited | Aviation | NA | NA | 1929 |
| 39 | China Eastern Airline Corporation (China Eastern) | Aviation | 13,289 (for year 2013) Source: marketrealist.com, US$1=CNY 6.64 | NA | 1988 |
| 40 | China Southern Airline Corporation (China Southern) | Aviation | 14,841 (for year 2013) Source: marketrealist.com, US$1 = CNY 6.64 | NA | 1988 |

(Continued)

| No. | Name of Chinese SOE | Industry | Revenue (USD million) for 2014 | Fortune Global 500 2015 ranking | Founding year |
|---|---|---|---|---|---|
| 41 | Sinochem Group | Chemicals | 80,635 | 105 | 1950 |
| 42 | COFCO Group | | 40,524 | 272 | 1952 |
| 43 | China Minmetals Corporation | Non-ferrous metal | 52,383 | 198 | 1950 |
| 44 | China General Technology (Group) Holding Corporation Limited | Engineering and construction | 27,670 | 426 | 1998 |
| 45 | The China State Construction Engineering Corporation | Engineering and construction | 129,887 | 37 | 1957 |
| 46 | China Grain Reserves Corporation (Sinograin) | Food administration | 27,026 (for year 2011) Source: audit.gov.cn, US$1=CNY6.64 | NA | 2000 |
| 47 | State Development and Investment Corporation | Investments in strategic sectors | NA | NA | 1995 |
| 48 | China Merchant Group | Investments in transport related industry | 106 (for year 2015) Source: markets.ft.com, US$1=HK$7.76 | NA | 1872 |
| 49 | China Resources (Holdings) Corporation Limited | Multisectors | 74,887 | 115 | 1983 |
| 50 | China National Travel Service (HK) Group Corporation | Travel | 7.530 (for year 2011) Source: www.hkcts.com, US$1=CNY6.64 | NA | 1928 |
| 51 | The Commercial Aircraft Corporation of China, Limited (Comac) | Aviation | NA | NA | 2008 |
| 52 | China Energy Conservation and Environmental Protection Group | Environmental protection | NA | NA | 2010 |
| 53 | China International Engineering Consulting Corporation | Power generating and communication equipment | NA | NA | 1982 |

| No. | Company name | Industry | Revenue | | Year |
|---|---|---|---|---|---|
| 54 | China Chengtong Holdings Group Limited | Paper manufacturing | NA | NA | 1992 |
| 55 | China National Coal Group Corporation | Coal | NA | NA | 1999 |
| 56 | China Coal Technology Engineering Group | Coal | 106 (company annual report) US$1= CNY6.64 | NA | 2008 |
| 57 | China Academy of Machinery Science and Technology | Machinery | NA | NA | 1956 |
| 58 | Sinosteel Corporation | Iron and steel | NA | NA | 1993 |
| 59 | China Iron and Steel Research Institute Group | Iron and steel | NA | NA | 2006 |
| 60 | China National Chemical Corporation (ChemChina) | Chemicals | 41,813 | 265 | 2004 |
| 61 | China National Chemical Engineering Corporation Limited | Chemicals | 8,885 (for year 2015) Source: markets.ft.com, US$1 = CNY6.64 | NA | 2008 |
| 62 | Sinolight Corporation | Technology for light industry | NA | NA | 2008 |
| 63 | China National Arts and Crafts (Group) Corporation | Arts and crafts | NA | NA | 2007 |
| 64 | China National Salt Industry Corporation (China Salt) | Salt | NA | NA | 1950 |
| 65 | China Hi-Tech Group Corporation | Textile | 164 (for year 2016) Source: www.reuters.com, US$1= CNY6.64 | NA | 1998 |
| 66 | China National Materials Group Corporation (Sinoma) | Non-ferrous metals | 8,012 (for year 2015) Source: markets.ft.com, US$1=HK$7.76 | NA | 1983 |
| 67 | China National Building Materials Group Corporation | Building materials | 40,644 | 270 | 1984 |

*(Continued)*

| No. | Name of Chinese SOE | Industry | Revenue (USD million) for 2014 | Fortune Global 500 2015 ranking | Founding year |
|---|---|---|---|---|---|
| 68 | China Non-ferrous Metal Mining (Group) Corporation Limited | Non-ferrous metals | 30,456 | 390 | 1983 |
| 69 | General Research Institute for Non-ferrous Metals | Non-ferrous metals | NA | NA | 1952 |
| 70 | Beijing General Research Institute of Mining & Metallurgy | Mining and metallurgy | NA | NA | 1956 |
| 71 | China International Intellectech Corporation | HR outsourcing provider | NA | NA | 1987 |
| 72 | China Academy of Building Research | Building research | NA | NA | 1953 |
| 73 | CRRC Corporation | Transportation: railway | 38,984 (for year 2015) Source: markets.ft.com, US$1=CNY6.64 | NA | 2014 |
| 74 | China Railway Signal and Communication Corp | Transportation: railway | NA | NA | 1953 |
| 75 | China Railway Engineering Corporation | Engineering and construction | 99,537 | 71 | 1950 |
| 76 | China Railway Construction Corporation | Engineering and construction | 96,395 | 79 | 1948 |
| 77 | China Communications Construction | Engineering and construction | 60,119 | 165 | 2005 |
| 78 | China Putian Corporation | Telecommunications | NA | NA | 1980 |
| 79 | Institute of Telecommunication Sciences and Technology | Telecommunications | NA | NA | 1957 |
| 80 | China National Agricultural Development Group Corporation Limited | Agribusiness | NA | NA | 2004 |
| 81 | Chinatex Corporation | Agribusiness | 6,701 (for year 2012) Source: company annual report, US$1=CNY6.64 | NA | 1951 |

| | | | | | |
|---|---|---|---|---|---|
| 82 | China Silk Corporation | Textile – silk | NA | NA | 1946 |
| 83 | China Forestry Group Corporation | Forestry | NA | NA | 1996 |
| 84 | China National Pharmaceutical Group Corporation (Sinopharm) | Pharmaceutical | 40,105 | 276 | 1998 |
| 85 | CITS Group Corporation | Travel | 973 (for year 2016) Source: www.reuters.com, US$1=CNY6.64 | NA | 1954 |
| 86 | China Poly Group Corporation | Real Estate | 26,046 | 457 | 1999 |
| 87 | China Architecture Design and Research Group | Architecture design and research | NA | NA | 2000 |
| 88 | China Metallurgical Geology Bureau | Metallurgy | NA | NA | 1952 |
| 89 | China National Administration of Coal Geology | Coal | NA | NA | 1953 |
| 90 | Xinxing Cathay International Group Co., Ltd. | Metals and materials | 34,497 | 344 | 1952 |
| 91 | TravelSky Technology Holding Company | Aviation | 823 (for year 2015) Source: markets.ft.com, US$1=HK$7.76 | NA | 2000 |
| 92 | China National Aviation Fuel Group | Aviation | 36,178 | 321 | 2002 |
| 93 | China Aviation Supplies Holding Company | Aviation | NA | NA | 2002 |
| 94 | Power Construction Corporation of China | Power construction | 34,090 (for year 2015) Source: markets.ft.com, US$1=CNY6.64 | NA | 2011 |
| 95 | China Energy Engineering Group Co., Ltd | Engineering and construction | 30,322 | 391 | 2011 |
| 96 | China National Gold Group Corporation | Commodity: Gold | 16,777 (for year 2013) Source: www.moodys.com, US$1=CNY6.64 | NA | 2003 |
| 97 | China National Cotton Reserves Corporation | Agriculture | NA | NA | 2003 |

(Continued)

| No. | Name of Chinese SOE | Industry | Revenue (USD million) for 2014 | Fortune Global 500 2015 ranking | Founding year |
|---|---|---|---|---|---|
| 98 | China General Nuclear Power Group | Power generation | NA | NA | 1994 |
| 99 | China Hualu Group Corporation Limited | Manufacturer: electronics | NA | NA | 1992 |
| 100 | Shanghai Bell Corp. Ltd (Alcatel-Lucent) | Telecommunications | NA | NA | 1984 |
| 101 | Wuhan Posts and Telecommunications Research Institute | Telecommunications | NA | NA | 1974 |
| 102 | Overseas Chinese Town Holdings Company (OCT Group) | Multisectors | 967 (for year 2015) Source: markets.ft.com, US$1= HK$7.76 | NA | 1985 |
| 103 | Nam Kwong Group | Multisectors | NA | NA | |
| 104 | China XD Group Corporation | Power equipment | 1,965 (for year 2015) Source: markets.ft.com, US$1= CNY6.64 | NA | 1959 |
| 105 | China Railway Materials Commercial Corporation | Transportation: railway | NA | NA | 1887 |
| 106 | China Reform Holdings Corporation Limited | Investments: asset management | NA | NA | 2010 |

Source: Unless otherwise specified, number and name of CSOE were sourced from SASAC (in Chinese), translated into English by Xinting Jia (web address: www.sasac.gov.cn/n86114/n86137/c1725422/content.html, accessed: 1 July 2016). Revenue and Fortune 500 ranking were sourced from Fortune (http://fortune.com/global500/, accessed 1 July 2016). Industry and founding year were sourced from company websites and various online sources.

# Notes

1. There are two types of tradable shares listed in the China's domestic stock market: A shares and B shares. A shares are denominated in Renminbi and traded primarily between domestic investors. Qualified Foreign Institutional Investors (QFIIs) are foreign investors that have been given permission by the Chinese government to trade in China's domestic market (Mobius, 2012). B shares represent Chinese companies with a face value in Renminbi, but listed for trading in US dollars to primarily international investors in Shanghai Stock Exchange and in Hong Kong Dollars in Shenzhen Stock Exchange (Mobius, 2012).
2. Based on Xinting Jia's interview with a staff member of National Social Security Fund (NSSF) in May 2012 in Beijing.
3. One of S. Kidman's cattle stations (Anna Creek station) is close to the Woomera weapons testing range, raising national security concerns if S. Kidman & Co. were to sell its cattle stations to a Chinese company.

# Bibliography

Arthur, C. 2012, *China's Huawei and ZTE pose national security threat, says US committee* [Online], available: www.theguardian.com/technology/2012/oct/08/china-huawei-zte-security-threat, accessed: 4 June 2016.

Bath, V. 2013, "National security and Chinese investment policy", *Harvard Business Law Review Online* [Online], available: www.hblr.org/wp-content/uploads/2013/03/Bath_National-Security1.pdf, accessed: 25 June 2016, pp. 81–91.

Berle, A. A. and Means, G. C. 1932, *The modern corporation and private property*, New York, The Macmillan Company.

Bloomberg 2016, *Cattle giant S Kidman & Co sold to Chinese interests led by Shanghai Pengxin Group* [Online], available: www.smh.com.au/business/cattle-giant-s-kidman--co-sold-to-chinese-interests-led-by-shanghai-pengxin-group-20160419-goa12z.html, accessed: 23 April 2016.

Boulter, J. 2013, *Food and water security China's most significant national challenge* [Online], available: www.futuredirections.org.au/publication/food-and-water-security-china-s-most-significant-national-challenge/, accessed: 20 June 2016.

Brandt, L. and Rawski, T. G. 2008, "China's great economic transformation", in Brandt, L. and Rawski, T. G. (eds.) *China's great economic transformation*, Cambridge University Press, Cambridge, pp. 1–26.

Brødsgaard, K. E. and Grünberg, N. 2014, "Key points of China's economic programme after the Third Plenum of the CPC", *China Report*, vol. 50, no. 4, pp. 343–359.

Burger, L. 2016, *China seeks food security with $43 billion bid for Syngenta* [Online], available: www.reuters.com/article/us-syngenta-ag-m-a-chemchina-idUSKCN0VB1D9, accessed: 24 April 2016.

Carey, K. 2012, *Australia's largest "food bowl" snared by China-based developer for ethanol* [Online], available: http://ausfoodnews.com.au/2012/11/14/australia%E2%80%99s-largest-%E2%80%9Cfood-bowl%E2%80%809D-snared-by-china-based-developer-for-ethanol.html, accessed: 25 June 2016.

Central Intelligence Agency 1959, *Comparison of the first five year plans of communist China and the USSR* [Online], available: www.foia.cia.gov/sites/default/files/document_conversions/89801/DOC_0000313443.pdf, accessed 9 July 2016.

China.org.cn 2014, *Decision of the Central Committee of the Communist Party of China on some major issues concerning comprehensively deepening the reform*

(English translation of 'Zhonggong zhongyang guanyu quanmian shenhua gaige ruogan zhongda wenti de jueding') [Online], available: http://lawprofessors.type pad.com/files/131112-third-plenum-decision---official-english-translation.pdf, accessed: 26 June 2016.

Connolly, A. J., Luo, L. S., Woolsey, M., Lyons, M. and Phillips-Connolly, K. 2016, "A blueprint for food safety in China", *China Agricultural Economic Review*, vol. 8, no. 1, pp. 129–147.

Du, M. 2014, "When China's national champions go global: Nothing to fear but fear itself?", *Journal of World Trade*, vol. 48, no. 6, pp. 1127–1166.

The Economist 2012, *The world in their hands: State capitalism looks outward as well as inward* [Online], available: www.economist.com/node/21542930, accessed: 23 June 2016.

Ellyatt, H. and Chatterley, J. 2016, *Syngenta: ChemChina deal 'not China nationalization'* [Online], available: www.cnbc.com/2016/02/02/syngenta-says-to-be-acquired-by-chemchina.html, accessed: 24 April 2016.

EY 2015, *Riding the silk road: China sees outbound investment boom: Outlook for China's outward foreign direct investment* [Online], available: www.ey.com/Pub lication/vwLUAssets/ey-china-outbound-investment-report-en/$FILE/ey-china-outbound-investment-report-en.pdf, accessed: 26 June 2016.

Firth, M., Lin, C. and Zou, H. 2010, "Friend or foe? The role of state and mutual fund ownership in the split share structure reform in China", *Journal of Financial and Quantitative Analysis*, vol. 45, no. 3, p. 22.

Foxnews.com 2014, *China surpasses U.S. to become largest world economy* [Online], available: www.foxnews.com/world/2014/12/06/china-surpasses-us-to-become-largest-world-economy.html, accessed: 1 May 2016.

Fu, J. and Nicoll, G. 2011, "The milk scandal and corporate governance in China", *Canberra Law Review*, vol. 10, no. 3, pp. 103–124.

Gallagher, K. P. and Irwin, A. 2014, "Exporting national champions: China's outward foreign direct investment finance in comparative perspective", *China and World Economy*, vol. 22, no. 6, p. 21.

Gao, S. 2013, *China's search for energy diversification policy and the Sino-Australian relations* [Online], available: www.library.uq.edu.au/ojs/index.php/asc/article/view/2031/1969, accessed: 26 June 2016.

Graham, E. M. and Marchick, D. M. 2006, *US national security and foreign direct investment*, Peterson Institute for International Economics, Washington, DC.

Greenpeace 2016, *ChinaChem to takeover Syngenta—Greenpeace statement* [Online], available: www.greenpeace.org/eastasia/press/releases/food-agricul ture/2016/ChinaChem-to-takeover-Syngenta---Greenpeace-statement/, accessed: 24 April 2016.

Guo, W. 2016, "Insights from the Fifth Plenary Session of the 18th CPC Central Committee on indigenisation of the path of development of social work in China", *China Journal of Social Work*, vol. 9, no. 1, pp. 92–95.

Hemphill, T. A. and White, III G. O. 2013, "China's national champions: The evolution of a national industrial policy—or a new era of economic protectionism?", *Thunderbird International Business Review*, vol. 55, no. 2, pp. 193–214.

Hou, W., Kuo J.-M. and Lee, E. 2012, "The impact of state ownership on share price informativeness: The case of the Split Share Structure Reform in China", *The British Accounting Review*, vol. 44, no. 4, pp. 248–261.

International Monetary Fund 2014, *World economic and financial surveys: World economic outlook database* [Online], available: www.imf.org/external/pubs/ft/weo/2014/02/weodata/index.aspx, accessed: 1 May 2016.

Jia, X. and Tomasic, R. 2010, *Corporate governance and resource security in China: The transformation of China's global resources companies*, Routledge, New York.

Jongbloed, W. P. F. S., Sachs, L. E. and Sauvant, K. P. 2012, "Sovereign investment: An introduction", in Sauvant, K. P., Sachs, L. E. and Jongbloed, W. P. F. S. (eds.) *Sovereign investment: Concerns and policy reactions*, Oxford Scholarship [Online], available: Victoria University Online Library, accessed: 25 June 2016, pp. 1–36.

Kay, J. 2012, *Kay Review of UK equity markets and long-term decision making* [Online], available: http://webarchive.nationalarchives.gov.uk/20121204121011/http://www.bis.gov.uk/assets/biscore/business-law/docs/k/12-996-kay-review-of-equity-markets-speech-and-presentation.pdf, accessed: 13 May.

Larsen, P. T. 2015, *Signs of spring* [Online], available: http://www.pressreader.com/india/business-standard/20151006/281964606541230, accessed: 12 June 2016.

Lee, J. 2013, *A long march for China's national champions* [Online], available: www.theaustralian.com.au/business/business-spectator/a-long-march-for-chinas-national-champions/news-story/4f2215462586493fe68bc30397dadf31, accessed: 6 May 2016.

Li, X. and Brødsgaard, K. E. 2013, "SOE reform in China: Past, present and future", *The Copenhagen Journal of Asian Studies*, vol. 31, no. 2, pp. 54–78.

Liao, L., Liu, B. and Wang, H. 2014, "China's secondary privatization: Perspectives from the split-share structure reform", *Journal of Financial Economics*, vol. 113, no. 3, pp. 500–518.

Lin, L.-W. and Milhaupt, C. J. 2013, "We are the (national) champions: Understanding the mechanisms of state capitalism in China", *Stanford Law Review*, vol. 65, no. 4, pp. 697–759.

Liu, G. S. and Garino, G. 2001, "China's two decades of economic reform: A special issue for the papers selected from the 10th conference of the Chinese Economic Association (UK)", *Economics of Planning*, vol. 34, nos. 1–2, pp. 1–4.

Ministry of Commerce PRC 2016, *The regular press conference of the ministry of commerce (March 17, 2016)* [Online], available: http://english.mofcom.gov.cn/article/newsrelease/press/201603/20160301278807.shtml, accessed: 22 April 2016.

Mobius, M. 2012, *The ABCs of China's share markets* [Online], available: www.cnbc.com/id/49441597, accessed: 6 May 2016.

Nottage, L., Wolff, L. and Anderson, K. (eds.) 2008. *Corporate governance in the 21st century: Japan's gradual transformation*, Edward Elgar, Cheltenham.

OECD 2015, *OECD guidelines on corporate governance of state-owned enterprises: 2015 edition* [Online], available: www.oecd.org/daf/ca/OECD-Guidelines-Corporate-Governance-SOEs-2015.pdf, accessed: 27 May 2016.

Patel, K. 2014, *China's food security dilemma* [Online], available: www.worldpolicy.org/blog/2014/06/04/chinas-food-security-dilemma, accessed: 20 June 2016.

people.com.cn 2007, *Overview of the Third Plenary Session of the 11th CPC Central Committee (Zhong Guo Gong Chan Dang Shi Yi Jie San Zhong Quan Hui Jian Jie)* [Online], available: http://cpc.people.com.cn/GB/64162/64168/64563/65371/4441896.html, accessed: 3 June 2016.

SASAC 2015, *List of CSOEs* [Online], available: www.sasac.gov.cn/n86114/n86137/index.html, accessed: 9 June 2016.

Schwartz, D., Vidot, A. and Jasper, C. 2016, *S Kidman and Co: Scott Morrison approves sale of cattle empire to Gina Rinehart, Chinese company* [Online], available: www.abc.net.au/news/2016-12-09/s-kidman-and-co-sale-to-rinehart-approved/8106694, accessed: 13 May.

Spegele, B. and Wu, K. 2017. "ChemChina seals $58bn deal", *The Australian*, 8 May 2017, p. 22.

Tam, O. K. 1999, *The development of corporate governance in China*, Edward Elgar, Northampton, MA.

Tomasic, R. and Xiong, P. 2016, "Globalization, legal culture, and handling of Sino-Australian commercial disputes", *The Chinese Journal of Comparative Law*, vol. 4, no. 1, pp. 149–171.

Umar, A. R. M. 2016, *Extractive industries and future of global resource governance* [Online], available: www.thejakartapost.com/news/2016/02/22/extractive-industries-and-future-global-resource-governance.html, accessed: 21 April 2016.

United Nations Conference on Trade and Development 2015, *World investment report 2015: reforming international investment governance* [Online], available: http://unctad.org/sections/dite_dir/docs/wir2015/wir15_fs_cn_en.pdf, accessed: 22 April 2016.

Wang, H. and Lu, M. 2016, *China goes global: The impact of Chinese overseas investment on its business enterprises*, Palgrave Macmillan, UK, Hampshire.

Wang, J., Guthrie, D. and Xiao, Z. 2011, "The rise of SASAC: Asset management, ownership concentration, and firm performance in China's capital markets", *Management and Organization Review*, vol. 8, no. 2, pp. 252–281.

Wei, Y. 2003, *Comparative corporate governance: A Chinese perspective*, Kluwer Law International, London.

Williams, P. 2016, *Australia blocks bids for Ausgrid, triggering warning from China* [Online], available: www.bloomberg.com/news/articles/2016-08-19/australia-bars-foreign-investors-from-buying-50-4-of-ausgrid-is1gmaue, accessed: 13 May.

Witt, M. A. and Redding, G. 2014, "China: Authoritarian capitalism", in Witt, M. A. and Redding, G. (eds.) *The Oxford handbook of Asian business systems*, Oxford University Press, Oxford.

Woetzel, J. and Towson, J. 2014, *It's a shame to let a China food scandal go to waste* [Online], available: www.scmp.com/comment/blogs/article/1571442/its-shame-let-china-food-scandal-go-waste, accessed: 29 June 2016.

World Bank 2016, *Overview* [Online], available: www.worldbank.org/en/country/china/overview, accessed: 1 May.

Xin, M., Qian, N. and Yared, P. 2015, "The institutional causes of China's Great Famine, 1959–1961", *Review of Economic Studies*, vol. 82, no. 4, pp. 1568–1611.

Yang, J., Chi, J. and Young, M. 2011, "A review of corporate governance in China", *Asian-Pacific Economic Literature*, vol. 25, no. 1, p. 14.

Zhao, H. 2006, *China names key industries for absolute state control* [Online], available: www.chinadaily.com.cn/china/2006-12/19/content_762056.htm, accessed: 9 June 2016.

# 2 Resource Security and Corporate Social Responsibility Norms in the Governance of Globally Active Chinese State-Owned Enterprises

*Roman Tomasic and Ping Xiong*

## 1. Introduction

With the rapid development of the Chinese economy in the past 40 years, China has become a country with increasing outbound investment. According to UNCTAD statistics and Chinese official sources, China has seen a steady increase of its outbound investment, reaching US$116 billion in 2014 (UNCTAD, 2015; Buckley et al. 2010: 143) and US$118 billion in 2015 (PRC Ministry of Commerce, 2016).[1] A report from the American Enterprise Institute (AEI) and the Heritage Foundation shows that Chinese foreign investment in Australia over the decade to 2016 comprised US$75.5 billion (American Enterprise Institute and the Heritage Foundation, 2005–2016). This investment includes investments from state-owned enterprises (SOEs) and from private sources. In 2015, a KPMG-Sydney University study estimated that Chinese investment in Australia over the next decade will be over US$90 billion (KPMG and the University of Sydney, 2015: 31).

Among all of these investments, the largest Chinese investments tend to be made in developing countries or those with substantial natural resources sectors (Nolan, 2012). Australia, as a country with rich natural resources, has received large amounts of Chinese investment, mainly from Chinese SOEs, which invested in the natural resources sector.

Australia has a long history in attracting foreign direct investment (FDI) to the natural resources sector; this includes British investment in the pastoral and mining industries in the nineteenth and early twentieth centuries, American investment after World War II in the manufacturing industries and resource sector, Japanese investment in the 1960s, largely in the mining industry and more recent acquisitions of Australian industries by British and American multinationals in the 1980s and 1990s (Huang and Austin, 2011: 4). Recently, China as another important investor, has invested heavily in Australia, including in the construction and resources sector (KPMG and the University of Sydney, 2016: 14).

Australia has benefited greatly from an influx of investment from China; much of this investment has come from Chinese SOEs. According to a KPMG-Sydney University study of Chinese investment into Australia between September 2006 and December 2012, capital investment by Chinese SOEs accounted for 80% by volume and 94% by transaction value of all Chinese investment (KPMG and the University of Sydney, 2013: 1). The China-Australia Free Trade Agreement signed in 2015 has further liberalised trade and investment between these countries and investment in Australia by Chinese SOEs continues to rise.

Functioning as China's so-called national champions, Chinese SOEs have been vehicles for the Chinese government efforts to obtain resources from the global market, to participate in international market competition and to expand China's national soft power (Nolan, 2012). They also allow Chinese SOEs to gain controlling interests in foreign companies, allowing them to open doors for other Chinese enterprises to sell goods and services in foreign countries; this is a pattern that is well established by other countries during prior eras of foreign investment in Australia.

However, the 'soft power' implications of China's investments in Australia have increasingly raised concern, especially where investment by Chinese SOEs is involved. It is interesting to note that such concerns with Chinese investment in Australia have most clearly been expressed by foreign governments and their representatives, especially by representatives of the United States.

As a result, we have begun to see the emergence of a more critical Australian response to some Chinese SOE investment in Australia. By and large, Chinese investment in Australia has been permitted, although national interest and securities issues have sometimes been raised to prevent foreign acquisitions taking place. A number of recent decisions by the Australian Federal Treasurer preventing acquisitions on national interest grounds have alarmed some Chinese investors. This was most evident in the blocking of the sale of Ausgrid (which controls a large electricity distribution network in eastern Australia) to State Grid Corporation of China, a large Chinese SOE; this was done on the grounds of national interest and national security (BBC News, 2016). China's State Grid had previously been allowed to acquire less strategic infrastructure assets in other parts of Australia but these purchases had not triggered security concerns.

The Australian government recognises that the corporate governance practices of foreign investors in Australia is important; it is also known that national interest considerations are considered as a fundamental criterion used by the Australian government in assessing proposed foreign investments (Huang and Austin, 2011: 182–183). In 2016, the Australian government's Foreign Investment Policy provided a detailed statement of factors for the assessment of national interest, among which the character of a foreign investor is a factor that will influence any national interest assessment; corporate governance is seen as an indicator of good investor character.[2] This policy paper also provided detailed criteria for foreign government investors, requiring that the foreign investment should be commercial in nature and questioning whether the proposed governance arrangement in the acquired entity could facilitate actual or potential control of an enterprise by a foreign government.

In addition, investments in the natural resources sectors by Chinese SOEs in Australia have been challenged on the basis of environmental protection issues, labour standards and respect for indigenous people's rights.[3] Chinese investment is also facing other management challenges, such as concern over management styles, human resources management, cross-cultural management, the use of business contractors and risk-management concerns (Huang and Austin, 2011: 186).

With the on-going development of China's socialist market economy, and in order to meet the challenges of modern corporate governance, China's SOEs have sought to enhance their corporate governance practices whilst the Chinese government has continued to try to reform its inefficient SOEs. As part of China's response to the challenges facing modern globally active companies, it has also adapted corporate social responsibility (CSR) ideas so as to better regulate its enterprises. This has often been supported by legislative mechanisms. With increasing outbound investment by Chinese SOEs, many SOEs have also developed their own CSR codes. CSR codes are non-binding voluntary rules for corporations that allow them to demonstrate their accountability in the marketplace.

This chapter will explore some CSR norms developed by the Chinese central government and its SOEs and examine how Chinese SOEs implement their CSR norms to protect non-economic interests in countries such as Australia. Section 2 explores the challenges faced by Chinese SOEs operating overseas, specifically in Australia; these have usually been motivated by Chinese government strategic policies such as the 'China go global' (CGG) policy and the 'One Belt, One Road' (OBOR) policy. Section 3 discusses some recent theories regarding corporate management and the control of risk in the context of the globalisation of multinationals and the emergence of CSR ideas in China. Section 4 examines the implementation overseas of CSR principles by Chinese government agencies, industry associations and SOEs. Finally, Section 5 offers some observations and conclusions.

## 2. Challenges Facing Chinese SOEs as China's SOEs Goes Global

### 2.1. *Chinese SOEs Abroad*

China's adoption of its "CGG" policy has encouraged many Chinese SOEs to go abroad to invest. The 'go global' strategy was adopted under the leadership of former president Hu Jingtao and the Decision on Several Important Issues to Improve the Socialist Market Economy promulgated during the Third Plenary Session of the Sixteenth National Congress of the CPC; this called on the government to continue to implement the 'go global' strategy and to improve its services to encourage Chinese investment abroad.[4] The

2007 Report of the Seventeenth National Congress of the CPC followed this strategy.[5] Some PRC domestic laws and regulations have been changed in order to provide incentives to Chinese companies to invest abroad under the influence of this policy (Drysdale, 2013; State Council, 2006).

The recent "OBOR" initiative proposed under President Xi Jinping's leadership has become a catalyst for Chinese SOEs to trade internationally and invest overseas.[6] Chinese investment overseas equips Chinese SOEs with local legal vehicles to exploit local resources and create more competitive advantages for China in international markets.

At the same time, the rapid expansion of SOEs abroad has raised concerns in many countries. The Trans-Pacific Partnership Agreement that had been proposed by the Obama Administration in the USA included a chapter dealing with the challenges presented by SOEs.[7] The summary provided by the USTR notes,

> Concerns about the role of SOEs have grown in recent years because SOEs that had previously operated almost exclusively within their own territories are increasingly engaged in international trade of goods and services or acting as investors in foreign markets. Their coverage in a specific TPP chapter is a new feature in U.S. trade agreements that will help us address emerging concerns, including financing and subsidization of SOEs involved in exporting, domestic competition for business and contracts; and regulatory policies which, by design or because of lack of transparency, create inherent advantages for SOEs favored by home governments. At the same time, TPP recognizes, defines, and ensures legitimate roles for SOEs in provision of public services.[8]

### 2.2. Some Challenges Faced by Chinese SOEs in Australia

Investment by Chinese SOEs in Australia faces many challenges. Usually a Chinese SOE will have to comply with Australian regulations in setting up a local subsidiary to operate its business in the country. Such companies are set up according to local regulations, however, they will always carry the "DNA" inherited from their Chinese parent companies, which may cause some friction with local businesses. Firstly, there may be tensions arising out of the conditions imposed on proposed investments in Australia by the Australian government, such as by the Foreign Investment Review Board, as detailed criteria for assessing investment from foreign governments are followed (Treasurer, 2016).[9]

Secondly, different legal and investment environments and a different social context in Australia may mean that the foreign investors will encounter differences in the management culture of a company in Australia. For example, a former partner in King and Wood Mallesons, an international law firm which has assisted with many Chinese ODIs in Australia, has noted that some Chinese investments in Australia fail for a variety of reasons:

> Dealing with a different legal and regulatory landscape in Australia may partly explain unsuccessful transactions; however, language and cultural differences play a part in understanding and negotiating new deal structures. Moreover, problems understandably arise in the implementation of deals if there is no pre-existing relationship with Australian targets and there are no strategies for dealing with cross-cultural integration and the management of expatriate staff.
>
> (Evans, 2013: 81)

Yancoal Australia (Australia's largest listed coal company), a company controlled by China's fourth largest coal company, Yanzhou Coal Mining, also at one time experienced these types of cultural and governance problems. Mr Murray Bailey, a former Australian CEO of Yancoal Australia, was reportedly frustrated by directors of Yancoal's Chinese parent company; his lack of understanding of the nuances in Chinese culture was reported as a reason for friction between Chinese and local staff (Freed and Chessell, 2013:17; also see, Mather and Yngvesson, 1980: 775–821).

A similar pattern of behavior that was evident from cultural conflicts also arose in regard to the activities of Sino Iron Pty Ltd, a subsidiary of a Hong Kong company CITIC Pacific, which at the time was itself owned by a major Chinese SOE. The former president of CITIC Pacific, Mr Zhang Jijing, was critical of another Australian company, Mineralogy Pty Ltd, which controlled port facilities in Western Australia through which Sino Iron had sought to export its iron ore to China and had held the mining licence upon which the CITIC mine was built. Zhang was frustrated with claims made by Mineralogy in a royalties dispute with its local partner. It had been alleged that CITIC had reportedly sought to 'steal' Australian resources (Ker, 2014a).

Earlier, it had been alleged that managers at CITIC Pacific "were hoping the government would pass a new law so that they could operate here under Chinese law". This sweeping and unfounded allegation was denied by a CITIC representative who stated that "Everything being done by CITIC is being done strictly under Australian law" (Kretser and Gerritsen, 2013). Zhang observed that CITIC had hoped to privately resolve its dispute with Mineralogy, but that in this case, this had been an unrealistic expectation (see further, Fitzgerald and Burrell, 2014: 1 and 44; and Fitzgerald and Packham, 2014:4; and Ker, 2014b: 1 and 12; and Gerritson, 2013:17).

The Sino Iron dispute with Mineralogy was increasingly played out in the Australian courts. A contract dispute over royalty payments arose before the Supreme Court of Western Australia. The Federal Court of Australia was also involved in hearing legal issues regarding the control of

Port Preston, in the Pilbara, through which Sino Iron's iron ore was being exported. This saw a Federal Court decision in 2014 in favour of Mineralogy in *Sino Iron Pty Ltd v Secretary of the Department of Infrastructure and Transport* ([2014] FCA 28) that was overturned on appeal by CITIC (Sino Iron). The Full Federal Court in *Sino Iron Pty Ltd & Ors v Secretary of the Department of Infrastructure and Transport and Mineralogy Pty Ltd* ([2014] FCA 28: para 14) subsequently reversed the decision at first instance and found that Mineralogy Pty Ltd "should not be designated as port operator."

The 2012 decision of the High Court of Australia in *Forrest v Australian Securities and Investments Commission*[10] provides another illustration of cultural differences in relation to understanding the nature of contracts involving Chinese SOEs and Australian mining companies. In finding that the market had not been misled by statements made by FMG's chairman and chief executive, Andrew Forest, when he announced to the stock market that agreements had been reached with a number of major Chinese SOEs to build FMGs new mine and associated port and railway facilities.

At the time of the announcement, Forrest had formally signed "framework agreements" with these SOEs in Beijing. ASIC alleged that under Australian law, such an agreement would not constitute a binding contract, as it did not contain provisions regarding enforcement of the contract in the event of a breach. This raised questions regarding contracting with Chinese SOEs. But those who were interested in large mining projects such as this involving Chinese SOEs would not have been misled. As the High Court observed,

> It was probable that Fortescue's target audience would consider that Fortescue's representation did not suggest that the agreement had terms which "forced" either the People's Republic of China or CREC to do anything, because even the tightest of terms would not do that. Instead the target audience probably took the representation to be that there was a binding contract containing machinery capable of procuring the result that CREC would voluntarily design, build, transfer and finance the railway even if it was impossible to force it to do so. The agreement was a binding contract containing that machinery—duties to conduct future negotiations leading to future agreements.
>
> ([2012] HCA 39 at para 107)

Thirdly, as China is infamous for its sweatshops, environmental pollution and other social problems involving its companies (Lin, 2010: 65), the higher Australian standards of protection for labour and the environment, as well as human rights (including the protection of indigenous Australians) may pose potential challenges to Chinese SOEs investing in Australian natural resources projects. This in part explains the preference of Chinese SOEs for investment in developing countries where legal regulations and legal institutions are less restrictive.

## 3. The Emergence of Corporate Social Responsibilities in China

### *3.1. The Emergence of Corporate Social Responsibility*

Corporate social responsibility (CSR) refers to a company's obligation to be accountable to its stakeholders in all its operations and activities with the aim of achieving sustainable development, not only in regard to economic and financial issues but also in regard to social and environmental issues. The earliest development of CSR can be traced back to the 1950s, but in the 1970s, some companies began social reporting, which accelerated the birth of CSR (Carroll, 2008). In 1989, the multinational oil company Exxon was called upon to demonstrate its CSR after Exxon Mobil's fuel carrier, the 'Valdez', ran aground on a reef in Alaska, causing one of the largest oil spills and clean-up operations in modern history.[11] At that time, approaches to CSR largely focused on the responsibilities of shareholders.

In the late 1980s, a broader approach to the CSR of stakeholders emerged and looked at other stakeholders apart from shareholders. The rapid expansion by US-based TNCs or MNCs gave an impetus to the development of broader CSR codes (Levy and Kaplan, 2008). Since then, company CSR reports have evolved and involve more sophisticated reporting procedures and accountability mechanisms, and have become an integral part of the public profile and investment strategies of many multinational corporations.

The focus upon CSR has emerged as a consequence of the development of new corporate governance techniques following frequent market failures. The development of 'new governance techniques' reflected the limits of government regulation and led to reliance upon more flexible principles-based rules regulating corporations, the use of risk-based regulation replacing a heavy-handed, top-down governmental regulatory structure, and the use of market-based mechanisms that rely on markets being self-balancing (Black, 2011: 3 and Black, 2015).

However, as a result of the turmoil that occurred in financial markets during the global financial crisis, it was apparent that these "new governance techniques" were ineffective (Black, 2011: 3–4). Consequently, CSR ideas have continued to be promoted; this can be seen as another strand of a new model of corporate regulation, although it is still too soon to reach definitive conclusion as to its effectiveness (see further, Horrigan, 2010; and Fleming and Jones, 2013).

CSR rules are generally regarded as a kind of 'soft law', and China's use of CSR ideas as new governance techniques shows the use of soft law approaches to replace its 'hard law' approach in its company law and corporate regulation. Soft law norms are of two broad types; first, those developed by states as part of international law; secondly, those developed by private actors such as multinational corporations, non-government organisations and individuals. Robilant is of the view that two origins can be found for the 'blossoming' of soft law, with one being medieval legal pluralism and the *lex mercatoria* and the other being the notions of social law and legal pluralism developed by European anti-formalist jurist at the end of the nineteenth century and beyond (Robilant, 2006: 501). In China, the use of soft law codes and principles has also been a creature of the state itself, and has even been reflected in statutes, such as the Company Law, 2005. Soft law has been seen as 'constitutionalising' spaces that are not readily governed by laws developed by nation states (Robe, Lyon Cazen and Vermac, 2016).

Soft law may be effective in regard to corporate governance, as soft law can adjust behaviour in advance of the hardening of soft law; at the same time, soft law is a source of information regarding the intentions of a law-making body (Gersen and Posner, 2008: 585). According to Gersen and Posner, the existence of international soft law arises from the lack of an authoritative interpreter to distinguish between communications "that comply with formalities and [those] that do not", and they note that states will comply with soft law norms when they have an interest in such compliance (Gersen and Posner, 2008: 617).

However, the implementation of CSR rules can be problematic, given the absence of coercive enforcement mechanisms associated with most soft law norms. In the Chinese context, ideas such as the use of meta-regulation and reflexive law may be considered as a solution to China's corporate law implementation problems (Coglianese and Mendelson, 2015; and Tomasic, 2015; also see Parker, 2002: 245–291). According to Teubner, reflexive law is characterised by a new kind of legal restraint, and such law is regarded as a kind of communication in the transformation of a legal system and, as an autopoietic system, create communication in law by itself (Teubner, 1983 and Teubner, 1993). As these regulatory techniques, were, however, developed in democratic societies, their effectiveness in a non-democratic society, such as China, will be a challenge (Zhao, 2014). This is especially so where Chinese SOEs invest overseas in major projects, such as those in the natural resources sector; the effectiveness of soft law rules in governing SOE subsidiaries can be problematic. It is therefore appropriate to examine the effectiveness of the implementation of CSR rules in Chinese SOEs operating overseas and investing in the natural resources sector.

### 3.2. China's Responses to CSR

There are different theories and approaches to CSR, and four main groups of CSR theories and related approaches have been identified in the literature (Garriga and Melé, 2004: 51–57):

> (1) instrumental theories, in which the corporation is seen as only an instrument for wealth creation, and its social activities are only a means to achieve economic results; (2) political theories, which concern themselves with the power of corporations in society and a responsible use

of this power in the political arena; (3) integrative theories, in which the corporation is focused on the satisfaction of social demands; and (4) ethical theories, based on ethical responsibilities of corporations to society.

These theories are therefore referred to as 'instrumental, political, integrative and value theories' representing different dimensions of CSR.

The benefits of CSR are also subject to differing assessments. Some see CSR as a means for corporations to balance societal interests against short-term financial gains and maximise shareholder value (Corbett, 2014: 414). This 'trade-off' requires corporations to take into account the interests of its stakeholders (communities, employees, suppliers and government) when making decisions, even if this impacts upon the corporation's 'bottom line' by possibly violating specific rights (Corbett, 2014: 414).

Others view CSR as a natural response to external changes in the business environment as external factors are key drivers in the emergence of CSR. Therefore, the role of a company's directors and senior officers will be subject to regulation, and, while making a decision, they have an obligation to ensure that the interests of stakeholders have been taken into account as well as to maximise the value of the company over the long term (Corbett, 2014: 415).

While it was argued that CSR was originally a concept derived from western countries, elements of these approaches can now be found in China's approach to CSR. Arguably, it was introduced into China primarily through codes of conduct and third-party audits "in the wake of sweatshop exposes of the 1990s" (Ho, 2013: 398). It was originally focused on the protection of the rights of labourers and employment issues; these issues were seriously questioned in China during the 1990s as many in China's leadership saw CSR as merely a tool that was used by foreign consumers, by NGOs and trading partners to place pressure upon Chinese businesses (Ho, 2013: 398). As a result, CSR in China has passed through a period of time without much development.

But, in the mid-2000s, President Hu Jintao articulated his new policy vision of building a "harmonious society"; this triggered a shift in attitudes to CSR amongst Chinese leaders (Zhao, 2014: 218–250). This approach was officially adopted as a policy mandate by the Central Committee of the PRC Communist Party in 2006 (Ho, 2013: 399; Yao, 2002). Also, in 2005, China amended its Company Law and inserted Article 5, which now endorses CSR ideas within the field of corporate regulation. However, the actual degree to which Article 5 of the Company Law has been directly applied remains unclear.

Although President Hu's concept of a 'harmonious society' may be regarded as a trigger for the emergence of the CSR movement in China, some argue that traditional Chinese culture has long has also had a parallel impact on the behaviour of individuals in China (Bu, 2015: 124). It is argued that Confucianism has also had a bearing on corporate governance in China, as it saw well-being as deriving from the social coexistence of rites and ethics and advocated wise rule by a patriarchal monarch over their subjects (He, 2002; Peerenboom, 2002). Thus, respect for existing hierarchies and the adherence to harmonious social relations, as embedded in traditional Confucian culture, may also account for the application of CSR ideas to Chinese firms (Bu, 2015: 124).

However, in his study of *Corporate Social Responsibility in Contemporary China*, Zhao is of the view that, although Confucian philosophy has helped companies to maintain a harmonious but competitive business environment, the social hierarchies emphasised by the Confucian philosophy have influenced the implementation of CSR in China, but with a strong degree of government interference (Zhao, 2014: 49–50). Such strong government interference has become a feature of CSR development and implementation in China.

The development of CSR in China has continued with more attention to it coming from the Chinese Communist Party (CCP) and its top political leaders. Thus, during the 2008 APEC summit meeting, President Hu Jingtao also proposed the concept of global responsibility, and Premier Wen Jiabao stressed that "Entrepreneurs should have moral blood running in their bodies." Later, at the Central Party's economic meeting held in 2012, the party explicitly sought to strengthen CSR (Xinhua New Group, 2012). In 2014, the CCP also proposed strengthening the legislative basis of CSR in China through its *Central Committee Decision Concerning Several Major Issues in Comprehensively Advancing Governance According to Law* (Decision of the CPC, 2014: para 2.4). On 24 August 2015, the CCP and the State Council issued the *Guiding Opinions on Deepening the Reform of State Owned Enterprises* to require SOEs to become models in voluntarily fulfilling CSR obligations (Guidelines of the State Council and CPC Central Committee, 2015).

The manner in which CSR has emerged in China shows the key role of the CCP and the top Chinese political leadership in formulating national policies and governance rules; SOEs are seen as fundamental vehicles that can be used to carry out the CCP's policies. The formalisation of CSR ideas in China through a legislative instrument such as the Company Law can be seen as the beginnings of efforts to implement the CCP's polices through the use of the state's legislative power.

The Chinese Company Law was first promulgated in 1993 and has gone through several revisions since that time. In the 2005 revision, China, like some other transitional economies (Sukmono, 2013; PWC and Confederation of Indian Industry, 2013), started to introduce CSR ideas.[12] The new CSR provision has now been carried over into the most recent revised version of the Company Law in 2014. Article 5 of the Company Law now mandates,

> In its operational activities, a company shall abide by laws and administrative regulations, observe *social morals and commercial ethics*, persist

in *honesty and good faith*, accept supervision by the government and the public, and *assume social responsibility*.

(Emphasis added)[13]

However, the inclusion of these broad 'soft law' principles within the 'hard law' legislative framework of the Company Law may deserve further contemplation. These 'soft law' principles have not been clearly articulated, and the meaning of their language is such that expressions such as observance of 'social morals and commercial ethics', 'good faith' and 'assume social responsibility' can be quite broad or nebulous. Perhaps traditional Chinese social norms and business ethics have also influenced the inclusion of this language in the Company Law. This would be consistent with ideas from relational contract theory which has emphasised the importance of informal business norms in understanding attitudes to business contracting (see, generally, Macaulay, 1963: 55–67). As Zhao has also pointed out, the influence of achieving a harmonious society and the emphasis on social hierarchies found in Confucian philosophy may have led to government interference in this area (Zhao, 2014). Former president Hu Jingtao's promotion of the concept of a 'harmonious society' may also be a reflection of the idea of strong government interference, and this may account for the inclusion of these ideas in the reformed Company Law.

Article 5 of the Company Law also uses the language of 'good faith" or bona fides. This is basically a civil law concept and may create difficulties in applying the law in judicial practice. Some have seen this idea as something of a 'legal irritant' when it is introduced into a common law system, but it may be less harmful in China given that China's legal system is a civil law inspired legal system (see further, Teubner, 1998 and Campbell, 2014).

The last of these concepts in Article 5, assuming 'social responsibility' can be seen as having been influenced by the western CSR movement. However, the actual implementation of these concepts requires more research. The following section will discuss the implementation CSR in China in greater depth with a focus on the implementation of CSR by Chinese SOEs in the natural resources sector.

## 4. The Implementation of CSR Norms

With the attention given to CSR principles by the CCP and by top Chinese political leaders, and the inclusion of CSR concepts in the Company Law, China began to implement CSR principles in a number of other contexts. The implementation of CSR has occurred both at the governmental level and at the enterprises level. Major Chinese ministries and business regulatory bodies and industry representational bodies and large corporate groups and corporate entities have all actively participated in this process. At the same time, while Chinese enterprises have increasingly been globally active under the central government's 'go global' policy (Tomasic, 2014:155–174), it is likely that soft law rules, such as CSR principles, will become more important and operate by way of private contracting (Lin, 2009: 711–744). Therefore, many Chinese SOEs operating outside China will also implement CSR ideas when they go abroad to invest in foreign countries.

### 4.1. Implementation of CSR by China's Government

According to Professor Ho, "Since 2006, numerous initiatives around CSR at the national level have been introduced into China, but no single State Council Ministry has yet asserted leadership over CSR as a broad policy domain" (Ho, 2013: 401). The Ministry of Commerce (MOFCOM), the State Assets Supervision and Administration Commission (SASAC), the Ministry of Environmental Protection (MEP), the People's Bank of China, the General Administration of Quality Supervision, Inspection and Quarantine (AQSIQ) and the Standardisation Administration of PRC (SAC) are the major government agencies to implement CSR and they actively promote CSR in some form within their respective areas of expertise. Also, other governmental regulatory agencies, such as the China Securities Regulatory Commission, have been active in issuing codes of conduct for industry. The 2001 *Code of Corporate Governance for Listed Companies in China* issued by the China Securities Regulatory Commission and the State Economic and Trade Commission seeks to enhance the 'moral standards' of directors and explains its goals (China Securities Regulatory Commission (CSRC) and the State Economic and Trade Commission (SETC), 2001). China also has an extensive system of information disclosure by companies that are listed on its stock exchanges; Zhao has suggested that such disclosure rules have promoted social responsibility on the part of Chinese listed companies (Zhao, 2014).

These government agencies have issued a series of policies and guidelines to promote CSR over the last two decades. In order to help Chinese companies 'go global' to invest and implement their projects overseas, these government agencies have also issued guidelines or policies to promote CSR ideas related to the Chinese companies' investment overseas. The appendix is a table that chronologically lists key policies and regulations regarding sustainable overseas development by Chinese companies.[14] These reflect CSR ideas to varying degrees.

These government-issued guidelines or policies, according to the focus of each document, can be categorised as corporate governance policies, economic policies, environmental policies, social policies and comprehensive polices.[15] For corporate governance polices, the guidelines or policies can be used to promote security and risk management, or corporate culture development or CSR management.[16]

SASAC, as the supervising government agency which holds state shares in SOEs, in 2008, issued its *Guidelines to the State-Owned Enterprises Directly under the Central Government on Fulfilling Corporate Social*

*Responsibilities Guidelines* (SASAC, Guidelines 2008). In 2011, SASAC issued *Implementation Guidelines for the Twelfth Five-Year Plan for the Harmonious Development of Central Enterprises*, emphasizing the need to reinforce the integrity, environmental awareness, security, vitality and accountability of central enterprises (SASAC, Implementation Guidelines, 2011). In 2012, the SASAC Steering Committee for Corporate Social Responsibility of Central Enterprises was formed in order to enhance the management of CSR activities and help central enterprises build more sophisticated CSR management systems. In 2015, SASAC initiated a study of CSR in Central SOEs during the thirteenth five-year plan.

MOFCOM has also focused on CSR programs for export-oriented and foreign-invested enterprises to promote CSR, and in 2013 it jointly issued the *Guidance on Environmental Protection in Foreign Investment and Cooperation* with the Ministry of Environment (MOFCOM, 2013). MOFCOM also issued *Provisions on Regulating Competition in Overseas Investment and Cooperation* in 2013 to promote sustainable development of overseas investment (MOFCOM, 2013).

Recently, AQSIQ and SAC jointly issued three national standards in respect of social responsibilities—namely, the *Guidelines on Social Responsibilities*, the *Guidelines for Compiling the Report of Social Responsibilities* and the *Guidelines for Classification of Performance Indication of Social Responsibilities*; these three standards have been in effect since 1 January 2016.[17] This is the first time that China has sought to standardise its CSR guidelines at a national level.

These guidelines frequently include references to China's key political concepts, such as 'adhering to the scientific development outlook' and to the writings of senior political leaders. The 2008 guidelines issued by SASAC still have the language of the "spirit of the 17th CPC National Congress and the Scientific Outlook on Development" (SASAC Guidelines, 2008),[18] and paragraph 5 of the guidelines proclaim (Guidelines by SASAC, 2008: para 5),[19]

> CSOEs should take Deng Xiaoping Theory and the Important Thought of Three Represents as the guiding principles, thoroughly apply the Scientific Outlook on Development, adhere to the demands of human-oriented policy and sustainable development strategy from the Central Government of China, enhance their awareness of social responsibility and sustainable development, make overall planning with due consideration of every aspect. They should actively embody their responsibilities and set up good examples for other enterprises in fulfilling CSR so as to promote the construction of a harmonious and well-off society.

The slogan-like language embedded in these guidelines may lead to CSR guidelines being seen as being more akin to political statements. However, the guidelines issued in 2015 by AQSIQ and SASAC seek to standardise

CSR nationally; they have offered very specific standards and criteria for measuring CSR compliance by Chinese companies, perhaps leading China to amend the trajectory of CSR from one of mere political lip service towards a more practical implementation of these principles.

### 4.2. Implementing CSR Through Industry Associations in Natural Resources Sector

Chinese industry associations have also been active in issuing their own CSR guidelines. These include the *Guidelines to Chinese Industrial Enterprises and Industrial Associations on Corporate Social Responsibilities* jointly issued by several industrial associations in 2008; (China Federation of Industrial Economics, the China National Coal Association, the China Machinery Industry Federation, the China Iron and Steel Industry Association, the China Petroleum and Chemical Industry Federation, the China National Light Industry Council, the China National Textile and Apparel Council, the China Building Material Federation, the China Nonferrous Metals Industry Association, the China Electricity Council and the China Mining Association, 2008).[20] The *Guidance to Chinese Banking Finance Institutions on Corporate Social Responsibilities* was issued by the Chinese Banking Association in 2009; (Chinese Banking Association, 2009)[21] the *Implementation Manual of the Guidelines to Chinese Industrial Enterprises and Industrial Associations on Corporate Social Responsibilities* was issued in 2011.[22]

With an increasing number of Chinese companies going abroad to invest, industry associations have also been actively promoting CSR among their members and applying these to their overseas investment projects. In 2010, the China International Contractors Association (CICA) became the first industry to issue its own CSR guidelines in regard to overseas investment. CICA issued voluntary standards for Chinese companies to enhance their CSR abroad. In 2012, CICA issued the "Guide on Social Responsibility for Chinese International Contractors", which was circulated by MOFCOM in the same year (CICA, 2012).[23] In 2014, CICA built on reports voluntarily submitted by 66 Chinese companies and their branches, and edited and released the *Survey Report on Localization Practice of China's International Contractors in Africa* (CICA, 2014).[24] The report shared the practical experience of China's international contractors in localizing their operations and provided suggestions on enhancing CSR awareness and practices.[25]

More importantly for the companies in the natural resources sector, in 2014, the China Chamber of Commerce of Metals, Minerals and Chemicals Importers and Exporters (CCCMC) issued its *Guidelines for Social Responsibility in Outbound Mining Investments* (China Chamber of Commerce of Metals, Minerals & Chemicals Importers & Exporters, 2014).[26] The CCCMC social responsibility guidelines cover matters such as organisational governance, operating practices, value chain management, human rights, labour issues, vocational health and safety, the environment and community involvement and engagement.

The CCCMC Guidelines provides six paragraphs with specific measures to implement the guidelines, which include the dissemination of the guidelines, provision of training, workshops, and exchanges to strengthen the capacities of companies, encouraging the assessment of CSR by companies, conducting an evaluation of CSR performance of Chinese companies engaged in outbound mining investments according to these guidelines and disseminate best practice, regular reports and reviews every three years (China Chamber of Commerce of Metals, Minerals & Chemicals Importers & Exporters, 2014: paras 3.1 to 3.6). For example, in order to evaluate CSR performance of companies, the CCCMC Guidelines specifically require the adherence to the principles provided in the guidelines. These principles are (i) to ensure compliance with all applicable laws and regulations, (ii) to adhere to ethical business practices, (iii) to respect human rights and protect the rights and interests of employees, (iv) to respect nature and protect the environment, (v) to respect stakeholders, (vi) to strengthen responsibility through the extractive industries value chain and (vii) to strive for transparency (China Chamber of Commerce of Metals, Minerals & Chemicals Importers & Exporters, 2014: paras 1.1 and 1.7).

Statements regarding the prevailing political context in China, as well as repeating some of the basic principles of CSR found in guidelines issued by governmental agencies, can always be found in the guidelines issued by Chinese industry associations. Chinese industry associations have a special status in China, as they were often formed by converting former government agencies into relevant industry associations, but their staff are sourced from these agencies and the structural organisations and functions as the same as those of their former supervising ministries. Most of their personnel are still officially 'affiliated' (*guakao*) with these government agencies (Zheng, 2010: 669–670).

One commentator has pointed out that industry associations in China are 'quasi-governmental entities' established during the governmental reforms in the 1990s in order to provide industrial coordination and self-regulation. (Zheng, 2010: 669; and Zheng, 2015: 454) Recently, the Chinese government has tried to ensure that industry associations can become civil entities with no links with government,[27] but industry associations are still widely believed to be quasi-governmental in character. Therefore, the unique status of industry associations may mean that the guidelines created by these various associations are in fact more like orders imposed by various government agencies and that Chinese SOEs will be encouraged to follow soft rules under the supervision of these associations.

## 4.3. Chinese SOEs in Natural Resources Sector Implementing Corporate Social Responsibility Codes Abroad

According to the Report on Sustainable Development of Chinese Enterprises Overseas, more and more Chinese companies are starting to recognise and implement CSR ideas, and nearly 90% of the companies "have established or plan to establish an overseas CSR management system".[28] Most of these companies have appointed special personnel or designated special departments to implement CSR.[29] This situation is also true for many Chinese SOEs in the natural resources sector. However, according to the same report, challenges also exist among the Chinese companies seeking to implement CSR overseas.[30]

- Chinese companies' knowledge of the specific international standards and guidelines on sustainable development needs to be enhanced.
- Chinese companies need to be motivated more by such external factors as expectations of their business partners, stakeholders and local communities.
- The effective connection between CSR management system and their overseas CSR implementation departments needs to be enhanced.
- Overseas CSR reports need to be released more frequently.
- Lack of professionals, financial support and incentive/punishment systems are the major factors affecting the implementation of CSR initiatives.

Chinese SOEs implement their CSR policies by attaching importance to the national development strategies of the host countries, transferring technologies and managing experiences to host countries, mitigating impacts to the environment and ecosystem and respecting the rights of their employees, community residents and other stakeholders.

### 4.3.1. Annual Reports

The annual reports of Chinese SOEs always include a statement regarding the implementation of CSR. Before SASAC released its CSR guidelines, some Chinese central SOEs even started to issue annual reports dealing with CSR issues (SASAC).[31] Since the release of the SASAC CSR guidelines, the annual reports issued by SOEs, such as the Annual CSR Reports issued by CNOOC (China National Offshore Oil Corporation), (SASAC)[32] by Sinoche (SASAC)[33] and by China Coal (SASAC)[34] would rely upon other reports, including United Nations documents (such as the Global Compact), the Global Reporting Initiative (GRI) and CSR guidelines issued by SASAC.[35] In addition, many Chinese companies including private companies have started to issue CSR reports.[36]

The CSR issues ranging from the protection of the interests of their employees and disclosure of information regarding their corporate governance practices to wider societal issues such as environmental protection, anti-corruption and the performance of charitable work are all encompassed in the annual reports.

CITIC is one large globally active Chinese SOE; it is a diverse, state-controlled entity and the largest Chinese conglomerate now registered in Hong Kong, but operating much more widely, including having major investments in Australia. The 2014 Annual Report of the CITIC Group contained the following message, delivered by the chairman of the board of directors, Chang Zhengming, to the shareholders, referring to the subject of SOE reform and SOE social responsibilities (CITIC):[37]

> The acquisition of CITIC Group's businesses and the further diversification of our ownership base are major steps in our efforts to be a world-class company and a leader in state-owned enterprise reform. Not only were these decisions the right ones for our company and our shareholders, they were also a positive development for corporate China and a vote of confidence in Hong Kong's capital markets and community.
>
> We are truly rooted here in Hong Kong, literally and figuratively. We are a key constituent of the Hang Seng Index. We operate tunnels that are the main arteries connecting Hong Kong Island to Kowloon, and CITIC Tower is a key part of the Hong Kong skyline. We have been an active member of the local corporate community for thirty years. In short, we are one of the anchors of corporate life in Hong Kong, and we are proud of that.
>
> We also want to be open and humble and challenge ourselves to do more for Hong Kong. The CITIC approach is that wherever we operate, we have a responsibility to that community. The geographic spread of our interests and projects is vast—from the bustling streets of Hong Kong to the remote country towns fringing the Australian outback. Our positive commitment to these communities has been consistent.

The 2015 Annual Report of the CITIC Group also showcased the CSR-related activities engaged in by CITIC Group's subsidiaries overseas (CITIC, 2015: 156–157). CITIC Pacific Mining is a company controlled by CITIC Limited and has business operations in Australia in exploiting iron ore. This company also commits to the improvement of health and safety, environment, community, heritage and local opportunities in their Sino Iron Project (CITIC).[38]

### 4.3.2. CSR Case Cameos[39]

THE CITIC CONSTRUCTION CO LTD (CITIC)[40]

This company built a 20,000-unit social housing project in Kilamba-Kiax, Luanda (the KK Project), in 2014 in accordance with the development policy of the Angolan government in order to restore Angola after its 27 years of civil war. The project not only provided housing, hospitals and schools, but it also boosted local employment and production of building materials by employing local people and building up factories to supply the materials needed for the building projects.

CHINA INTERNATIONAL TELECOMMUNICATION CONSTRUCTION
CORPORATION (CITCC) AND (CITCC)[41]

CITCC has completed several fiber optic networks projects since 2009 to
help Tanzania become an IT and communication hub. The projects include
five phased projects and so far the CITCC has completed Phase I, Phase
II and stage I of Phase III of the whole project with an aggregate contract value of the (now completed) first two phases of the project valued
at $170 million. The total of 7,560 kilometers of fiber optic cable laid
by CITCC has lowered local communication costs and has prompted an
explosive growth of users, which has enabled Tanzanians to enjoy sustainable electronic services and facilitated technology spillover and inter-
regional communication.

CHINA MACHINERY ENGINEERING CORPORATION (CMEC)[42]

CMEC has provided power supplies in Sri Lanka after the completion of
construction projects of various power plants. CMEC also offered electrical
technician training program in Sri Lanka and organised training to ensure
sound operation and maintenance of these power plants. The executive secretary of the Ministry of Power and Energy of Sri Lanka spoke in praise of
these developments: "By helping us train a pool of electric power specialists,
CMEC has assisted Sri Lanka in laying a solid foundation for the development of its power industry."

CHINA NATIONAL PETROLEUM CORPORATION (CNPC)[43] AND SINOPEC (SINOPEC)[44]

These companies established a joint venture, Andes Petroleum Ecuador
Ltd., to operate oilfield in Ecuador. Early in 1997, CNPC adopted the
ISO140001 standards for environmental management system. Therefore,
it developed and implemented strict safety and environmental protection
systems and processes in accordance with the highest industrial standards
to operate the oilfields in Ecuador, including developing a series of environmental management rules and plans to ensure the implementation of
an effective environmental management system, emission reduction indicators, monitoring and evaluation system. It adopted a three-year rainforest
pollution control plan regarding management of oilfield operations and
stipulated that Andes Petroleum submit environmental reports at every link
of its production.

CHINA NONFERROUS METAL MINING (GROUP) CO., LTD.
(CNMC OR THE "GROUP") (CNMC)[45]

CNMC has invested more than $2.6 billion in Zambia, paid nearly $300 million in taxes, created 10,000 local jobs and has donated $20 million locally.
CNMC has specifically established a safety and environmental protection

department dedicated to environmental management and employed a qualified environmental officer to take charge of related work. CNMC also adopted green circular economy initiatives that have produced remarkable results in energy conservation and emission reduction.

MINERALS AND METALS GROUP AND CMC[46]

MMG is an affiliate of China Minmetals Corporation, which has extensive mining operations in Australia, Laos and Democratic Republic of Congo. MMG invested in the Sepon mine located in Southern Laos, but also supported and engaged with local communities. It has established community development funds to improve infrastructure and has funded education in local communities. It has also built a cultural museum to preserve the cultural heritage of the indigenous people.

## 5. Observations and Conclusions

The adoption of CSR norms and policies by Chinese SOEs abroad is, firstly, a response to the requirements of modern corporate governance and the requirements of the international and local legal environment. The rise of the new *lex mercatoria*, as have been suggested by a number of leading scholars, has provided the greatest prospects for the rising importance of CSR principles in the globalised space (see further, Backer, 2016; Michaels, 2007; Teubner, 2002; Tamanaha, 2008; and Zumbansen, 2011). The creation of multilateral codes of conduct for corporations, such as the *OECD Guidelines for Multinational Enterprises*, will inevitably influence non-OECD countries; this has seen China's use of the *OECD Principles of Corporate Governance* as the model for its own code of corporate governance for listed companies (CSRC: 2001). With the increasing investment by Chinese SOEs overseas, these SOEs have been exposed to a more challenging legal and investment foreign environment so that they are constantly under scrutiny by foreign regulators. The fear of losing their reputations or even their investment opportunities has driven Chinese SOEs to turn to CSR to regulate themselves internally.

However, the implementation of CSR by Chinese SOEs abroad still remains under the influence of the party-state. The party-state control is a strong feature of Chinese SOEs, (Tomasic and Xiong, 2015; also see Lin and Milhaupt, 2013) and while implementing CSR abroad by Chinese SOEs, SOEs will be subject to the control of the Chinese government. According to Professor Ho (2013: 432–433), China has adopted a state-centric model of CSR, which contrasts with the market-based CSR model adopted by the United States and the relational model promoted in the EU. This top-down model of CSR implementation is a reflection of the dominant feature of party-state control of Chinese SOEs. The large number of CSR-related guidelines and provisions issued by various Chinese ministries or state administrative agencies is a manifestation of the Chinese government's

*Table 2.1* Key Policies and Regulations Regarding Sustainable Overseas Development by Chinese Companies

| Issue Date | Issuer | Title |
|---|---|---|
| 2001 | China Securities Regulatory Commission and the State Economic and Trade Commission | *Code of Corporate Governance for Listed Companies in China* |
| 2002 | Ministry of Foreign Trade and Economic Cooperation (MFTEC) | *Comprehensive Evaluation Measures for the Performance of Overseas Investments (Trial)* |
| 2002 | MFTEC, State Administration of Foreign Exchange (SAFE) | *Interim Measures for Joint Annual Inspection of Overseas Investment* |
| 2004 | Ministry of Commerce (MOFCOM) | *Measures for the Administration of Training of Workers Dispatched Overseas* |
| 2004 | MOFCOM | *Reporting System for Investment and Operation Obstacles in Foreign Countries* |
| 2005 | MOFCOM | *Notice of the State Administration of Foreign Exchange Regarding Adjustment to the Administration of Financing Guarantee from Domestic Banks for Enterprises with Foreign Investment* |
| 2005 | State Administration of Work Safety (SAWS), Ministry of Foreign Affairs (MFA), MOFCOM, State-Owned Assets Supervision and Administration Commission (SASAC) | *Notice of the State Administration of Work Safety, Ministry of Foreign Affairs, Ministry of Commerce, State-owned Assets Supervision and Administration Commission on Improving Work Safety Supervision of Overseas Chinese Enterprises* |
| 2005 | General Office of the State Council | *Opinions on Strengthening the Security and Protection of Overseas Chinese Enterprises and Staff* |
| 2007 | MOFCOM, Ministry of Finance, People's Bank of China, All-China Federation of Industry and Commerce (ACFIC) | *Opinions of the Ministry of Commerce, the Ministry of Finance, the People's Bank of China and All-China Federation of Industry and Commerce on Encouraging and Guiding Overseas Investment and Cooperation by Private Enterprises* |
| 2007 | State Forestry Administration (SFA), MOFCOM | *Guidelines on Sustainable Forest Cultivation for Chinese Enterprises Overseas* |
| 2007 | SASAC | *Guidelines to the State-Owned Enterprises Directly under the Central Government on Fulfilling Corporate Social Responsibilities Guidelines* |

| Issue Date | Issuer | Title |
|---|---|---|
| 2008 | MOFCOM, MFA, SASAC | *Notice of the Ministry of Commerce, Ministry of Foreign Affairs, State-owned Assets Supervision and Administration Commission on Further Regulating Overseas Investment and Cooperation of Chinese Enterprises* |
| 2008 | State Council | *Administrative Rules for Overseas Contracting* |
| 2009 | SFA, MOFCOM | *Guidelines on Sustainable Operation and Utilization of Overseas Forests by Chinese Enterprises* |
| 2009 | MOFCOM, Ministry of Housing and Urban-Rural Development (MOHURD) | *Measures for the Administration of Overseas Contracting Qualification* |
| 2010 | Ministry of Finance | *Guidelines No. 4 of Internal Enterprises Control Application – Social Responsibilities* |
| 2010 | MOFCOM, China Export and Credit Insurance Corporation | *Notice on Strengthening Risk Prevention in Overseas Economic and Trade Cooperation Zones* |
| 2010 | MOFCOM, MFA, National Development and Reform Commission (NDRC) | Ministry of Public Security (MPS), SASAC, SAWS, ACFIC<br>*Provisions on the Security Management of Overseas Chinese Institutions and Staff* |
| 2010 | MOFCOM | *Overseas Security Risk Warning and Information Notification System in Overseas Investment and Cooperation* |
| 2011 | MOFCOM, MFA, SASAC, ACFIC | *Guidelines on Security Management of Overseas Chinese Enterprises (Institutions) and Staff* |
| 2011 | SASAC | *Interim Measures for the Administration of Overseas State-owned Property Rights of Central Enterprises* |
| 2011 | SASAC | *Interim Measures for the Supervision and Administration of Overseas Assets of Central Enterprises* |
| 2012 | MOFCOM | *Guidelines on Security Management of Overseas Chinese Enterprises and Staff* |
| 2012 | China Banking Regulatory Commission | Green Credit Policy |
| 2012 | MOFCOM, International Communication Office of the CPC Central Committee, MFA, NDRC, SASAC, National Bureau of Corruption Prevention, ACFIC | *Opinions on Corporate Culture Development of Chinese Enterprises Overseas* |

(*Continued*)

*Table 2.1* (Continued)

| Issue Date | Issuer | Title |
|---|---|---|
| 2012 | SASAC | *Interim Measures for the Supervision and Administration of Overseas Investment of Central Enterprises* |
| 2013 | MOFCOM, SAWS, MFA, NDRC, MOHURD, SASAC | *Notice of the Ministry of Commerce, State Administration of Work Safety, Ministry of Foreign Affairs, National Development and Reform Commission, Ministry of Housing and Urban & Rural Development, State-owned Assets Supervision and Administration Commission on General Inspection of Work Safety Governance of Chinese Enterprises Overseas* |
| 2013 | MOFCOM, Ministry of Environmental Protection | *Guidelines on Environmental Protection in Overseas Investment and Cooperation* |
| 2013 | SASAC | *Interim Measures for Emergency Management of Central Enterprises* |
| 2013 | MOFCOM | *Provisions on Regulating Competition in Overseas Investment and Cooperation* |
| 2013 | MOFCOM, MFA, MOHURD, National Health and Family Planning Commission, SASAC, SAWS | *Provisions on Responding to and Addressing Security Incidents in Overseas Investment and Cooperation* |
| 2013 | MOFCOM, MFA, MPS, MOHURD, General Administration of Customs, State Administration of Taxation, State Administration for Industry and Commerce, General Administration of Quality Supervision, Inspection and Quarantine, SAFE | *Trial Measures for Negative Credit Record in Overseas Investment, Cooperation and Foreign Trade* |
| 2013 | MOFCOM | *Notice of the Ministry of Commerce on Strengthening the Categorized Administration of Chinese Personnel Dispatched Overseas for Overseas Investment and Cooperation* |
| 2014 | MOFCOM | *Guidelines on Intellectual Property Right of Overseas Enterprises* |
| 2014 | MOFCOM | *Measures for the Administration of Overseas Investment* |
| 2015 | China Insurance Regulatory Commission | *Guidelines on the Fulfilling Corporate Social Responsibilities of Chinese Insurance Companies* |

| Issue Date | Issuer | Title |
|---|---|---|
| 2015 | NDRC, MFA, MOFCOM | *Vision and Proposed Actions Outlined on Jointly Building Silk Road Economic Belt and 21st-Century Maritime Silk Road* |
| 2016 | AQSIQ and the SAC | *Guidelines on Social Responsibilities, Guidelines for Compiling the Report of Social Responsibilities Guidelines for Classification of Performance Indication of Social Responsibilities* |

Source: Table 2.1 is based on the 2015 *Report on the Sustainable Development of Chinese Enterprises Overseas* (Chinese Academy of International Trade and Economic Cooperation Ministry of Commerce; Research Center of the State-Owned Assets Supervision and Administration Commission of the State Council; United Nations Development Programme China); pp. 15–17.

control over the implementation of CSR. Although the top-down approach to the implementation of CSR can, on the one hand, facilitate CSR implementation by SOEs, the actual implementation of CSR ideas by Chinese SOEs may remain somewhat cosmetic. The slogan-laden language used in the Annual Reports of some Chinese SOEs is the result of this kind of top-down approach to regulation.

Nevertheless, the implementation of CSR by Chinese SOEs operating abroad has actually created some limited positive outcomes for SOEs and may to some degree help Chinese SOEs meet the investment and legal challenges that they face abroad. However, the effectiveness of the implementation of CSR by Chinese SOEs abroad is yet to be established due to a lack of more detailed case studies, especially more case studies of the implementation of CSR in OECD countries where higher legal and investment standards for non-economic interests are usually imposed. The party-state controls over Chinese SOEs will inevitably cause Chinese SOEs to face more challenges and create more obstacles to their investment overseas, but the adoption and implementation of CSR may ease these kinds of difficulties if the implementation of CSR by SOEs abroad can be real and effective. Therefore, a more effective implementation of CSR in countries such as Australia can potentially facilitate the more successful investment outcomes by Chinese SOEs abroad. Table 2.1 provides a list of the key PRC policies and regulations regarding sustainable overseas development by Chinese companies.

## Notes

1. PRC, Ministry of Commerce, <http://hzs.mofcom.gov.cn/article/aa/201601/20160101236264.shtml> (last accessed on 10 November 2016).

2. Australia's Foreign Investment Policy (last updated 1 July 2016 by the Treasurer) 8–11, available at <http://firb.gov.au/files/2015/09/Australias-Foreign-Invest ment-Policy-2016-2017.pdf>. It provides "the Government considers the extent to which the investor operates on a transparent commercial basis and is subject to adequate and transparent regulation and supervision. The Government also considers the corporate governance practices of foreign investors."

3. Submission to the Department of Foreign Affairs and Trade Concerning Negotiating Priorities for the Proposed Australia-China FTA, 2005 and Opportunities and Challenges: Australia's relationship with China, 2005. The Australian Conservation Foundation raised the issue of Australian government's narrow economic focus in its feasibility study on Australia—China Free Trade Agreement. See Submission to the Department of Foreign Affairs and Trade Concerning Negotiating Priorities for the Proposed Australia-China FTA (June 2005, Prepared by Michael Kerr, ACF Adviser on Trade). Also see "Opportunities and Challenges: Australia's Relationship with China" (Commonwealth Government of Australia, 10 November 2005), Chapter 14. Available at www.aph.gov.au/ Parliamentary_Business/Committees/Senate/Foreign_Affairs_Defence_and_Trade/ Completed_inquiries/2004-07/china/report01/index.

4. See further, para 27 of the Decision on the Several Important Issues to Improve the Socialist Market Economy (adopted by the Third Plenary Session of the Sixteenth National Congress of CPC, 23 October 2003). [关于完善社会主义市场经济体制的若干重大问题的决定].

5. See for example the State Council has promulgated the [关于鼓励和规范我国企业对外投资合作的意见] [*Opinion on the Encouragement and Standardization of the Domestic Enterprises to Invest and Cooperate Abroad*] (State Council, October, 2006). The change of domestic laws can be found in the more favourable tax support and more favourable finance support from the government.

6. For the Belt and Road Initiative, see the State Council of PRC website, available at <http://english.gov.cn/beltAndRoad/>.

7. See further, Chapter 17 of draft TPP, available at <https://ustr.gov/sites/default/ files/TPP-Final-Text-State-Owned-Enterprises-and-Designated-Monopolies.pdf>.

8. See further, <https://ustr.gov/sites/default/files/TPP-Chapter-Summary-State-Owned-Enterprises.pdf> at pp. 4–5.

9. See further at Australia's Foreign Investment Policy (last updated 1 July 2016 by the Treasurer) 8–11, available at: <http://firb.gov.au/files/2015/09/Australias-Foreign-Investment-Policy-2016-2017.pdf>.

10. [2012] HCA 39.

11. The Alaska Oil Spill Commission Final Report, *Spill—The Wreck of the Exxon Valdez*, February 1990 at <www.arlis.org/docs/vol1/B/33339870.pdf.>.

12. For example, India and Indonesia have both introduced CSR laws. In the case of Indonesia, it has enacted mandatory corporate social responsibility provisions in statutes applicable respectively with mining companies, foreign investment and state-owned enterprises; for example, Article 74(1) of the *Indonesian Limited Liability Company Law* (Law No 40/2007) imposes an obligation on natural resources companies to engage in environmental social responsibility.

13. The Company Law of the People's Republic of China (revised and adopted at the Eighteenth Meeting of the Standing Committee of the Tenth National People's Congress of the People's Republic of China on 27 October 2005, and promulgated and effective as of 1 January 2006).

14. 2015 Report on the Sustainable Development of Chinese Enterprises Overseas (Chinese Academy of International Trade and Economic Cooperation Ministry of Commerce; Research Center of the State-owned Assets Supervision and Administration Commission of the State Council; United Nations Development Programme China) 15–17.

15. Ibid, 18–123.

16. Ibid, 18–19.
17. *Guidelines on Social Responsibilities* [社会责任指南] GB/T 36000–32015), *Guidelines for Compiling the Report of Social Responsibilities* [《社会责任报告编写指南》] (GB/T 36001–32015), *Guidelines for Classification of Performance Indication of Social Responsibilities* 《 [社会责任绩效分类指引] (GB/T 36002–32015; available at: www.cnis.gov.cn/ . . . /P020140512224950804830.pdf.
18. Preamble of the Guidelines, available at:<http://en.sasac.gov.cn/n1408035/c1477196/content.html.>.
19. See further at <http://en.sasac.gov.cn/n1408035/c1477196/content.html>.
20. This was jointly issued by the China Federation of Industrial Economics, the China National Coal Association, the China Machinery Industry Federation, the China Iron and Steel Industry Association, the China Petroleum and Chemical Industry Federation, the China National Light Industry Council, the China National Textile and Apparel Council, the China Building Material Federation, the China Nonferrous Metals Industry Association, the China Electricity Council and the China Mining Association. Now the second version prevails. See images.mofcom.gov.cn/csr/ . . . /1281064433802.pdf.
21. *Guidance to Chinese Banking Finance Institutions on Corporate Social Responsibilities*, (Chinese Banking Association, 12 January 2009). [中国银行业金融机构企业社会责任指引].
22. See further at: <www.cfie.org.cn/2710757099819/2724937977050/1336/2724937977199.html> [中国工业协会社会责任指南实施手册].
23. See further at: <www.mofcom.gov.cn/article/ae/ai/201209/20120908364916.shtml>
24. Survey Report on Localization Practice of China's International Contractors in Africa [中国国际承包商非洲本土化实践调查报告]; Available at <www.mofcom.gov.cn/article/huiyuan/xuehuidongtai/201403/20140300526463.shtml>.
25. 2015 Report on the Sustainable Development of Chinese Enterprises Overseas (Chinese Academy of International Trade and Economic Cooperation Ministry of Commerce; Research Center of the State-owned Assets Supervision and Administration Commission of the State Council; United Nations Development Programme China) 24.
26. *Guidelines for Social Responsibility in Outbound Mining Investments* (China Chamber of Commerce of Metals, Minerals & Chemicals Importers & Exporters, 2014).
27. For example, in 1997, in order to establish of more self-governed industrial associations, the National Economic and Trade Committee issued *Plans for Choosing Several Cities for Pilot Industrial Associations* [关于选择若干城市进行行业协会试点的方案]. In 2007, the General Office of the State Council issued *Several Opinions on Quickening the Reforms of Industrial Associations* [国务院办公厅关于加快推进行业协会商会改革和发展的若干意见]. In 2009, the State Council even started to draft the *Law on Industrial Associations and Chambers of Commerce*; See at <http://news.xinhuanet.com/politics/2009-12/06/content_12598306.htm>. In 2015, the State Council established a Working Group to deal with separating Industrial Associations from Government Agencies; see the Circular of the State Council on Establishing Working Group to Separate Industrial Associations from Government Agencies, (6 July 2015, State Council of PRC) [国务院办公厅关于成立行业协会商会与行政机关脱钩联合工作组的通知].
28. Report on Sustainable Development of Chinese Enterprises Overseas (Chinese Academy of International Trade and Economic Cooperation Ministry of Commerce; Research Center of the State-owned Assets Supervision and Administration Commission of the State Council; United Nations Development Programme China, 2015) 103.
29. Ibid.
30. Ibid.

31. See further at: <www.sasac.gov.cn/n1180/n4175042/n4175059/>.
32. See further at: <www.sasac.gov.cn/2010rdzt/yjj/zhy2009.pdf>.
33. See further at: <www.sasac.gov.cn/2010rdzt/yjj/zh2009.pdf>.
34. See further at: <www.sasac.gov.cn/2010rdzt/yjj/zm2009.pdf>.
35. Other such reports of SOEs can be found at www.sasac.gov.cn/n1180/n4175042/n4175059/>.
36. The information can be found here <www.csrreport.cn>.
37. See further at <www.citic.com/Managed/Resources/docs/FinancialReports/ENG/ar2014e.pdf
38. See www.citicpacificmining.com/our-responsibilities/health-safety/>.
39. The source of the following information is from 2015 Report on the Sustainable Development of Chinese Enterprises Overseas (Chinese Academy of International Trade and Economic Cooperation Ministry of Commerce; Research Center of the State-owned Assets Supervision and Administration Commission of the State Council; United Nations Development Programme China).
40. CITIC Construction Co., Ltd. [中信建设有限责任公司] <www.construction.citic/iwcm/cici/en/ns:LHQ6MTYyLGY6NDM3LGM6LHA6LGE6LG06/channel.vsml>.
     China International Telecommunication Construction Corporation (CITCC) [中国通信建设集团有限公司]; <www.citcc.cn/worldwide/en/index.aspx>.
41. China International Telecommunication Construction Corporation (CITCC) [中国通信建设集团有限公司]; <www.citcc.cn/worldwide/en/index.aspx>.
42. China Machinery Engineering Corporation ("CMEC") [中国机械设备工程股份有限公司]; <www.cmec.com/html/>.
43. China National Petroleum Corporation (CNPC) [中国石油天然气集团公司]; <www.cnpc.com.cn/en/>.
44. China Petrochemical Corporation (Sinopec Group) [中国石油化工集团公司]; <www.sinopecgroup.com/group/en/>.
45. China Nonferrous Metal Mining (Group) Co., Ltd. (CNMC) [中国有色集团]; <www.cnmc.com.cn/outlineen.jsp?column_no=12>.
46. China Minmetals Corporation (CMC) [五矿资源有限公司]; <www.mmg.com/>.

# References

American Enterprise Institute and the Heritage Foundation 2005–2016, "China global investment tracker", available: www.aei.org/china-global-investment-tracker/.

Backer, LC. 2016, "A lex mercatoria for corporate social responsibility codes without the state?: On the regulatory character of private corporate codes", *Indiana Journal of Global Legal Studies,* vol. 23, no. 2, p. 1–26.

BBC News 2016, "Australia blocks Ausgrid energy grid sale to Chinese companies", 19 August 2016, available: www.bbc.com/news/business-37129047.

Black, J. 2011, "The rise, fall and fate of principles based regulation", in Moloney, N. and Alexander, K. (eds.) *Law reform and financial markets*, Edward Elgar, Cheltenham.

Black, J. 2015, "Regulatory styles and supervisory strategies", in Moloney, N., Ferran, E. and Payne, J. (eds.) *The Oxford handbook of financial regulation*, Oxford University Press, Oxford, pp. 217–253.

Bu, Q. 2015, "Will Chinese legal culture constrain its corporate governance-related laws?" *Journal of Corporate Law Studies*, vol. 15, p. 103.

Buckley, P. J., Cross, A., Tan, H., Liu, X. and Voss, H. 2010, "Chapter 7: Historic and emergent trends in Chinese outward direct investment", in Buckley, P. J. (ed.)

*Foreign direct investment, China and the world economy*, Palgrave Macmillan, Houndmills.

Campbell, D. 2014, "Good faith and the ubiquity of the 'relational contract'", *Modern Law Review*, vol. 77, p. 475–492.

Carroll, A. B. 2008, "A history of corporate social responsibility: Concepts and practices", in Crane, A., Matten, D., McWilliams, A., Moon, J. and Siegel, D. S. (eds.) *The Oxford handbook of corporate social responsibility*: Oxford Handbook [Online], available: www.oxfordhandbooks.com/view/10.1093/oxfordhb/9780199211593.001.0001/oxfordhb-9780199211593-e-002.

China Chamber of Commerce of Metals, Minerals & Chemicals Importers & Exporters 2014, *Guidelines for social responsibility in outbound mining investments*.

Chinese Academy of International Trade and Economic Cooperation Ministry of Commerce; Research Center of the State-owned Assets Supervision and Administration Commission of the State Council; United Nations Development Programme China 2015, *Report on sustainable development of Chinese enterprises overseas*.

Chinese Banking Association 2009, *Guidance to Chinese banking finance institutions on corporate social responsibilities* [中国银行业金融机构企业社会责任指引].

CICA 2012, *Guide on social responsibility for Chinese international contractors* [中国对外承包工程行业社会责任指引].

CICA 2014, *Survey report on localization practice of China's international contractors in Africa* [中国国际承包商非洲本土化实践调查报告], available: http://www.mofcom.gov.cn/article/huiyuan/xuehuidongtai/201403/20140300526463.shtml.

CITIC 2015, *CITIC annual report 2015*, available: www.citic.com/Managed/Resources/docs/FinancialReports/ENG/fy2015e.pdf.

Coglianese, C. and Mendelson, E. 2015, "Meta-regulation and self-regulation", in Baldwin, R., Cave, M. and Lodge (ed.) *The Oxford handbook of regulation*, Oxford University Press, Oxford.

Corbett, A. 2014, "Corporate social responsibility: Do we have good cause to be sceptical about it?" *Griffith Law Review*, vol. 17, no. 413.

CPC 2003, *Decision on the several important issues to improve the socialist market economy* [关于完善社会主义市场经济体制的若干重大问题的决定].

CPC 2014, *Central committee decision concerning several major issues in comprehensively advancing governance according to law* [中共中央关于全面推进依法治国若干重大问题的决定].

CPC and the State Council of PRC 2015, *Guideline to deepen reforms of state-owned enterprises (SOEs)* [中共中央、国务院关于深化国有企业改革的指导意见].

CSRC 2001, *Code of corporate governance for listed companies in China*, Issued by the China Securities Regulatory Commission and the State Economic and Trade Commission, January 7, 2001 (Zhengjianfa No.1 of 2002), available: www.ecgi.org/codes/documents/code_en.pdf.

CSRC 2001, *Guidelines for introducing independent directors to the board of directors of listed companies* (Zhengjianfa [2001]) No. 102, available: www.csrc.gov.cn/pub/csrc_en/newsfacts/release/200708/t20070810_69191.html.

CSRC and SETC, [China Securities Regulatory Commission (CSRC) and the State Economic and Trade Commission (SETC)] 2001, *Code of corporate governance* for listed companies in China (Zhengjianfa No.1 of 2002), available: www.ecgi. org/codes/documents/code_en.pdf.

Drysdale, P. 2013, "Foreword", in Nicoll, G., Brennan, G. and Golley, J. (ed.) *The Australia-China investment relationship: Law, governance and policy*, Australian Centre on China and the World, ANU, Canberra.

Evans, N. W. 2013, "Recent Australian transactions", in Nicoll, G., Brennan, G. and Golley, J. (eds.) *The Australia-China investment relationship*, Australian Centre on China in the World, ANU, Canberra, p. 65.

Fitzgerald, B. and Burrell, A. 2014, "Palmer inflames fight with Chinese", *The Australian*, 7 February 2014.

Fitzgerald, B. and Packham, B. 2014, "Clive Steps Up Attack, Robb Warns on Fallout", *The Weekend Australian*, 8–9 February 2014.

Fleming, P. and Jones, M. T. 2013, *The end of corporate social responsibility: Crisis and critique*, Sage Publications Ltd., London.

Freed, J. and Chessell, J. 2013, "Yancoal Chief Executive Now Required", *The Australian Financial Review*, 11 February 2013.

Garriga, E. and Melé, D. 2004, "Corporate social responsibility theories: Mapping the territory", *Journal of Business Ethics*, vol. 53, no. 1, p. 51.

Gerritson, N. 2013, "Palmer takes on CITIC over port 'Obstruction'", *The Australian Financial Review*, 26 April 2013.

Gersen, J. E. and Posner, E. A. 2008, "Soft law: Lessons from congressional practice", *Stanford Law Review*, vol. 61, no. 573, p. 573–627.

He, W. 2002, *In the name of justice—striving for the rule of law in China*, Brookings Institution Press, Washington, DC.

Ho, V. H. 2013, "Beyond regulation: A comparative look at state-centric corporate social responsibility and the law in China", *Vanderbilt Journal of Transnational Law*, vol. 46, p. 375.

Horrigan, B. 2010, *Corporate social responsibility in the 21st century*, Edward Elgar, Cheltenham.

Huang, X. and Austin, I. 2011, *Chinese investment in Australia: Unique insights from the mining industry.* Palgrave Macmillan, London, UK.

Ker, P. 2014a, "Palmer accuses China's CITIC of 'Stealing Australian Resources'", *The Sydney Morning Herald*, Sydney.

Ker, P. 2014b, "Palmer spat risks China investment", *The Australian Financial Review*, 7 February 2014.

KPMG and the University of Sydney 2013, *Demystifying Chinese Investment in Australia.*

KPMG and the University of Sydney 2015, *Demystifying Chinese Investment in Australia.*

KPMG and the University of Sydney 2016, *Demystifying Chinese Investment in Australia.*

Kretser, A. de and Gerritsen, N. 2013, "Chinese going too far: Palmer", *The Australian Financial Review*, (22 April 2013).

Levy, D. L. and Kaplan, R. 2008, "Corporate social responsibility and theories of global governance: Strategic contestation in global issue arenas", in Crane, A., Matten, D., McWilliams, A., Moon, J. and Siegel, D. S. (eds.) *The Oxford handbook of corporate social responsibility*, Oxford University Press, Oxford, pp. 432–451.

Lin, L. W. 2009, "Legal transplants through private contracting: Codes of vendor conduct in global supply chains as an example", *American Journal of Comparative Law*, vol. 57, p. 711.

Lin, L-W. 2010, "Corporate social responsibility in China: Window dressing or structural change?" *Berkeley Journal of International Law*, vol. 28, no. 64, p. 64–100.

Lin, L-W. and Milhaupt, C. 2013, "We are the (national) champions: Understanding the mechanisms of state capitalism in China", *Stanford Law Review*, vol. 65, p. 697.

Macaulay, S. 1963, "Non-Contractual relations in business", *American Sociological Review*, vol. 28, no. 1, p. 55–67.

Mather, L. and Yngvesson, B. 1980, "Language, audience and the transformation of disputes", *Law & Society Review*, vol. 15, p. 775–821.

Michaels, R. 2007 "The true lex mercatoria: Law beyond the state", *Indiana Journal of Global Legal Studies*, vol. 14, no. 2, p. 447–468.

Ministry of Commerce of PRC 2016, *Ministry of commerce of the people's republic of China department of outward investment and economic cooperation*, A Talk by the Responsible Chief of the Department Outward Investment and Economic Cooperation about the Situation of Outward Investment and Economic Cooperation [商务部合作司负责人谈2015年我国对外投资合作情况], available: http://hzs.mofcom.gov.cn/article/aa/201601/20160101236264.shtml, accessed on 10 November 2016.

MOFCOM 2013, *Guidance on environmental protection in foreign investment and cooperation*, available: http://english.mofcom.gov.cn/article/newsrelease/significant news/201303/20130300043146.shtml, available: http://hzs.mofcom.gov.cn/article/zcfb/b/201302/20130200039909.shtml.

MOFCOM 2013, *Provisions on regulating competition in overseas investment and cooperation*, issued by the Ministry of Commerce on 18 March 2013 [Shang He Fa (2013) No. 88], available: www.mofcom.gov.cn/article/b/g/201309/20130900322914.shtml.

Nolan, P. 2012, *Is China buying the world?* Polity Press, Cambridge.

Parker, Christine 2002, "Meta-regulation: The regulation of self-regulation", in Parker, C. (ed.) *The open corporation—Effective self-regulation and democracy*, Cambridge University Press, Cambridge, pp. 245–291.

Peerenboom, R. 2002, *China's long March toward rule of law*, Cambridge University Press, Cambridge.

PWC and Confederation of Indian Industry 2013, *Handbook on corporate social responsibility in India*, available: www.pwc.in/assets/pdfs/publications/2013/handbook-on-corporate-social-responsibility-in-india.pdf

Robe, J. P., Lyon-Cazen, A. and Vermac, S. (eds.) 2016, *Multinationals and the Constitutionalization of the world power system*, Routledge, Abingdon.

Robilant, A. D. 2006, "Genealogies of soft law", *The American Journal of Comparative Law*, vol. 54, p. 499.

SASAC 2008, *Guidelines to the state-owned enterprises directly under the central government on fulfilling corporate social responsibilities*, available: http://en.sasac.gov.cn/n1408035/c1477196/content.html.

SASAC 2011, *Implementation guidelines for the twelfth five-year plan for the harmonious development of central enterprises* [中央企业"十二五"和谐发展战略

实施纲要], available: www.sasac.gov.cn/n85463/n327265/n327567/n327598/c1657262/content.html

State Council 2006, *Opinion on the encouragement and standardization of the domestic enterprises to invest and cooperate abroad* [关于鼓励和规范我国企业对外投资合作的意见].

Sukmono, A. F. 2013, "The legal framework of CSR in Indonesia", in Lambooy, T., Kusumadara, A., Argyrou, A. and Istiqomah, M. (eds.) *CSR in Indonesia: Legislative developments and case studies*, Konstitusi Press, Utrecht University and Brawijaya University, Malang, Indonesia, available at SSRN: http://ssrn.com/abstract=2270580.

Tamanaha, B. Z. 2008, "Understanding legal pluralism past to resent, local to global", 30 *Sydney Law Review*, vol. 30, p. 375–411.

Teubner, G. 1983, "Substantive and reflexive elements in modern law", *Law and Society Review*, vol. 17, no. 2, p. 239.

Teubner, G. 1993, *Law as an autopoietic system*, Blackwell Publishers, Oxford.

Teubner, G. 1998, "Legal irritants: Good faith in British law or how unifying law ends up in new divergences", *Modern Law Review*, vol. 61, no. 1, pp. 11–32.

Teubner, G, 2002, "Breaking frames: Economic globalization and the emergence of lex mercatoria", *European Journal of Social Theory*, vol. 5, no. 2, p. 199–217.

Tomasic, R. 2014, "Corporate governance in Chinese-listed companies going global", *The Chinese Journal of Comparative Law*, vol. 2, no. 1, p. 155.

Tomasic, R. 2015, "Company law implementation in the PRC—the rule of law in the shadow of the state", *The Journal of Corporate Law Studies*, vol. 15, no. 2, pp. 285–309.

Tomasic, R. and Xiong, P. 2015, "Chinese state-owned enterprises in Australia - Legal and investment challenges", *Australian Journal of Corporate Law*, vol. 30, no. 2, p. 151–176.

Treasurer, G. 2016, *Australia's foreign investment policy*, available: http://firb.gov.au/files/2015/09/Australias-Foreign-Investment-Policy-2016-2017.pdf.

UNCTAD 2015, *World investment report 2015: Reforming international investment governance*, available: http://unctad.org/en/pages/PublicationWebflyer.aspx?publicationid=1245

Xinhua New Group 2012, "中央经济会议闭幕 明确提出改革总体方案", (The economic meeting of the central committee has been closed and a general reform plan was proposed) available at: http://finance.people.com.cn/n/2012/1216/c1004-19913110.html.

Yao, X. 2002, *An introduction to Confucianism*, Cambridge University Press, Cambridge.

Zhao, J. 2014, *Corporate social responsibility in contemporary China*, Edward Elgar, Cheltenham.

Zheng, W. 2010, "Transplanting antitrust in China: Economic transition, market structure, and state control", *University of Pennsylvania Journal of International Law*, vol. 32, p. 643.

Zheng, W. 2015, "Competition law in China", in Duns, J., Duke, A. and Sweeney, B. (eds.) *Comparative competition law (Research handbook)*, Edward Elgar, Cheltenham, p. 443.

Zumbansen, P. 2011, "Neither 'public' nor 'private', 'national' nor 'international'; transnational corporate governance from a legal pluralist perspective", *Journal of Law and Society*, vol. 38, no. 1, p. 50–75.

# 3 Extractive Governance, Environmental Management and Community Engagement
## China Versus Global

*Xinting Jia*

## 1. Introduction

Operating in a high-risk sector, extractive companies often face more challenges than companies in other sectors in terms of balancing economic interest, protecting the environment and engaging with the communities that they are operating within. The globalisation of China's extractive companies through acquisition of assets worldwide makes it important to understand how social and environmental risks are managed by these companies. The government controlled nature of these companies also suggests that the major shareholder—i.e., the Chinese government—could play an important role in shaping the environmental, social and community practices of these companies.

In order to help us gain a better understanding of how China's global resources companies are managing their environmental and social obligations, this chapter employs a comparative approach and reviews environmental and community practices of leading Chinese extractive companies and compares these with those of their global peers.

The sheer size of mining projects and the complexity in managing relationships with a host government, as well as with the community, make it an important subject to study. To facilitate a better understanding of the practices of China's global extractive companies, this chapter will first generally discuss the development of 'social' responsibility of companies, followed by a review of the stakeholders' role in the governance of extractive companies in China as well as globally. Key issues and risks in the extractive sector, as well as global and Chinese specific principles addressing these issues will be examined. This chapter will then look at environmental and social practices of China's global extractive companies, such as PetroChina and MMG, and compare those with practices at global extractive companies BHP and Anglo American.

## 2. Does the Extractive Sector Have a 'Social' Responsibility?

First of all, it is important to provide some background on the development of corporate social responsibility (CSR) and in particular the evolving view of what should be the role of companies in our society.

It is worth noting that the argument over "whether companies should have a responsibility to society" is not new. In fact, more than 80 years ago, two famous Harvard scholars, Berle and Dodd, started a heated debate over what a company's responsibilities should be. While Berle (1932) suggested that the role of a company is solely to serve its shareholder and make profits, Dodd argued that it is actually in a company's best self-interest for it to take other stakeholders' interests into account, including those of employees' and communities'. Corporations have a responsibility not just to their stockholders, but also to the wider society they are operating within, in order to survive for the longer term. In addition, the public expects corporations, sometimes referred to as 'corporate citizens', to be more 'socially responsible'. As Dodd noted (1932:1153),

> We are undergoing a substantial change in our public opinion with regard to the obligations of business to the community, it is natural to expect that this change of opinion will have some effect upon the attitude of those who manage business. If, therefore, the managers of modern businesses were also its owners, the development of a public opinion to the effect that business has responsibilities to its employees and its customers would, quite apart from any legal compulsion, tend to affect the conduct of the better type of business man. The principal object of legal compulsion might then be to keep those who failed to catch the new spirit up to the standards which their more enlightened competitors would desire to adopt voluntarily.

Despite the strong arguments of Dodd, economists who strongly support 'free' market capitalism hold a similar view to that of Berle. For example, Nobel Laureate Milton Friedman was a strong believer of free-market capitalism, and one of his famous quotes was that "the social responsibility of business is to increase its profits" (Friedman, 1970). Specifically in regard to in regard to the mining sector, Bruce Harvey,[1] a mining expert on community engagement, argued that extractive companies have a responsibility to create value for their shareholders and that "social development will not deliver a social licence to operate for the extractive sector" (Harvey, 2014:7).

However, regardless of these contrary views, more recent opinions point in a different direction. Scholars have emphasised the importance of managing relationships with key stakeholders of companies and becoming a good 'corporate citizen' in order to build a good reputation and obtain the 'social license to operate' (Carroll and Buchholtz, 2003, Carroll, 1991, Clarkson, 1995). Many companies in the extractive sector have drawn attention to the intertwining nature of mining work with the community they are operating within, and more importantly, that the way they deal with the community will not only affect community and company operations, it will also affect a company's reputation in the market place, and therefore the long-term value of the company. Some companies, like Anglo

American, even go further to claim that the community work should be its major focus.

> We can change the lives of communities forever. We can go from being an extractive industry to a development industry.
> (Mark Cutifani, CEO, Anglo American, quoted by Wong, 2013:4)

While it is difficult to judge from a single quote how committed Anglo American is to community development, it certainly shows that the company's CEO at least feels that it is important to acknowledge the value of engaging with communities that the company is operating within, as the general this public would expect from a good 'corporate citizen' and, therefore, it is in the company's best interest to properly manage its relationship with the community and other stakeholders.

## 3. Governance of the Extractive Sector: China Versus Global

To gain a better understanding of the environmental and social practices of China's global extractive companies, it is important to understand the idiosyncracies of how China's extractive sector is governed and the roles of major stakeholders, such as government, major shareholder(s), the community and NGOs.

### 3.1. The Role of Government

Large Chinese extractive companies are mainly controlled by their government as a result of their being categorised as state-owned enterprises (SOEs). For SOEs that are operating in the oil sector, they have also been referred to as national oil companies (NOCs). Extractive companies like NOCs are controlled by government and most are listed on stock exchanges in China as well as overseas. Unlike their global peers, such as BHP and Anglo American, whose operations are more or less guided by their commercial environment, China's global extractive companies/NOCs are some of the major agents for carrying out government policy such as the 'go global' policy aimed at acquiring assets overseas and at securing energy supply for the growing Chinese economy (Lao, 2015).

The different treatment of Chinese investments by host countries also reflects the relationship between the Chinese government and the government of the host country. For countries such as the United States and Australia, potential acquisition of assets by Chinese extractive companies in these countries often face additional scrutiny from the host government due to 'national security' concerns (Du, 2014). On the other hand, Chinese acquisitions in African countries are often welcomed and facilitated by host African governments. This is due to the long-term cooperative relationship deliberately built by the Chinese government with these African govern-ments (Brautigam, 2009).

To understand the unique characteristics of Chinese extractive firms oper-ating overseas, it is important to understand how government policy directs company behaviour in China as well as overseas. Chinese investment over-seas is guided by broader government policy as well as by its foreign policy. For example, in resource rich Africa, major acquisitions are carried out following the broader principles of 'Sino-African' cooperation, and these acquisitions are also complemented by generous infrastructure projects (Alden and Alves, 2009). This model is quite distinct from the model based on pure business relationship and is often branded as the 'Angola mode'[2]—i.e., trading infrastructure for resources (Alden and Alves, 2009). This is very different from Chinese acquisitions in Australia and the United States, which are assessed on commercial as well as national security terms.

### 3.2. The Role of Major Shareholders

With the Chinese government as the major shareholder of most large listed Chinese extractive companies, the governance of these companies is quite different from that of their western counterparts. While in the case of west-ern companies one could argue that the improvement of corporate social and environmental practices in recent years are partly due to the engage-ment from active shareholders, especially institutional investors, that are signatories to the Principles for Responsible Investment (PRI)[3] and other collaborative initiatives that aim to improve long-term sustainability/CSR practices of companies.

In China's case, since most large listed extractive companies are also listed on overseas stock exchanges, they have become the engagement targets for global institutional investors who can be major minority shareholders in these companies. However, as these companies are controlled by the Chinese government, engagement with these companies on CSR issues effectively means engaging with the Chinese government, posing greater challenges for foreign investors. In this situation, corporate governance is closely inter-twined with public sector governance (Jia and Tomasic, 2010). Despite the potential difficulty of engaging with the Chinese government on CSR issues, on the flip side, it also means that if foreign investors could solicit support from the major shareholder, the Chinese government issues such as environ-mental management and protection of the local community are likely to be resolved more efficiently and effectively.

### 3.3. The Role of NGOs and Communities

Any discussion of governance of extractive companies would not be com-plete without mentioning NGOs' role in community and mining develop-ment. NGOs have long been active in supporting communities and engaging with mining companies to protect community interests. The movement of mining companies towards better social and environmental practices due to the pressure from the public, as well as engagement from their major share-holders, has in a way facilitated a gradual migration of mining companies towards better management of social and environmental issues. There has also been a gradual change of NGOs' engagement practices. Some NGOs have realised the potential important roles that companies can contribute to community development and have therefore slowly moved away from purely focusing on advocacy. Rather than taking a 'win-lose' approach, NGOs can come to the table as 'critical friends' of mining companies and sought to facilitate better partnerships between mining companies and their communities.

The global reach of large Chinese mining companies and the potential impact of their operations on society places these companies under con-stant public scrutiny. Shareholder activism in the past decade has also seen major institutional investors actively engaging with extractive companies demanding better social and environmental practices.[4] In contrast to min-ing companies, NGOs are advocates of community interests and have often been working alongside communities to support their development for some time. Under contemporary thinking, NGOs act as 'critical' friends of mining companies and can help facilitate community work which can benefit both the community and the company operating along side it.

Examples of NGO involvement in mining development include Oxfam's long-time engagement with the mining sector as well as World Vision's support of the Nyiyaparli traditional owners to use the payments received from mining companies for the long-term benefit of the community (World Vision Australia, 2013). In addition, World Vision Australia has also worked in partnership with BHP Billiton to provide AU$5 million worth of support to improve early childhood development in the East Pil-bara region of Western Australia (Business News, 2009, Mineral Council of Australia, 2011).

Overall, NGO engagement, together with the demand from major institu-tional investors for better management of social and environmental risks of extractive companies, have facilitated a gradual movement of mining com-panies towards better disclosure and improved practices.

## 4. Overview: General Challenges for the Sector—Key Community-Related Social and Environmental Issues

Given the complexity of the mining sector, it is important to understand the major social and environmental risks faced by the sector, the especially related to communities they are operating within. Overall, these risks can be grouped into the following categories: resettlement, changing social dynam-ics of the community, potential negative environmental impacts such as climate change and damage of fresh water source, and mine lifecycle man-agement including mine rehabilitation (Oxfam, 2016b). In most cases, these issues are closely related.

Resettlement of a community for land acquisition can create a huge challenge for both the mining company and the community. Resettlement, especially involuntary resettlement, can cause severe long-term hardship, impoverishment for the community as well as environmental damage (World Bank, 2001:1). For example, resettlement could not only shock the community by changing its social fabric, but also affect economic development of the community especially if the community's main livelihood was from farming/agriculture on the land that was now being used by mining companies for a totally different purpose. Even if the community can continue with farming in a region close by, mining can adversely affect nearby farming activities through pollution and changes to a local aquifer. At the same time, mining could provide new employment opportunities, but sustaining local economies after mine closure is also problematic.

From a company's perspective, if not managed properly, resettlement problems could adversely affect the company's operation, as well as its reputation (Owen and Kemp, 2016). Communities need to be consulted and closely involved in any resettlement planning. Free, Prior and Informed Consent (FPIC) is an effective strategy to engage a community in the decision making process of large mining projects (Oxfam, 2016a). FPIC aims to achieve "a fairer treatment of indigenous and other affected people in development and resource interventions" (Mahanty and McDermott, 2013: 407) as, arguably, it could prevent "coercion, intimidation or manipulation", provide access to "sufficient and appropriate information" and enough time for decision making (Mahanty and McDermott, 2013: 407).

In addition, the host government plays an important role in the land acquisition and community resettlement process. Both the host government and the extractive companies need to be monitored to ensure proper disclosure of 'facilitation' fees paid by extractive companies to the recipient government for accessing the land and mining licenses. It is important for extractive companies to disclose payments paid to the host government to improve transparency and build trust with its stakeholders (EY, 2016).

Other issues include the likelihood of changes to the social fabric of the community due to resettlement and most importantly due to potential environmental risks such as pollution, and contaminated water resources. Mine rehabilitation after closure also needs to be managed properly to minimise negative impact on the community and the environment.

In addition, the potential economic benefit often associated with the richness in resources could easily be translated into a natural 'resource curse' or the so-called 'Dutch Disease', if not managed properly (Forstater et al., 2010). Where rich resources are acquired by different interest groups, can cause social unrest, war and loss of social cohesiveness in the local community. Mining activities could also have a negative impact on the local subsistence economy and make the community much worse off (Forstater et al., 2010).

These issues illustrate the complexity of managing community-related social and environmental risks. In recent years, community concerns have also gained better traction in the 'community—mining company' relationship and demonstrated that companies cannot merely pay 'lip' service in order to gain the 'social license to operate'. For example, in the case of the Conga project in Peru, this US$5 billion project has been held up for years by community activism (Holland, 2014).

Despite the sophistication needed to manage these risks, it is possible for the company and the local community to work together in order to achieve optimal outcomes for both the community and the company involved. If managed properly, company and community partnerships can create economic benefits for both the company (through increased income) and the local community (through job increase), and at the same time minimise the negative impact on the ecosystem and the local communities (World Bank and International Finance Corporation, 2002).

Another issue that is closely related to community and mining companies is artisanal and small-scale mining (ASM).[5] ASM is largely driven by poverty and is mainly carried out by women and children in developing country in order to economically support themselves and their families (or 'earn a living') (Hentschel et al., 2003). ASM has evolved from justifying its existence in the 1970s to a new focus on managing specific issues related to mining companies, such as gender and child labour issues, as well as community-related issues and achieving sustainable livelihoods (Hentschel et al., 2003). The legitimation of ASM will not only support all stakeholders to work together, it may also help alleviate environmental and health issues related to ASM, as well as provide better protection of women and children's rights (UNICEF, 2015). For mining companies, it is also important to conduct social due diligence to help manage child labour risks when drawing upon ASM by following best practices, such as IFC (the International Finance Corporation) Performance Standards on Environmental and Social Sustainability (UNICEF, 2015).

## 5. Global Principles and Voluntary Standards to Help Address Social and Environmental Issues in the Extractive Sector

For global extractive companies operating in a complex multi-stakeholder commercial environment, just meeting the regulatory requirement and obtain a formal license from the government is no longer sufficient (Zhang and Moffat, 2015). Companies also need to move beyond 'do no harm' in order to obtain the 'social license to operate'. To help protect a local community from being exploited by large extractive companies, various organisations, including NGOs, have promoted key principles for improving mining and community engagement in order to achieve an optimal result for all stakeholders.

To address social and environmental issues in extractive industry and to help companies in this industry to improve their social and environmental performance, governments, research houses and supranational organisations have come up with principles and standards to guide these companies towards more sustainable and responsible mining.

In 1999, as part of the Mining, Minerals and Sustainable Development (MMSD) project, the World Business Council for Sustainable Development (WBCSD) engaged with the International Institute for Environment and Development (IIED) to explore mining's role in sustainable development; this topic was revisited in 2012. The conclusion reached was that while the extractive sector had made major advances towards sustainability, more work needed to be done in this sector in order to achieve inclusive and sustainable mining (International Institute for Environment and Development, 2016).

In 2001, International Council on Mining and Metals (ICMM) was formed as one of the initiatives raised by the MMSD project in order to improve the social and environmental performance of the extractive sector. ICMM's members include 23 mining and metals companies and 34 regional and commodities associations (International Council on Mining and Metals, 2016a). In 2003, ten principles were developed based on the recommendation of the MMSD project.

These ten principles are (International Council on Mining and Metals, 2015) as follows:

> *Principle 1: Apply ethical business practices and sound systems of corporate governance and transparency to support sustainable development*
>
> *Principle 2: Integrate sustainable development in corporate strategy and decision-making processes*
>
> **Principle 3: Respect human rights and the interests, cultures, customs and values of employees and communities affected by our activities**
>
> *Principle 4: Implement effective risk-management strategies and systems based on sound science and which account for stakeholder perceptions of risks*
>
> *Principle 5: Pursue continual improvement in health and safety performance with the ultimate goal of zero harm*
>
> **Principle 6: Pursue continual improvement in environmental performance issues, such as water stewardship, energy use and climate change**
>
> **Principle 7: Contribute to the conservation of biodiversity and integrated approaches to land-use planning**
>
> *Principle 8: Facilitate and support the knowledge base and systems for responsible design, use, re-use, recycling and disposal of products containing metals and minerals*
>
> **Principle 9: Pursue continual improvement in social performance and contribute to the social, economic and institutional development of host countries and communities**

*Principle 10: Proactively engage key stakeholders on sustainable development challenges and opportunities in an open and transparent manner. Effectively report and independently verify progress and performance*

Among these ten principles, Principles 3, 6, 7 and 9 are closely related to communities.

The member companies were committed to disclosure of their sustainable practices following the Global Reporting Initiative (GRI) G4 guidelines, as well as reporting specifically against Mining and Metals sector specific standards (International Council on Mining and Metals, 2016b). Member companies of ICMM included major miners such as BHP Billion, Rio Tinto and Anglo American. MMG, a majority-owned subsidiary of China Minmetals, has also been a member since 2009.

In addition, the OECD *Due Diligence Guidance for Responsible Supply Chains of Minerals from Conflict-Affected and High-Risk Areas: Second Edition* has made specific provisions on ASM, in order to protect artisanal and small-scale miners as well as to provide economic and development opportunities for these miners (OECD, 2013).

Another important initiative is the Extractive Industry Transparency Initiative (EITI). EITI was established in 2003 with the aim of enhancing transparency of payments in the extractive industry. Together with other rules, including the Dodd-Frank Act Section 1504 SEC Rule 13(q), the EU Accounting and Transparency Directive, Canada's Extractive Sector Transparency Measures Act and Australia's Publish What You Pay Private Senator's Bill, have helped to drive better disclosure from the extractive sector (EY, 2016).

## 6. Chinese Government Policy in CSR and Responsible Mining

In 2008, China's State-Owned Assets Supervision and Administration Commission of the State Council (SASAC) issued the *Guidelines to the State-Owned Enterprises Directly under the Central Government on Fulfilling Corporate Social Responsibilities*, which apply to all centrally controlled state-owned enterprises (CSOEs) (SASAC, 2008, Forstater et al., 2010). In addition, in parallel to global developments in the mining sector, China has introduced its own requirements on social responsibility for Chinese miners who invest overseas. *Guidelines for Social Responsibility in Outbound Mining Investments* were released in June 2015 and have broadly mirrored the ICMM principles, adding further details on implementation (China Chamber of Commerce of Metals Minerals & Chemicals Importers & Exporters, 2015). For example, these Chinese guidelines discussed the importance of complying with EITI and the disclosure of all payment (cash and in-kind payment to foreign government) paid to access mineral rights

(China Chamber of Commerce of Metals Minerals & Chemicals Importers & Exporters, 2015:32–33).

The guidelines also discussed other standards such as *OECD Due Diligence Guidance for Responsible Supply Chains of Minerals from Conflict-Affected and High-Risk Areas* to help with conducting proper due diligence with minerals sourced from conflicted areas, specifically the so-called 3TG minerals (tin, tantalum, tungsten and gold) sourced from the African Great Lakes Region (China Chamber of Commerce of Metals Minerals & Chemicals Importers & Exporters, 2015:35–36). The Chinese guidelines also support the signing of FPIC protocols before any work is carried out (China Chamber of Commerce of Metals Minerals & Chemicals Importers & Exporters, 2015:35).

Subsequently, China released its own version of due diligence guidelines for outbound mineral investment, *Chinese Due Diligence Guidelines for Responsible Mineral Supply Chain*, following the major principles included in the UN *Guiding Principles on Business and Human Rights* and the *OECD Due Diligence Guidance on Responsible Supply Chains of Minerals from Conflict-Affected and High-Risk Areas*. Chinese due diligence guidelines have clearly defined risks in mining in conflict-affected area as well as included provisions for working with the local community, such as seeking FPIC approval, proper remuneration for local employee, no child labour and managing environmental risks (China Chamber of Commerce of Metals Minerals & Chemicals Importers & Exporters, 2016).

In regards to ASM, *Guidelines for Social Responsibility in Outbound Mining Investments* has specifically covered areas such as the requirement that (Chinese) companies should seek to build a productive relationship with artisanal and small-scale miners as well as assess risks in ASM operations including forced labour, child labour, unsafe working conditions, uncontrolled use of hazardous substances and other significant environmental impacts (China Chamber of Commerce of Metals Minerals & Chemicals Importers & Exporters, 2015: 33–34).

## 7. Environmental and Social Management of Global Extractive Companies

To-date, various principles and guidelines, in addition to engagement from NGOs and institutional investors, have helped drive the improvement of environmental and social management in the extractive sector. To help us gain a better understanding of the similarities and variations in environmental, social and community practices of Chinese companies when compared with global companies, this section focuses on case studies of two global mining companies, BHP Billiton and Anglo American, and compares their practices with two Chinese companies PetroChina and MMG. Each case study is also focused on different aspects of environmental and social management to provide a broader picture across the whole sector.

## 7.1. The Case of BHP Billiton: From OK Tedi to Samarco

BHP Billiton, hereinafter refer to as BHP, is a member of ICMM and commits to the 2013 ICMM Position Statement on Indigenous Peoples and Mining (BHP Billiton, 2015b). BHP has also been a member of the EITI since its inception (BHP Billiton, 2015b).

The case of BHP is focused on environmental issues (tailings management and climate change issues) and community engagement. As a member of ICMM, BHP has participated in the global tailings review led by ICMM, together with 22 other mining companies including Anglo American and MMG (Mining review Africa, 2015). Proper management of tailing is an integral part of mining management and if not managed properly can create enormous environmental impact. A notable case was BHP's damage to the environment and community in Ok Tedi in Papua New Guinea (PNG) due to inappropriate dealing with tailings (Sharp, 2007, Siang and Chu, 2001).

Since the start of this century, BHP has improved its environmental practices and mended their relationship with communities through better community engagement and environmental management, and remains as a leader of good environmental management in the extractive sector. However, a recent incident in Brazil—the breach of a tailings dam operated by Samarco Mineracao, a company jointly owned by BHP and Vale—has seen fatalities of employees and community members, discharge of minerals and the destruction of a village near the dam (Chambers, 2015)

The social and environmental consequences of this are enormous as the breach of the dam wall of not only destroyed lives and infrastructure of a nearby village, the discharge of hazardous tailings into the area could also cause enormous damage to wild life and the environment. Financially, experts estimated that the cost of remediation could be around $1.4 billion (Stevens, 2015), not to mention the reputational cost to the company which has wiped out the share price gains accumulated since the China-export boom in 2005 (Saunders et al., 2015a). What is more disturbing is that an engineering report two years previously had warned the company management that the dam was likely to burst, indicating that there could be serious mismanagement and a failure of public trust if BHP and Vale's management were found to be aware of the report (Saunders et al., 2015b). Recently, in order to restore public trust, BHP has started to run a public campaign with the slogan 'think big' and is planning to drop Billiton from its name (Chambers, 2017).

In terms of community engagement, BHP supports the use of FPIC and has worked closely with the Nyiyaparli community in the Pilbara region in partnership to improve early childhood development (Business News, 2009).

To address the concerns of institutional investors and other stakeholders regarding climate change risk, BHP released a report in 2015 which sought evaluate the impact of climate change on its portfolio of assets and to explore possible strategies to facilitate transition to a low carbon economy

(BHP Billiton, 2015a). In addition, BHP has engaged with different stake-holder groups including the Climate Group (China), Renewable Energy Agency Australia, Alliance for Responsible Mining as well as Oxfam to dis-cuss responsible mining and stakeholder management in its corporate social responsibility forum in late 2014 (BHP Billiton, 2015b). BHP also supports the water stewardship program (BHP Billiton, 2015b).

Despite BHP's leadership in driving better environmental and community management across the extractive sector through its membership of ICMM and engagement with NGOs and communities, the case study illustrates that operating in a high-risk sector and with a large footprint globally, the company needs to embed its social and environmental management strate-gies across its operations as well as the operations of its joint ventures to ensure that risks are managed properly at the group level.

### 7.2. *The Case of Anglo American*

Headquartered in London, United Kingdom, Anglo American has signifi-cant operations in South Africa as well as globally. Anglo American is a founding member of ICMM and its Socio-Economic Assessment Toolbox (SEAT) has won the International Association for Impact Assessment's (IAIA) 2012 "Corporate Initiative Award" (ICMM, 2012). Anglo American has publicly endorsed its compliance with ICMM Sustainable Development Principles including settlement, land rehabilitation and climate change as well as produced annual reports following its GRI G4 Sustainability Report-ing Guidelines (Anglo American, 2016b). Other external principles Anglo American subscribes to include the UN Guiding Principles on Business and Human Rights, the UN Resolution on access to water, the UN Global Com-pact, EITI and the Responsible Jewellery Council (RJC) and certification to the RJC's Code of Practice, to name but a few (Anglo American, 2016b).

Despite Anglo American's public stance of supporting community devel-opment (Wong, 2013) and integrating biodiversity in its operations (IUCN and ICMM, 2004), it has been involved in some projects that have caused environmental concern. For example, NGOs including Greenpeace, the Deep Sea Mining Campaign, and Friends of the Earth have criticised Anglo Ameri-can for investing into the deep-sea mining project (the Solwara 1 Project) in PNG, which could have serious environmental consequences including releas-ing mining waste back in to sea and reducing the fish population (RepRisk, 2015). In addition, Anglo American's Grosvenor Phase 2 coal project was among a list of projects that if it went ahead could contribute significantly to greenhouse gas emission and climate change (Greenpeace, 2013).

In terms of social and community management, due to record low iron ore and coal prices, at the end of 2015, Anglo American announced that it was cutting 85,000 employees to reduce its workforce from 135,000 to 50,000 (The Chemical Engineer, 2015) and restructuring and selling assets to other companies (The Chemical Engineer, 2015). The selling of assets to other companies adds other potential risks to communities since if the counter-parties of Anglo American—the potential new owners of Anglo American's mines and development projects—have a lower standard of environmental, social and community practices, communities will also be much worse off. In addition, the local workers employed at the mines are more likely to be the locals that have given up their land on farming and instead redeveloped their skills and worked at the mine. The reduction of the workforce will have a tremendous impact on their well-being since it could be difficult for retrenched workers to find similar jobs close by and be retrained for new work. The social risk inherent in job cutting in mining operations, can often be substantial and have a material impact on the local community, as well as affecting the social fabric of the region. In 2012, after Anglo American announced cutting 14,000 jobs in its platinum division in South Africa, a strike broke out in its Marikana platinum mine (Schwartz and Comer, 2015). Police opened fire on workers on strike, injuring 112 and killing 34 (Davies, 2015).

The environmental risk can also be high. In 2017, in order to prepare for the Drayton coal mine disclosure in the Hunter Valley in Australia, Anglo America started trial grazing at rehabilitated land at the mine in 2015 (Latimer, 2015). However, the global restructuring to cut 85,000 employees has put raised doubt concerning the company's ability to carry out the rehabilitation of land with the total mine closure estimated to cost around AUD 275 million (Hagemann, 2016).

Water risk is also high in the mining industry. In terms of water risk, the company has acknowledged that its Minas-Rio iron ore operation in Brazil and its Grosvenor coal project in Australia had a significant impact on water and energy consumption and that the company was trying to mitigate its high water and energy footprint in these two operations with savings from other mines (Anglo American, 2016b). The company is also promoting good resource stewardship through engaging with government departments and participating in multi-stakeholder events (Anglo American, 2016b). Water issues were also prevalent at the union mine, while communities of Malepetleke and Sekgoboko protested at shortages of water (Anglo American, 2016b).

On a positive note, Anglo American's HIV AIDS programs has reached over 90% of its employees and contractors (Anglo American, 2012). In regard to transparency and disclosure, Anglo American has been a member of EITI since 2002. In terms of improving disclosure, Anglo American has worked closely with the Peruvian government, and together with 18 hydrocarbon companies and 40 mining companies—the high conciliation rate for the Peru EITI report—makes Peru the first in Americas to reach EITI compliant status (Anglo American, 2016a).

In addition, Anglo American incorporated FPIC when dealing with indigenous people. Anglo American also promoted responsible sourcing and is supporting artisanal and small-scale miners through providing grants to the Diamond Development Initiative (Diamond Development Initiative, 2015).

## 8. China's Mining Companies

Chinese companies have also demonstrated a reasonable level of compliance with global policies such as ISO140001 (Dong, 2012). In addition, Chinese companies' CSR practices are also mainly driven by their major shareholder—the Chinese government. For example, PetroChina has declared that it is government support that has helped it achieve Sustainable Development Goals (Dong, 2012). Other companies, such as Yancoal mining, has also stated in its 2010 annual report that the company aimed to improve mine safety, and the quality of mine closure and rehabilitation in order to achieve the goals of the government's twelfth five-year plan (Dong, 2012: 14).

While it is too early to tell how the Chinese version of responsible mining principles have been implemented, we can gain a good understanding of the practices of Chinese extractive sector environmental, social and community practices by reviewing the cases of PetroChina and MMG.

### 8.1. PetroChina/CNPC: Carrying Out Government Policy

PetroChina is ranked number four in Fortune Global 500 Companies in 2015 and is controlled by the China National Petroleum Corporation (CNPC), a state-owned enterprise under the direct control of the central government (CSOE) via the State-Owned Assets Supervision and Administration Commission (SASAC). PetroChina is also a NOC.

In its 2015 Sustainability Report, PetroChina stated that the company was forging closer ties with countries that were included in China's 'One Belt, One Road' initiative,[6] and as government controlled listed company, it was arrying out the Chinese government's 'go global' policy to secure energy resources overseas (PetroChina, 2016).

Specifically related to African countries, such as Angola, which supplied one-quarter of China's oil imports in 2010 (Burgos and Ear, 2012), China has provided loans and resources to help the country build government office buildings, hospitals, roads and bridges (Burgos and Ear, 2012). This has helped PetroChina and Sinopec gain access to oil supplies in future years and helped Angola solve some of its social problems. As noted by Yang Guang, the director-general of the Institute of West-Asian and African Studies of the Chinese Academy of Social Sciences (IWAAS–CASS),

> When Chinese companies are going to Africa their CSR is positively contributing to solving social problems. They are hiring local people. Many large companies have good environmental protection policy. But they need to quantify and collect data. CSR is still a new concept for Chinese companies. There is a lot of potential.
>
> (Forstater et al., 2010: 9)

While the common perception is that Chinese companies are less transparent than their western counterparts they will report less on payments made to host governments in order to access resources; but some Chinese companies such as PetroChina/CNPC have disclosed more information than required since 2013 by publishing project level information (Global Witness, 2013, EITI, 2016). Lack of disclosure is also found in some non-Chinese companies; other companies operating in some African countries do not report payments made to governments due to difficulty in reporting (EITI, 2016).

Despite the company's recognition of climate change as one of the biggest risks related to the energy industry, the company is looking to further develop natural gas as the 'cleaner' type of energy as well as unconventional sources such as shale gas (PetroChina, 2016), which could have high environmental risks. In addition, environmental damage, by CNPC in Chad has caused the withdrawal of mining licenses by the Chad government (EITI, 2016). Other environmental issues related to the company include building a gas pipe line across Tibet in 2011 without any a prior impact assessments, causing NGOs to demand that BP, one of its shareholders, divested (Greenpeace, 2001).

## 8.2. MMG: A New Generation of Chinese Controlled Extractive Companies[7]

MMG is majority owned by the China Minmetals Corporation (CMC), a CSOE owned by the Chinese government. MMG was listed on the Hong Kong Stock Exchange in 2012 and obtained a second listing on the Australian Securities Exchange in 2015 (MMG, 2015b). MMG explores copper, zinc and other base metals in Australia, the Democratic Republic of Congo (DRC), the Lao PDR and Peru. MMG also has exploration projects in Australia, Africa and the Americas (MMG, 2016).

### 8.2.1. Overview of MMG Environmental and Social Practices

MMG has been a member of ICMM since 2009 and its CEO Andrew Michelmore became the Chair of ICMM in October 2015 (MMG, 2015a). Through its membership of ICMM, MMG has participated in EITI and disclosed its payments to the Congo, Mauritania and Peru governments (MMG) (EITI, 2016). MMG's sustainability report follows G4 standards issued by the GRI (MMG, 2016). MMG's sustainability report has also been independently certified by Ernst and Young (EY) (MMG, 2016).

According to MMG's 2015 Sustainability report, MMG has designed a Life-of-Asset Plan for each mining operation focusing on social and environmental management. In terms of social practice, each operation has its specific Community Investment Plan and the Plan is in line with its Life-of-asset

Plan (MMG, 2016). The company's community investment plan can has four pillars: education, essentials for life, health and well-being (MMG, 2016). Local development programs, such as investing in training and education, are an essential part of the company's life-of-asset commitment (MMG, 2016).

MMG also manages its environmental footprint including water access, usage, security, waste water discharge, land management and rehabilitation, social and economic impact of mine closure guided by its Life-of-asset Plan (MMG, 2016).

The degree to which MMG has implemented its environmental and social plans is explored through the following case studies.

### 8.2.2. Las Bambas Mine in Peru—Conflict with the Community

Located in the Apurimac region of Peru, Las Bambas mine is jointly owned by MMG (62.5%), Guoxin International Investment Co. Ltd (22.5%) and CITIC Metal Co. Ltd (15.0%) (MMG, 2016). According to MMG, the development of the Las Bambas mine has demonstrated proper management of social and environmental impact of mining activities including conducting mining Environmental Impact Study in 2011, which was approved by the Peruvian government. Further amendment to the mine development includes the relocation of the molybdenum and filter plants and the replacement of the slurry pipeline with a bimodal ore transport system (road and railway), which was also approved by the Peruvian government (MMG, 2016).

The company has sought FPIC of affected individuals and communities for land access, and has also developed a social investment plan for communities affected by the mine (MMG, 2016). In addition, MMG stated that the development projects at the Las Bambas mine is managed in line with Sustainable Development Goals (SDGs). For example, it has developed a Local Entrepreneur Development Program for the local community and achieved positive resettlement outcome through the company's Livelihood Restoration Program (MMG, 2016).

Despite the seemingly good environmental and social management practices adopted by the company to manage the Las Bambas mine, other data shows that there has been serious disagreement between the community and the company, and MMG needs to employ private security contractors and public security forces to protect its operation (MMG, 2016). There has been severe conflicts between community and the armed police over the dispute that the community were not consulted on changes made to the previous Environmental Impact Assessment (Global Witness, 2015). The conflicts have also resulted in the death of four protesters (Global Witness, 2015). After the incidence, MMG's management team in Las Bambas worked with the Peruvian government and the local community to establish a Otabambas Dialogue Table to develop a series of agreements in order to maintain social peace and additional security (MMG, 2016: 15).

In addition, the Las Bambas mine seems to have received a lot of complaints. Of the 341 complaints received by the company in 2015, over half (197) were related to local employment and procurement matters at Las Bambas (MMG, 2016).

It shows that MMG needs to further improve its social and environmental practices in order to obtain the 'license to operate'; it also illustrates the high-risk nature and the complexity of mining operations and the growing importance of working collaboratively with the community to achieve desired outcome. Nevertheless, the fact that most of this information is reported by the company demonstrated that there has been significant improvement over the past decade by mining companies to continue to improve its disclosure.

### 8.2.3. The '1000 Day' Project to Improve Child Nutrition— Community Development in the Sepon Mine in Laos

A child's first 1,000 days is the most critical time for growth and development.
(UNICEF)

Partnering with the United Nations Children's Fund (UNICEF) and the Laos Ministry of Health, MMG has contributed to the improvement of child nutrition for the first 1,000 days of life. MMG has pledged $1.4 million over a three-year period to help distribute about four million micronutrient sachets which contain important vitamins, zinc and other nutrients to around 180,000 children aged 6–9 months (MMG, 2012).

### 8.2.4. Kinsevere Mine in Democratic Republic of Congo: From Food for Life to Food for Livelihoods

To improve social and economic conditions for the locals, MMG has developed the Kinsevere Farmers Assistance Program (FAP). The FAP program is a modified microfinance program which seeks to help farmers obtain technical knowledge in order to transform their lives from relying on subsistence farming to have a sustainable livelihood through commercial cropping (MMG, 2016).

Despite of the MMG's efforts to work with the local community, at the Kinsevere mine, the company has experienced weak a weak rule of law system, and needs to employ private security contractors and public security forces on-site. In 2015, its security management plan for the mine was been improved by adding relevant elements of the Voluntary Principles on Security and Human Rights on risk assessment and public and private security (MMG, 2016).

*8.2.5. MMG's Involvement with Local Communities in Australia*

Apart from its community engagement activities in developing countries, MMG has closely engaged with communities through social activities such as sponsoring arts, culture events and sports, as well as supporting education through after school activities for the communities in its Rosebery operation in Australia (Huang and Staples, 2014). MMG's involvement with indigenous communities is also reflected in its provision of the Indigenous Pre-employment Training Program in Bayalgu in the Midwest region of Western Australia, which is part of its golden grove operations (Huang and Staples, 2014: 23).

In summary, despite differences in the ownership structure of Chinese extractive companies when compared to its global peers, MMG has started to show signs of convergence with its global peers in reporting environmental and social practices. In addition, comparing MMG's reporting with that of PetroChina, MMG's reporting is similar to its western counterparts and is less focused on its role of carrying out government policy.

## 9. Conclusion

The case studies discussed above have highlight significant environmental and social risks embedded in mining operations. The selected companies are deemed to be leaders in their respective sectors and have supported major international developments, such as ICMM, and are committed to better environmental and community management, yet their operations could still have a dramatic negative impact/footprint on the environment and the community. In addition, the seeming lack of stark contrast between the practices of global mining companies when compared with Chinese large extractive companies shows that Chinese companies have generally progressed well in their globalisation journeys. In addition, it is clear that the Chinese government has had a strong influence in pushing for the adoption of good social and environmental practices among large Chinese global companies.

The dynamic regulatory and market environment in which extractive companies are operating has seen these companies become more reactive to engagement of institutional investors and NGOs, which has helped them improve their environmental and social practices.

Going forward the increasing public awareness of environmental, climate change, social and community risks, and human rights issues, will place extractive companies under more public scrutiny, its major shareholders and media. It is therefore in these companies' best interest to have appropriate environmental and social practices and to improve their transparency in communicating their practices to the general public. Good environmental and social practices will not only help extractive companies gain the 'social license to operate' but may also support them in building a good reputation and in improving their long-term value.

In addition, to further demonstrate their commitment to community development and good corporate citizenship, extractive companies should consider reporting on how their operations can help achieve SDGs supported by the United Nations Development Programme (UNDP). This will ultimately help companies collaborate with all their stakeholders including communities to create 'shared value' together.

## Acronyms

| | |
|---|---|
| ASM | Artisanal and small-scale mining |
| CNPC | China National Petroleum Corporation |
| CSR | Corporate social responsibility |
| DDI | Diamond Development Initiative |
| DRC | Democratic Republic of Congo |
| EITI | Extractive Industries Transparency Initiative |
| ESG | Environmental, Social and Corporate Governance |
| FAP | Farmers Assistance Program |
| FPIC | Free, Prior and Informed Consent |
| GRI | Global Reporting Initiative |
| IAIA | International Association for Impact Assessment |
| ICMM | International Council on Mining and Metals |
| IFC | The International Finance Corporation |
| IIED | International Institute for Environment and Development |
| IWAAS—CASS | the Institute of West-Asian and African Studies of the Chinese Academy of Social Sciences |
| MMSD | Mining, Minerals and Sustainable Development |
| NOCs | National Oil Companies |
| PRI | Principles for Responsible Investment |
| RJC | Responsible Jewellery Council |
| SDGs | Sustainable Development Goals |
| SEAT | Socio-Economic Assessment Toolbox |
| SOEs | State-owned Enterprises |
| UNDP | United Nations Development Program |
| UNICEF | United Nations Children's Fund |
| WBCSD | World Business Council for Sustainable Development |

## Notes

1. Bruce Harvey is ex-global practice leader, Communities and Social Performance at Rio Tinto.
2. 'Anglo mode' refers to packaging infrastructure finance with natural resource development (Foster et al., 2008).
3. PRI (Principles for Responsible Investment), a collaborative initiative established in 2006. By May 2017, it has more than 1700 signatories including 343 asset owners and 1142 investment managers. The main aim of PRI is to promote integrating environmental, social and corporate governance (ESG) analysis and active ownership into investment processes. For further information, go to www.unpri. org/about.

4. Artisanal and small scale mining (ASM) refers to formal or informal mining operations with predominantly simplified forms of exploration, extraction, processing and transportation. ASM is normally low capital intensive and uses high labour intensive technology. "ASM" can include men and women working on an individual basis as well as those working in family groups, in partnership, or as members of cooperatives or other types of legal associations and enterprises involving hundreds or even thousands of miners. For example, it is common for work groups of four to ten individuals, sometimes in family units, to share tasks at one single point of mineral extraction (e.g. excavating one tunnel). At the organisational level, groups of 30–300 miners are common, extracting jointly one mineral deposit (e.g. working in different tunnels), and sometimes sharing processing facilities (OECD, 2013: 65)
5. Institutional investors especially the signatories to the Principles for Responsible Investment (PRI) have been very active in engaging with investee companies to make sure ESG risks are managed properly with the belief that these risks could have material impact on the long-term share price performance of these companies.
6. 'One Belt, One Road' Initiative (also known as the Belt and Road Initiative or BRI) refers to the creation of an economic land belt that includes countries on the original Silk Road through Central Asia, West Asia, the Middle East and Europe and a maritime road that links China's port facilities with the African coast (CLSA, 2015)
7. Unless otherwise specified, this section is sourced from MMG's 2015 Sustainability Report (MMG, 2016)

## Bibliography

Alden, C. and Alves, A. C. 2009, "China and Africa's natural resources: The challenges and implications for development and governance", available: www.voltairenet.org/IMG/pdf/China_and_Africa_s_Natural_Resources.pdf, accessed: 20 August 2016, pp. 1–28.

Anglo American 2012, *Anglo American HIV/AIDS employee testing programme reaches highest ever participation rate of 90%* [Online], available: http://south-africa.angloamerican.com/media/press-releases/2012/03-12-2012.aspx, accessed: 22 May 2017.

Anglo American 2016a, *Peru's journey: The importance of transparency in the extractive sector* [Online], available: www.angloamerican.com/media/our-stories/perus-progress-eiti-importance-of-transparency, accessed: 16 September 2016.

Anglo American 2016b, "Sustainability report 2015: Driving change, defining our future", available: www.angloamerican.com/~/media/Files/A/Anglo-American-PLC-V2/documents/aa-sdreport-2015.pdf, accessed: 16 September 2016, pp. 1–89.

Berle, A. A. 1932, "For whom corporate managers are trustees: A note", *Harvard Law Review*, vol. 45, no. 7, pp. 1365–1372.

BHP Billiton 2015a, "Climate change portfolio analysis", available: www.bhpbilliton.com/~/media/5874999cef0a41a59403d13e3f8de4ee.ashx, accessed: 22 May 2017, pp. 1–20.

BHP Billiton 2015b, "Taking the long view: Sustainability report 2015", available: www.bhpbilliton.com/~/media/bhp/documents/investors/annual-reports/2015/bhpbillitonsustainabilityreport2015_interactive.pdf, accessed: 22 May 2017, pp. 1–74.

Brautigam, D. 2009, *The Dragon's gift: The real story of China in Africa*, Oxford University Press, Oxford.

Burgos, S. and Ear, S. 2012, "China's oil hunger in Angola: History and perspective", *Journal of Contemporary China*, vol. 21, no. 74, pp. 351–367.

Business News 2009, *BHP, World vision in $5m Pilbara program* [Online], available: www.businessnews.com.au/article/BHP-World-Vision-in-5m-Pilbara-program, accessed: 14 August 2016.

Carroll, A. B. 1991, "The pyramid of corporate social responsibility: Towards the moral management of organizational stakeholders", *Business Horizons*, vol. 34, no. 4, pp. 39–48.

Carroll, A. B. and Buchholtz, A. K. 2003, *Business and society: Ethics and stakeholder management*, South-Western, Mason, OH.

Chambers, M. 2015, *Fatalities rise after BHP dam burst* [Online], available: www.businessspectator.com.au/news/2015/11/6/resources-and-energy/fatalities-rise-after-bhp-dam-burst, accessed: 9 November 2015.

Chambers, M. 2017, "Billiton buried in BHP makeover", *The Australian*, 15 May 2017, p. 1.

The Chemical Engineer 2015, "Anglo American to cut 85,000 workers", *The Chemical Engineer*, no. 894/895, December 2015/January 2016, p. 14.

China Chamber of Commerce of Metals Minerals & Chemicals Importers & Exporters 2015, "Guidelines for social responsibility in outbound mining investments", available: www.estellelevin.com/wp-content/uploads/2015/06/CCCMC_Guidelines_for_Social_Responsibility_in_Outbound_Mining_Operations_EN.pdf, accessed: 22 May 2017, pp. 1–31.

China Chamber of Commerce of Metals Minerals & Chemicals Importers & Exporters 2016, "Chinese due diligence guidelines for responsible mineral supply chains", available: www.techuk.org/insights/news/item/6734-china-publishes-guidelines-for-responsible-mineral-supply-chains, accessed: 20 August 2016, pp. 1–41.

Clarkson, M. B. E. 1995, "A stakeholder framework for analyzing and evaluating corporate social performance", *Academy of Management Review*, vol. 20, no. 1, pp. 92–117.

CLSA 2015, *A brilliant plan: One belt, one road* [Online], available: www.clsa.com/special/onebeltoneroad/, accessed: 18 September 2016.

Davies, N. 2015, *Marikana massacre: The untold story of the strike leader who died for workers' rights* [Online], available: www.theguardian.com/world/2015/may/19/marikana-massacre-untold-story-strike-leader-died-workers-rights, accessed: 16 September 2016.

Diamond Development Initiative 2015, *Anglo American Group Foundation provides grant to diamond development initiative* [Online], available: www.ddiglobal.org/news/news/anglo-american-group-foundation-provides-grant-to-diamond-development-initiative, accessed: 16 September 2016.

Dodd, E. M. 1932, "For whom are corporate managers trustees?", *Harvard Law Review*, vol. 45, no. 7, pp. 1145–1163.

Dong, S. 2012, "An assessment of CSR reporting practices in China's mining and minerals industry", available: www.unisa.edu.au/Global/business/centres/cags/docs/seminars/Paper%20Shidi.pdf, accessed: 19 September 2016, pp. 1–34.

Du, M. 2014, "When China's national champions go global: Nothing to fear but fear itself?", *Journal of World Trade*, vol. 48, no. 6, pp. 1127–1166.

EITI 2016, "Chinese companies reporting in EITI countries: Review of the engagement of Chinese firms in countries implementing EITI", available: https://eiti.

org/sites/default/files/documents/eiti_chinese_companies_reporting_updated_feb2016.pdf, accessed: 28 August 2016, pp. 1–16.

EY 2016, "Disclosing payments to governments: Mining and metals in an era of transparency", available: https://eiti.org/sites/default/files/documents/ey-mining-and-metals-in-an-era-of-transparency.pdf, accessed: 13 August 2016, pp. 1–22.

Forstater, M., Zadek, S., Yang, G., Yu, K., Chen, X. and George, M. 2010, "Corporate responsibility in African development: Insights from an emerging dialog", available: www.hks.harvard.edu/m-rcbg/CSRI/publications/workingpaper_60.pdf, accessed: 23 August 2016, pp. 1–55.

Foster, V., Butterfield, W., Chen, C. and Pushak, N. 2008, "Building bridges: China's growing role as infrastructure financier for Sub-Saharan Africa", available: http://siteresources.worldbank.org/INTAFRICA/Resources/BB_Final_Exec_summary_English_July08_Wo-Embg.pdf, accessed: 18 September 2016, pp. 1–9.

Friedman, M. 1970, "The social responsibility of business is to increase its profits", *The New York Times Magazine*, 13 September.

Global Witness 2013, "Transparency matters: Disclosure of payments to governments by Chinese extractive companies", available: www.globalwitness.org/sites/default/files/library/transparency_matters_lr.pdf, accessed: 28 August 2016, pp. 1–44.

Global Witness 2015, *Deaths of four anti-mining protesters: a catastrophic consequence of Peru's weakened environmental safeguards, warns global witness* [Online], available: www.globalwitness.org/en/press-releases/deaths-four-anti-mining-protesters/, accessed: 27 August 2016.

Greenpeace 2001, *Greenpeace challenges oil industry to outline route map to renewable energy future* [Online], available: www.greenpeace.org.uk/media/press-releases/greenpeace-challenges-oil-industry-to-outline-routemap-to-renewable-energy-future, accessed: 16 September 2016.

Greenpeace 2013, "The critical list: 91 coal projects Australia can't afford", available: www.greenpeace.org/australia/Global/australia/assets/The%20Critical%20List.pdf, accessed: 16 September 2016, pp. 1–9.

Hagemann, B. 2016, *Rehab fears for Drayton coal* [Online], available: www.australianmining.com.au/news/rehab-fears-for-drayton-coal/, accessed: 16 September 2016.

Harvey, B. 2014, "Social development will not deliver social license to operate for the extractive sector", *The Extractive Industry and Society*, vol. 1, no. 1, pp. 7–11.

Hentschel, T., Hruschka, F. and Priester, M. 2003, "Artisanal and small-scale mining: Challenges and opportunities", available: http://pubs.iied.org/pdfs/9268IIED.pdf, accessed: 12 September 2016, pp. 1–94.

Holland, N. 2014, "Gold mining and shared value: Contributing to development and communities", available: http://ecdpm.org/great-insights/extractive-sector-african-perspectives/sharing-benefits-gold-mining/, accessed: 28 August 2016.

Huang, X. and Staples, W. 2014, "Community engagement by Chinese firms in Australia: Practices and benefits", available: http://mams.rmit.edu.au/xnjztnvvfxek.pdf, accessed: 1 September 2016.

ICMM 2012, *Anglo American wins international award for Socio-Economic Assessment Toolbox (SEAT)* [Online], available: www.icmm.com/en-gb/news/anglo-american-wins-international-award-for-socio-economic-assessment-toolbox-seat-, accessed: 16 September 2016.

International Council on Mining and Metals 2015, *ICMM 10 principles* [Online], available: www.icmm.com/en-gb/about-us/icmm-10-principles/the-principles, accessed: 11 August 2016.

International Council on Mining and Metals 2016a, *About us* [Online], available: www.icmm.com/en-gb/about-us, accessed: 12 August 2016.

International Institute for Environment and Development 2016, *Mining, Minerals and Sustainable Development (MMSD)* [Online], available: www.iied.org/mining-minerals-sustainable-development-mmsd, accessed: 12 August 2016.

International Council on Mining and Metals 2016b, *Member reporting and performance* [Online], available: www.icmm.com/en-gb/members/member-reporting-and-performance, accessed: 12 August 2016.

IUCN and ICMM 2004, "Integrating mining and biodiversity conservation: Case studies from around the world", available: www.icmm.com/publications/pdfs/4. pdf, accessed: 16 September 2016, pp. 1–52.

Jia, X. and Tomasic, R. 2010, *Corporate governance and resource security in China: The transformation of China's global resources companies*, Routledge, New York.

Lao, J. X. 2015, "The Chinese government and the national oil companies (NOCs): Who is the principal?", *Asia Pacific Business Review*, vol. 21, no. 1, pp. 44–59.

Latimer, C. 2015, *Anglo American start grazing trial on rehabilitated mine* [Online], available: www.australianmining.com.au/news/%E2%80%8Banglo-american-start-grazing-trial-on-rehabilitated-mine/, accessed: 16 September.

Mahanty, S. and McDermott, C. L. 2013, "How does 'Free, Prior and Informed Consent' (FPIC) impact social equity? Lessons from mining and forestry and their implications for REDD+", *Land Use Policy*, vol. 35, November, pp. 406–416.

Mineral Council of Australia 2011, "Minerals industry: Indigenous economic development strategy", available: www.minerals.org.au/file_upload/files/publications/Minerals-Industry-Indigenous-Economic-Development-Strategy-17-10-11-Final-laser(b).pdf, accessed: 14 August 2016, pp. 1–20.

Mining review Africa 2015, *ICMM commences global tailings management review* [Online], available: www.miningreview.com/news/icmm-commences-global-tailings-management-review/, accessed: 17 September 2016.

MMG 2012, *Announcement: The 1000 Day Project—improving the nutritional status of children in Laos* [Online], available: www.mmg.com.

MMG 2015a, *MMG CEO Andrew Michelmore to lead ICMM* [Online], available: www.mmg.com/en/Investors-and-Media/News/2015/10/16/MMG-CEO-Andrew-Michelmore-to-lead-ICMM.aspx?backitem=BA5603A202CE4D1E848FAB A9D1339247, accessed: 27 August 2016.

MMG 2015b, *Our history* [Online], available: www.mmg.com/en/About-Us/Company-Overview/Our-history.aspx, accessed: 27 August 2016.

MMG 2016, "Sustainability report 2015", available: www.mmg.com/en/Sustainability-and-Community/~/media/Files/sustainability%20and%20community/2016/MMG%20Sustainability%20Report%202015.pdf, accessed: 27 August 2016, pp. 1–40.

OECD 2013, "OECD due diligence guidance for responsible supply chains of minerals from conflict-affected and high-risk areas: Second edition", available: www.oecd.org/corporate/mne/GuidanceEdition2.pdf, accessed: 12 September 2016, pp. 1–122.

Owen, J. R. and Kemp, D. 2016, "The weakness of resettlement safeguards in mining", *Forced Migration Review*, vol. 52, May, pp. 78–81.

Oxfam 2016a, *Free, prior and informed consent* [Online], available: www.oxfam. org.au/what-we-do/mining/free-prior-and-informed-consent/, accessed: 13 August 2016.

Oxfam 2016b, *Impacts of mining* [Online], available: www.oxfam.org.au/what-we-do/mining/impacts-of-mining/, accessed: 11 August 2016.

PetroChina 2016, "2015 sustainability report", available: www.petrochina.com. cn/petrochina/xhtml/images/shyhj/2015kcxfzbgen02.pdf, accessed: 16 September 2016, pp. 1–38.

RepRisk 2015, "RepRisk special report: Deep sea extractive activities: seabed mining and deep sea drilling", available: www.reprisk.com/content/5-publications/1-special-reports/36-2015-06-02-reprisk-special-report-on-seabed-mining-and-deep/2015–2006–2002-reprisk-special-report-on-seabed-mining-and-deep.pdf, accessed: 16 September 2016, pp. 1–9.

SASAC 2008, *Guidelines to the state-owned enterprises directly under the central government on fulfilling corporate social responsibilities* [Online], available: http:// en.sasac.gov.cn/n1408035/c1477196/content.html, accessed: 23 August 2016.

Saunders, A., Lia, T. and Stevens, M. 2015b, "BHP dam was flawed, experts said", *The Australian Financial Review*, 12 November 2015.

Saunders, A., Stevens, M. and Chenoweth, N. 2015a, "BHP falls erase China boom gains", *The Australian Financial Review*, 13 November 2015.

Schwartz, M. and Comer, D. R. 2015, "De Beers, Anglo American and Optima magazine", *Business and Society Review*, vol. 120, no. 3, pp. 329–341.

Sharp, B. 2007, "Ok Tedi case study: 'If this were your village . . .?' ", available: www.scribd.com/doc/314559799/ok-tedi-cases-pdf, pp. 1–41.

Siang, B. and Chu, P. 2001, "The BHP and OK Tedi case, 1984–2000: Issues, outcomes and implications for corporate social reporting", available: www.unisa. edu.au/Global/business/centres/cags/docs/apcea/APCEA_2001_7(1)_Chu.pdf, pp. 1–10.

Stevens, M. 2015, "Has BHP become too stretched?" *The Australian Financial Review*, 11 November 2015.

UNICEF 2015, "Children's rights and the mining sector: UNICEF extractive pilot", available: www.unicef.org/csr/files/UNICEF_REPORT_ON_CHILD_RIGHTS_ AND_THE_MINING_SECTOR_APRIL_27.pdf, accessed: 12 September 2016, pp. 1–42.

Wong, A. 2013, "Responsible mineral development initiative (RMDI): Maximising the value of extractives for development", available: https://ec.europa.eu/ growth/tools-databases/eip-raw-materials/sites/rawmaterials/files/Responsible%20Mineral%20Development%20Initiative%20(RMDI)%20-%20AW. pdf, pp. 1–18.

World Bank 2001, *OP 4.12 - Involuntary resettlement* [Online], available: https://policies.worldbank.org/sites/ppf3/PPFDocuments/Forms/DispPage. aspx?docid=1572&ver=current, accessed: 22 May 2017.

World Bank & International Finance Corporation 2002, "Large mines and local communities: Forging partnerships, building sustainability", available: http:// siteresources.worldbank.org/INTOGMC/Resources/largemineslocalcommunities. pdf, accessed: 22 May 2017, pp. 1–32.

World Vision Australia 2013, "World Vision Australia 2013 reconciliation action plan report", available: www.reconciliation.org.au/raphub/wp-content/uploads/raps/community/word%20vision%20australia%202013%20rap%20report.pdf, accessed: 14 August 2016, pp. 1–30.

Zhang, A. and Moffat, K. 2015, "A balancing act: The role of benefits, impacts and confidence in governance in predicting acceptance of mining in Australia", *Resources Policy*, vol. 44, June, pp. 25–34.

# 4 CSR-Related Risk Management in the Overseas Investments of Chinese Companies

## Context, Dimensions and Effectiveness

*Zhirong Duan[1] and Peiyuan Guo[2]*

## 1. Introduction

According to data released by the National Bureau of Statistics of China (NBS), in 2016 alone, Chinese firms have made direct investment in 7961 non-financial sector projects, reaching 164 countries/areas, and amounted to more than 170 billion US dollars, an increase of 44.1% compared to the total investment amount in 2015. The NBS also reported that over the years, sectors such as mining and resources, infrastructure, manufacturing and agriculture have all grown strongly in Chinese outbound direct investment. A lot of these investments are located in Southeast Asia, Africa and Latin America, where risks are traditionally considered very high. In addition to the traditional political and economic risks, increased awareness of social and environmental cost associated with economic development has put a lot of pressures on companies investing in these regions, and as a result, corporate social responsibility (CSR) practices of Chinese investments in host countries have attracted public attention (such as from regulatory agencies, industry associations, think tanks and media) in both host and home countries, as well as from international organisations. With governance as one of the key issues, the so-called ESG (i.e. environmental, social and governance) factors became the focus of public attention. This new trend has strong implications for both macro-level policy makers as well as for business managers.

Failed cases and negative news of Chinese overseas investment projects included on China Overseas Investment Risk Map website show that environmental protection, conflicts with labor forces and local community have constantly been the underlying issues. Not only have bad reputations of Chinese firms grown around these topics, they also have become reasons for overdue and cancelled projects. The challenge is to identify these risks, understand their context and learn to manage similar situations effectively; this will be the objective of this chapter.

## 2. CSR-Related Risks and FDI

### 2.1. CSR-Related Risks

CSR entered the area of risk management long before its formal inclusion in risk-management theories. The negative impact of not fulfilling CSR requirements can be disastrous, especially for the reputations of companies. Bad news travels a lot faster than good news. This is probably why in the early years CSR was always connected to marketing and public relations. However, the strategic influence of CSR, though underestimated at the very beginning, has later gained more attention from scholars, as well as from practitioners. For example, Husted (2005) proposed a real option model on the link between CSR and risk management, which suggests that CSR should be negatively related to the firm's *ex ante* downside business risk. According to strategic management scholars who identified and researched the 'risk-return paradox', unlike the commonly accepted notion in investment that high return are expected with high-risk projects, Bowman (1980) has shown that there existed a negative relationship between CSR and risk at the firm level. The implication of Husted's real option model is that risk management is no longer a pure financial issue but a strategic issue as well.

Under growing attention from the public, on the one hand, stakeholders have applauded CSR activities such as CSR reporting and corporate philanthropy; on the other, companies are pushed for acting more responsibly towards their impacts on social and environmental issues as well as contributing to the general governance structure of the society, such as anti-corruption efforts. However, stakeholders' expectations are not always met, which could lead to conflicts and other undesirable consequences for businesses.

When undesirable events happen, people normally would attribute them to risks. Unlike many other risks, risks emerging from social responsibility issues cannot be completely reflected in the legal system or in economic terms. Instead of requirements set by law, these are mostly public pressures. For example, in case studies by Gunningham et al. (2004), pulp mills workers told the interviewers that they would react to complaints regarding odours from the mill after 'there is sustained public pressure'; this was despite the fact that odour control could be costly and was not required by law. It is therefore important to analyse the context as contextualisation and categorisation of risks are necessary to understand the differences between various types of risks in order to form corresponding strategies.

### 2.2. Contextualisation: Focal Issues and Foreign Direct Investment

There are many ways to contextualise risk analysis and hence risk management. For example, industry is one of the main distinctive features of the context. Industry characteristics shape firm behaviours when facing uncertainty towards undesirable events. Another widely used feature in contextualisation involves country issues.

One of the long-time academic puzzles is the problem of linking macro-level signals with micro-level activities and vice versa. Would characteristics identified at country level be transformed into firm or project level risks? Is it viable to call any country assessment measure a CSR-risk indicator? Looking into the construction sector, Wang et al. (2004) observed that among the risks of three hierarchical levels: country, market and project. Country-level risks are the most dominant risks; this was confirmed by their survey results.

Given the importance of foreign direct investment (FDI) in any modern economy, it is important to take "country"-related issues as the basis for contextualisation. On the one hand, there are the capital, skills and expertise that are much-needed for local community development in host countries. On the other hand, this needs to be balanced with profit making, as sometimes the speed of commercialisation could lead to problems in the near future.

Gunningham et al. (2004) touched upon the interactions between social, economic and legal actors in the context of stakeholder relationships and social license for businesses. This has deeper implications. Although people tend to distinguish between the dimensions of the triple-bottom-line, social aspects sometimes seems to be interwoven with economic considerations; once this occurs, social issues such as unemployment and labor relationships can become more complicated.

The current inquiry is among a series of research conducted on CSR issues in relation to outbound direct investment by Chinese firms. Starting with the mining industry and moving on to agriculture and infrastructure construction projects, this experience urged us to respond to the need for a new risk-management scheme embracing CSR perspectives.

One visit to the local community in rural Indonesia revealed that a Chinese firm formed a partnership with local investors and built a farm. The joint venture made many efforts to gain trust and cooperation from the local community. One of the initiatives was an economic cooperative where peasants in the villages where the farm was located could rent small patches of land from the farm and the farm guaranteed that it would buy back all of their outputs at a fair price. Other CSR initiatives include the payment to school teachers and sometimes the construction of roads, but nothing could be compared to the livelihood provided by the cooperative. We found that despite the funding provided to schools and mosques, some villages that were not included in the economic cooperative demanded similar arrangements; however, this was not economically feasible for the joint-venture farm. Although the farm only overlaps marginally with the village, the villagers could exercise some leverage as some of the roads connecting the farm to the outside world pass through their village. So, on a few occasions, unsatisfied villagers blocked these roads until their demands were fulfilled.

Another example of prevalent social problems that emerged from our field studies in Southeast Asia is the selection of plants to be used in the investments. High production corn in northern Myanmar and bananas in Laos provide examples of such plant selection problems. In both cases, the introduced plants dominated the field after some time of plantation, either because the new plants had grown rapidly or the farmers had planted the plants abundantly or both. Either way, when the market fluctuated, the demand level became lower than the breakeven point, as a consequence, the outside investors were no longer interested and left the farmers with unmarketable production.

Throughout our investigations, we found that there were common features of CSR-related risks for various industry sectors. Industries with heavy capital investment, and hence huge economic stakes, could face the same type of conflict with stakeholders as those faced by the agriculture farms; therefore, stakeholder engagement at community level is necessary for both large and small investment projects. Land and water usage, and waste handling, are the three main topics that faced by foreign infrastructure builders, miners and farm managers.

### 2.3. Dimensions of the CSR-Related Risk Space

There is a need for a new risk-management scheme involving CSR that can be contextualised in the actual situation of FDI. At the same time, it is necessary to be very cautious about considering CSR as a single dimensional term in Chinese foreign investments.

For the past decade, ESG/CSR considerations have become standard aspects in disclosure requirements set by stock exchanges for listed companies. Before they became accepted corporate terminologies, ESG and CSR were topics that were part of broader discussions due to their implications for the welfare of society; this occurred in the context of demand for economic development while also dealing with its negative impacts, defining its boundaries and probably also pointing to the limitations of a pure economic initiative. Social license is one of the mechanisms that reflect how the boundaries are defined. As Gunningham et al. (2004: 307) have stated, the corporate social license "governs the extent to which a corporation is constrained to meet societal expectations and avoid activities that societies (or influential elements within them) deem unacceptable, whether or not those expectations are embodied in law".

Governing through environmental and social issues, certain factors are more salient than others. It was not until some of the responsibilities turn into risks that firms realise how closely their operations are related to the demands and expectations of their stakeholders, particularly those who could be connected to the local community. Some stakeholders are at the arm's length, but others have subtle relationships and engagements, which could be a challenge for foreign firms. From a strategic point of view, stakeholders are providers of resources and this means that a firm has to constantly scan and map the stakeholder space so that important stakeholders are not ignored.

Finding dimensionality is a major concern in developing a new risk-management tool partly due to information explosion problems. Sources of information are complex in overseas investments when compared to purely domestic operations. Many governments sponsor data collection and analysis relevant to outbound direct investment. These efforts are well justified as regardless of the types of risk, this information is critical for agencies such as export insurance, for policy banks and many types of businesses. However, all too often, companies are so confused by the many sources of information related to the risks they face that they give up and ignore these risks entirely. Some guideline or criteria are thus needed for Chinese companies to help them make informed decisions.

It is essential that companies have an integrated framework of risk and CSR in the context of FDI. CSR-related risks in the form of conflicts are undesirable because they increase the costs for all parties and create obstacles to future development. As shown by the United Nations Sustainable Development Goals (SDGs), it is necessary to align the interests of businesses and stakeholders in host countries through appropriate CSR-risk management; it is possible to have a concise while effective framework that all parties can refer to for the purpose of sustainable development, creating a new angle for public governance.

## 3. Development of Country Responsibility Risk Index

Unlike most of indices published by international organisations, this Country Responsibility Risk Index is intended to be used as a management tool and, in particular, as a risk-management tool for Chinese companies. Although it is a targeted tool, it has much broader implications for multinational companies facing increasing challenges in regard to corporate social responsibility.

Integrating a risk-management framework sensitive to CSR considerations, a systematic funnelling approach was adopted to develop the index consisting of four steps: (a) building a pool of indicators, (b) finding dimensionality, (c) screening and verification and (d) weighting. The order of the steps is chosen deliberately to ensure a wide enough coverage of indicators and to keep it open for future verification processes for different types of companies and industry sectors.

### 3.1. Country Assessment Indices

The first step in constructing this index was to build a pool of globally adopted country assessment indicators. An important source of information is provided by statistics issued by national governments. These statistics would normally fulfill the needs for understanding the general economic situation of a country. Some countries also regularly publish their trade and FDI figures. In addition to data from individual countries, international organisations and research institutes also conduct a variety of survey and evaluations in different countries, covering many aspects of interest for businesses operating around the world. The indicators generated by these organisations have established their credibility over the years and have been adopted by various studies as country measures.

Starting with the most widely adopted databases, a number of indicators from the CSR perspective were added to the index. In addition to the more economic-oriented data available from the World Bank, the Global Competitiveness Index (GCI) (World Economic Forum 2016) and Standard & Poor's Global Rating (S&P), the index included various databases concerning ESG such as Environmental Performance Index (EPI) (Hsu et al. 2016), Hofstede Cultural Distance Index (Hofstede et al. 2010) and the Worldwide Governance Indicators (WGI) (World Bank 2016).

### 3.2. Distance Measures and Effectiveness

Since investment risks are being examined from the Chinese firms' perspective, it makes sense to start with 'distance' measures. Arguing that distance still matters, the CAGE framework, which has been used in analysing the international strategy of firms, emphasises the importance of cultural, administrative, geographic and economic differences between home and host countries (Ghemawat 2001). Established measures can be found in the academic literature on institutional distance and cultural distance (e.g. Berry et al. 2010).

A comparison between Chinese and Australian firms found that cross-national differences had an impact on how managers dealt with conflicts in the host country (Chen & Li 2005). Culture also influences corporate risk-taking behaviour as shown in a study using data from 35 countries (Li et al. 2013).

In contrast to 'distance' is the variable dealing with 'connectedness' among countries. We are aware of the DHL Global Connectedness Index (Ghemawat & Altman 2016), but since it is a synthesised index, which means it would overlap with other indicators, and also because it has a different focus than CSR and risk issues, we would echo some of the fundamental analytical schemes (i.e. the CAGE framework) while adopting a set of connectedness measures of our own developed for this purpose.

Distance matters because it may cause misunderstanding and improper activities or movement in the context of FDI. However, constant communication and adaptive behaviour may help alleviate distance effects, avoid conflicts and reduce risks. In a CSR-related study, researchers have identified 'interactional trust' as one of the contributing paths to gaining social license with cases from the mining industry, where 'interactional trust' was defined as "the perception that the company and its management listens, responds, keeps promises, engages in mutual dialogue, and exhibits reciprocity in its interactions" (Boutilier & Thomson 2014: 4). Social licenses that demand ESG benefits can be moderated by economic reliance among the stakeholders (Gunningham et al. 2004). This kind of interaction at the country level is also of relevance to evaluating country-specific risks/gains. Recently, empirical evidence was found on how bilateral political relations affect corporate decision making and, ultimately, the premium that was paid in cross-border acquisition deals (Bertrand et al., 2016). In light of the earlier discussion, the bilateral relations measures were introduced into the pool. Indicators in this category seek to measure both transactional exchanges and the relational activities promoted by either or both countries.

In a fast changing environment, it is important to build dynamism into the tracking indicators. Some macroeconomic indicators are published on a yearly basis; some may be updated every two or three years, and others could appear only once. Although some characteristics of a country might remain stable over a very long period of time, it is desirable to have a stringent set of predictors in any screening and verification model, so the designated year has been attached to each indicator and a pool of panel indicators thereby created. The panel covers the years from 2010–2015. A list of the chosen indicators is shown in Table 4.1.

### 3.3. Dimensionality of the Index Space

Despite the large number of existing country evaluation indicators generated by international organisations and research institutes over the years, given the high visibility and huge amount of capital at stake, new indicators in relation to FDI are still adding to the index space. This continuous growth of data highlighted two problems, information overload and measurement validity. In other words, how does one help decision-makers process information so that efficiency and effectiveness can be achieved? This can be approached through dimensionality analysis.

Factor analysis is a traditional dimensionality reduction technique. The exploratory nature of factor analysis fits well with our research question. With multiple categories of indicators from various sources, in particular with newly added measures from CSR perspectives, it is important to know whether indicators that are set to measure similar constructs would converge to a few key factors, and furthermore, whether any new structure involving a more explicit presentation of ESG dimensions would emerge.

A preliminary commonality test excluded two indicators: "change of government" and "coverage of primary education". Principal components analysis of the panel of 25 selected indicators revealed seven factors with eigenvalues greater than one, explaining 74.8% of the variance. Table 4.2 shows the varimax-rotated solution of indicators with absolute value of

*Table 4.1* Selected Indicators for Assessment of (Host) Country

| Original Categories | Indicators | Source |
|---|---|---|
| Economic and Financial | GDP growth rate | World Bank |
| | GDP per capita | World Bank |
| | Inflation | World Bank |
| | Stability of currency exchange rate | Calculated from World Bank data |
| | Country credit rating | S&P |
| | Effect of taxation on incentives to invest | GCI |
| | Local supplier quantity | GCI |
| | Local supplier quality | GCI |
| | Infrastructure | GCI |
| Governance | Change of government (time elapsed to election) | Coded from news in media |
| | Political stability and absence of violence | WGI |
| | Control of corruption | WGI |
| | Burden of government regulation | GCI |
| | Efficiency of legal framework in challenging regulations | GCI |
| | Number of procedures required to start a business | GCI |
| | Business impact of rules on FDI | GCI |
| Bilateral Relationship | Stock of FDI from China | China National Bureau of Statistics |
| | Trade (total amount of trade with China as a percentage of GDP) | China Bureau of Customs/ World Bank |
| | Diplomatic connectedness (official visits to each other by political leaders) | Ministry of Foreign Affairs, China |
| Social | Unemployment | World Bank |
| | Irregular payments and bribes | GCI |
| | Prevalence of foreign ownership | GCI |
| | Voice and accountability | WGI |
| | Cultural distance between China and the host country | Hofstede |
| | Primary education enrollment rate | GCI |
| Environmental | Environmental health | EPI |
| | Ecosystem vitality | EPI |

loading above 0.5. As expected, some measures seemed to be quite isolated, far from the larger groups as well as from each other, but for those that did converge, the actual validities of each factor were quite high. The only exception was factor 7 (F7), which was then treated as two factors.

From a methodological perspective, the advantages and disadvantages of using factor analysis to detect structure and dimensionality were both

Table 4.2 Factor Structure of Risk Indicators

| Risk Indicators | Factor | | | | | | |
|---|---|---|---|---|---|---|---|
| | $F_1$ | $F_2$ | $F_3$ | $F_4$ | $F_5$ | $F_6$ | $F_7$ |
| Law efficiency | 0.926 | | | | | | |
| Infrastructure | 0.854 | | | | | | |
| Supplier quantity | 0.853 | | | | | | |
| Bribe | 0.841 | | | | | | |
| Regulation | 0.828 | | | | | | |
| FDI law | 0.811 | | | | | | |
| Credit rating | −0.785 | | | | | | |
| Tax incentives | 0.779 | | | | | | |
| Supplier quality | 0.754 | | | | | | |
| FDI prevalence | 0.710 | | | | | | |
| GDP per capita | 0.607 | | | | | | |
| Business procedure | −0.601 | | | | | | |
| Inflation | −0.505 | | | | | | |
| Environment health | | 0.740 | | | | | |
| GDP growth | | −0.734 | | | | | |
| Ecosystem vitality | | 0.661 | | | | | |
| Corruption control | | | 0.884 | | | | |
| Political stability | | | 0.829 | | | | |
| Voice | | | 0.754 | | | | |
| FDI stock | | | | 0.846 | | | |
| Trade | | | | 0.828 | | | |
| Cultural distance | | | | | 0.737 | | |
| Exchange volatility | | | | | | 0.872 | |
| Diplomatic visits | | | | | | | −0.668 |
| Unemployment | | | | | | | 0.645 |

very obvious in our case. For one thing, it makes possible for the use of indicators from different sources to be mapped in the same space and shows relatively converged observations on similar constructs such as friendliness of general business environment towards FDI, the maturity of an environmentally healthy ecosystem, the maturity of political environment and economic connectedness. The internal validity of these factors is shown in Table 4.3 (all four composite factors have a Cronbach's alpha of above 0.7).

At the same time, results from the use of factor analysis also show how different environmental, social (unemployment), governance (political stability, corruption control and freedom) and connectedness measures could reflect the general business environment and each other. Even for connectedness alone, economic, cultural and diplomatic connectedness all fall on different dimensions. The implication of this is that maybe that they should not be treated in the same way in decision making. Differentiated treatments of various dimensions would require a test on a real sample, which leads to

*Table 4.3* Reliability Test of Composite Factors

| Factor | Label (Indicators) | Cronbach's α |
|---|---|---|
| $F_1$ | General Business Environment Towards Foreign Direct Investment ("*Inflation*", "*Credit rating*", "*Supplier quantity*", "*Supplier quality*", "*Regulation*", "*Law efficiency*", "*Business procedures*", "*FDI law*", "*Bribe*", "*FDI prevalence*", "*Tax incentives*", "*GDP per capita*", "*Infrastructure*") | 0.753 |
| $F_2$ | Maturity of an Environmentally Healthy Ecosystem ("*GDP growth*", "*Environmental health*", "*Ecosystem vitality*") | 0.716 |
| $F_3$ | Maturity of Political Environment ("*Political stability*", "*Corruption control*", "*Voice and accountability*") | 0.768 |
| $F_4$ | Economic Connectedness ("*FDI Stock*", "*Trade*") | 0.709 |

the next step for this investigation. A verification model was used to try to solve the issue of effectiveness.

### 3.4. Screening and Verification

There is a lack of generalisable empirical evidence for what actually leads to risks in the host country. Previous studies have tended to focus on the amount of FDI into the destination country, which is a little problematic in the context of risk management. There can be a range of reasons contributing to a company's decision whether to invest in one country, with the size of investments leading to complexity. Using the FDI amount as a dependent variable can at most explain risk-aversion behaviours of companies; this is not exactly risk management.

Following theories and conceptualisation of social license, CSR-related risk (or responsibility risk) can be defined as the possibility of conflicts taking place between the business and its stakeholders due to unfulfilled expectations. Hence, the probability of a risk incident is observed could be explained by the actual predictors. A responsibility risk incident is observed when negative news reports appear concerning topics such as stakeholder relations, including, but not limit to, worker strike behaviour, land-use disputes, conflicts with the local community, protests and the cancellation or postponement of investment projects.

A logit model was employed for this purpose. In doing so, a sample of overseas construction projects was used; these involved leading Chinese companies in the construction sector. These leading Chinese companies were identified through the Engineering News-Record top contractors list.

The China Global Investment Tracker database was used as the initial data source. The database was provided by the AEI, an independent research institute founded in 1938. The unit of analysis was the project, and the time frame used was from 2010–2015. Only projects of over 100 million dollars by the aforementioned top Chinese contractors were selected through information published on their websites and the accuracy of the data was cross-checked with a news search using Google (for English and Spanish news) and Baidu (for Chinese news). A sample of 787 projects involving 118 host countries was collected with information on value of the deal/project, size of the company (capitalisation) and status of the project (whether or not there is a responsibility risk incident). A further cleaning process to ensure completeness of each variable yielded the final dataset for analysis of 605 projects investing in 59 countries.

In evaluating the representativeness of the sample, the sample was compared with information from the China National Bureau of Statistics for the years 2010–2015, and it was found that the geographical distribution of the sample was fairly consistent with that in the overall data (as shown in Figures 4.1 and 4.2). Figure 4.1 sets out the distribution of Chinese construction projects in the sample (2010–2015); Figure 4.2 sets out the geographical distribution of projects by reference to their overall contracting value (2010–2015). The total amount of the sample projects represents a little over 60% of the overall Chinese investment in construction projects according to official records from China National Bureau of Statistics during the same period.

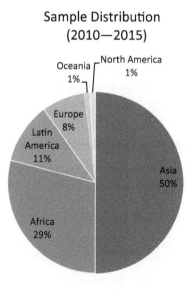

*Figure 4.1* Distribution of Chinese Construction Projects in Sample (2010–2015)

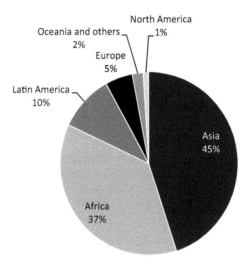

*Figure 4.2* Geographical Distribution of Overall Contracting Value (2010–2015)

Eight risk factors were revealed in factor analysis and the two individual indicators that had been excluded from the factor analysis became the predictors of the model. The sample was controlled for the two project-specific variables, deal value and company size. After applying logistic regression on the sample using risk incident as a dependent variable, four risk factors/indicators emerged as strong predictors – namely, 'general business environment towards FDI' (F1), 'maturity of an environmentally healthy ecosystem' (F2), 'change of government' and 'unemployment'. The results are shown in Table 4.4.

### 3.5. Country Responsibility Risk Index 2017 (CRRI 2017)

The four dimensions derived from the sample verification process become the components of the final index. Laying out concisely the economic, environmental, social and governance dimensions, these components have implications for their practical application and for theoretical development.

### 3.5.1. Component 1: General FDI Environment

First, the component labelled as 'general FDI environment' includes the most important general requirements needed for businesses involving

Table 4.4 Results of Logistic Regression on Responsibility Risk Incidence

| Variable | (1) | (2) | (3) | (4) | (5) | (6) | (7) | (8) | (9) | (10) | (11) |
|---|---|---|---|---|---|---|---|---|---|---|---|
| *Diplomatic connectedness* | | | | | | | | -0.054 | 0.023 | 0.034 | 0.175 |
| | | | | | | | | (0.176) | (0.182) | (0.184) | (0.197) |
| *Unemployment* | | | | | | | | | 0.330** | 0.336 | 0.330** |
| | | | | | | | | | (0.140) | (0.141) | (0.147) |
| *Primary education* | | | | | | | | | | -0.165 | -0.195 |
| | | | | | | | | | | (0.182) | (0.186) |
| *Change of government* | | | | | | | | | | | -0.894*** |
| | | | | | | | | | | | (0.237) |
| Constant | -2.759 | -3.007 | -2.986 | -2.989 | -2.991 | -3.018 | -3.056 | -3.058 | -3.111 | -3.125 | -3.386 |
| | (0.175) | (0.213) | (0.205) | (0.206) | (0.206) | (0.212) | (0.221) | (0.221) | (0.228) | (0.230) | (0.266) |
| Nagelkerke $R^2$ | 0.11 | 0.088 | 0.103 | 0.104 | 0.104 | 0.109 | 0.115 | 0.115 | 0.136 | 0.139 | 0.213 |
| p | 0.000 | 0.000 | 0.000 | 0.000 | 0.000 | 0.000 | 0.000 | 0.000 | 0.000 | 0.000 | 0.000 |

foreign ownership to survive and succeed in the host country. Its consistently significant predictive power shows how important the fundamental business environment is for operations including CSR initiatives. It is of interest to all parties to ensure a healthy investment environment. Contrary to the popularly held notion, none of the connectedness measures were significant in predicting CSR-related risk incidents, which indicates that to prevent or solve CSR-related conflicts, communications or interactions should get down to the ground and take place at the community level.

### 3.5.2. Component 2: Environmental Ecosystem

The second component, the 'environmental ecosystem', consists of three indicators: the two policy objectives evaluated in the EPI, 'environmental health' and 'ecosystem vitality', and an indicator outside of the environmental performance evaluation framework, 'GDP growth rate'. Although this is a relatively weak predictor in the full model of all factors and indicators included in this study, it shows strength in three of the embedded models. An interpretation for this component is that the more matured a country's environmental ecosystem, the higher the demand for environmental health and ecosystem vitality support, the lesser motivation for GDP growth, and the more likely that local stakeholders would have a higher expectation on environmental performance of the firm.

### 3.5.3. Component 3: Unemployment (Focal Social Issue)

The third component, 'unemployment', is currently a single indicator component. However, as employment to a large extent can be attributed to livelihood, this is a focal social issue that has been observed in many countries, and since its significance in the verification model is reduced when an education indicator is included, the component is a good representation of social considerations. The implications arising from this component is that higher CSR-related risks can be attached to a country with a higher unemployment rate, and CSR initiatives focusing on job creation or job-related training could probably alleviate the resistance of the local community and reduce the risk of investment.

### 3.5.4. Component 4: Change of Government (Governance System)

'Change of government' is more powerful than the other political stability measures and becomes the fourth component of the proposed composite index. After all, in state nations, there is literally no bigger change in the governance system than a change of government itself.

These indices constitute the output of the Country Responsibility Risk Index for Chinese Overseas Investment 2017. This index should be kept open to accommodate future amendments and alternative verification procedures, but to date, and on best available knowledge, this is the first index based upon empirical evidence that uses actual risk incidents in relation to CSR as the matched outcome.

### 3.5.5. Index Scores

As indicators have been standardised, and inconsistent and insignificant measures in relation to CSR-related risks have been screened out, a summated scale can be created to represent the Country Responsibility Risk Index. However, due to the skewed observation towards 'healthy' projects in the sample, it is desirable to highlight the most useful information so as to improve the effectiveness of the index. As a result, the 'entropy' weight concept was borrowed from information theory (Shannon 1948). In the current context, an indicator's entropy increases when its uncertainty or diversity goes up so that an indicator with higher entropy carries more effective information on risks than that one with a lower level of entropy. The Theil index (Summers & Heston 1991) was used as the entropy measure in this study. A robust check showed that its explanatory power of indices increased after the indicators were weighted with entropy.

In summary, the final composite index of CRRI 2017 comprises a weighted average of all the 18 indicators that stood out from the screening and verification process. The same method was used on the four component indices. Scores were transformed onto a scale of 20–100 so that a country with a lower risk would have a lower score. Final scores of the 81 countries with available information are shown in the appendix to this chapter.

## 4. Conclusions

Country-specific risks are critical for the success of multinational companies undertaking foreign investments. In recent years, with the increasing awareness of social and environmental impacts of businesses, questions have arisen as to how best to align CSR initiatives with risk management in cross-border investment; this has become an important topic for businesses as well as their stakeholders.

Using risk incidents of outbound direct investment of Chinese companies, this chapter has traced the roots of CSR-related risks, explored the emergence of ESG dimensions in the risk index space and proposed a composite index that would effectively highlight the trends in country-specific aspects which (Chinese) companies could use in order to avoid risks in stakeholder relationships. Such an index provides a reference for all stakeholders involved so that targeted strategies can be developed in the future for better managing CSR-related risks by Chinese investors in host countries.

## Acknowledgement

The authors wish to thank research team members from Tsinghua University School of Economics and Management and the SynTao consultancy for their contributions to the work, in particular, Bonan Lin for data processing and Hongfu Zhang, Haoxue Liu, Siran Huang and Yueyang Cao for inputs and fieldwork supports.

## Notes

1. School of Economics and Management, Tsinghua University, Beijing, China.
2. CEO, SynTao consultancy, Beijing; see further, www.syntao.com/AboutUs/AboutSyntao_EN.asp.

## References

Berry, H., Guillén, M. F. and Zhou, N. 2010, "An institutional approach to cross-national distance", *Journal of International Business Studies*, vol. 41, no. 9, pp. 1460–1480.

Bertrand, O., Betschinger, M.-A. and Settles, A. 2016, "The relevance of political affinity for the initial acquisition premium in cross-border acquisitions", *Strategic Management Journal*, vol. 37, no. 10, pp. 2071–2091.

Boutilier, R. G. and Thomson, I. 2014, "Modeling and measuring the social license to operate: Fruits of a dialogue between theory and practice", doi: 10.4000/vertigo.15139, www.researchgate.net/publication/276333081.

Bowman, E. H. 1980, "A risk/return paradox for strategic management", *Sloan Management Review*, vol. 21, no. 3, pp. 17–31.

Chen, X.-P. and Li, S. 2005, "Cross-national differences in cooperative decision-making in mixed-motive business contexts: The mediating effect of vertical and horizontal individualism", *Journal of International Business Studies*, vol. 36, no. 6, pp. 622–636.

Ghemawat, P. 2001, "Distance still matters", *Harvard Business Review*, vol. 79, no. 8, pp. 137–147.

Ghemawat, P. and Altman, S. A. 2016, *DHL global connectedness index 2016: The state of globalization in an age of ambiguity*, Deutsche Post DHL Group, Headquarters, Bonn, Germany.

Gunningham, N., Kagan, R. and Thornton, D. 2004, "Social license and environmental protection: Why businesses go beyond compliance", *Law and Social Inquiry*, vol. 29, no. 2, pp. 307–341.

Hofstede, G., Hofstede, G. J. and Minkov, M. 2010, *Cultures and organizations: Software of the mind*. Revised and Expanded 3rd Edition. New York: McGraw-Hill.

Hsu, A. et al. 2016, *2016 environmental performance index*. New Haven, CT: Yale University, available: www.epi.yale.edu.

Husted, B. W. 2005, "Risk management, real options, corporate social responsibility", *Journal of Business Ethics*, vol. 60, no. 2, pp. 175–183.

Li, K., Griffin, D., Yue, H. and Zhao, L. 2013, "How does culture influence corporate risk-taking?" *Journal of Corporate Finance*, vol. 23, pp. 1–22.

Shannon, C. E. 1948, "A mathematical theory of communication", *Bell System Technical Journal*, vol. 27, pp. 379–423, pp. 623–666.

Summers, R. and Heston, A. 1991, "The Penn world table (Mark 5): An expanded set of international comparisons, 1950–1988", *The Quarterly Journal of Economics*, vol. 106, no. 2, pp. 327–368.

Wang, S. Q., Dulaimi, M. D. and Aguria, M. Y. 2004, "Risk management framework for construction projects in developing countries", *Construction Management and Economics*, vol. 22, no. 3, pp. 237–252.

World Bank, *World development indicators 1960–2016*, available: https://data.worldbank.org/data-catalog/world-development-indicators.

World Bank, *Worldwide governance indicators 1996–2015*, available: https://data.worldbank.org/data-catalog/worldwide-governance-indicators.

World Economic Forum, 2016, *The global competitiveness report 2016–2017*.

# Appendix

Country Responsibility Risk Index
2017 for Chinese Overseas Investment

Composite and Component Scores (20–100)

| Rank | Country | Composite Score | General FDI Environment | Environmental Ecosystem | Unemployment | Change of Government |
|---|---|---|---|---|---|---|
| 1 | Qatar | 20 | 20 | 37 | 20 | 47 |
| 2 | Norway | 21 | 21 | 33 | 26 | 20 |
| 3 | Singapore | 40 | 30 | 20 | 21 | 100 |
| 4 | United Arab Emirates | 41 | 38 | 31 | 23 | 73 |
| 5 | Denmark | 46 | 38 | 39 | 25 | 87 |
| 6 | Australia | 47 | 40 | 36 | 21 | 87 |
| 7 | United Kingdom | 49 | 42 | 41 | 25 | 87 |
| 8 | Canada | 50 | 41 | 26 | 21 | 100 |
| 9 | United States | 51 | 45 | 43 | 21 | 87 |
| 10 | France | 54 | 50 | 46 | 20 | 73 |
| 11 | Israel | 57 | 55 | 44 | 23 | 73 |
| 12 | Kuwait | 61 | 61 | 70 | 22 | 73 |
| 13 | Brunei | 63 | 57 | 76 | 21 | 100 |
| 14 | Saudi Arabia | 63 | 58 | 51 | 23 | 100 |
| 15 | Oman | 64 | 60 | 40 | 20 | 100 |
| 16 | Panama | 64 | 67 | 37 | 21 | 47 |
| 17 | Malaysia | 65 | 59 | 22 | 23 | 100 |
| 18 | Barbados | 65 | 68 | 51 | 21 | 60 |
| 19 | Italy | 66 | 67 | 54 | 20 | 60 |
| 20 | Botswana | 68 | 70 | 60 | 27 | 60 |
| 21 | South Africa | 69 | 71 | 46 | 29 | 60 |
| 22 | Jordan | 71 | 73 | 44 | 25 | 60 |
| 23 | Senegal | 71 | 78 | 34 | 24 | 47 |
| 24 | Indonesia | 72 | 77 | 54 | 30 | 47 |
| 25 | Poland | 72 | 67 | 43 | 23 | 100 |
| 26 | Greece | 74 | 75 | 50 | 20 | 60 |

(Continued)

| Rank | Country | Composite Score | General FDI Environment | Environmental Ecosystem | Unemployment | Change of Government |
|---|---|---|---|---|---|---|
| 27 | Costa Rica | 74 | 75 | 59 | 24 | 60 |
| 28 | Philippines | 74 | 81 | 79 | 23 | 33 |
| 29 | India | 74 | 77 | 58 | 25 | 73 |
| 30 | Namibia | 74 | 74 | 55 | 29 | 73 |
| 31 | Trinidad Tobago | 75 | 69 | 50 | 25 | 100 |
| 32 | Turkey | 75 | 74 | 47 | 22 | 87 |
| 33 | Brazil | 75 | 84 | 79 | 22 | 20 |
| 34 | Laos | 75 | 77 | 39 | 21 | 87 |
| 35 | Morocco | 75 | 73 | 40 | 27 | 87 |
| 36 | Russian Federation | 75 | 76 | 46 | 24 | 60 |
| 37 | Thailand | 76 | 73 | 39 | 20 | 100 |
| 38 | Cameroon | 76 | 82 | 41 | 24 | 60 |
| 39 | Sri Lanka | 76 | 76 | 53 | 21 | 87 |
| 40 | Congo (Democratic Republic of) | 76 | 84 | 41 | 24 | 60 |
| 41 | Madagascar | 77 | 85 | 39 | 22 | 60 |
| 42 | Cambodia | 77 | 83 | 59 | 20 | 60 |
| 43 | Guatemala | 77 | 76 | 43 | 26 | 87 |
| 44 | Pakistan | 77 | 85 | 58 | 28 | 47 |
| 45 | Bulgaria | 77 | 75 | 40 | 33 | 73 |
| 46 | Kenya | 78 | 82 | 54 | 27 | 60 |
| 47 | Zambia | 78 | 77 | 40 | 26 | 87 |
| 48 | Mexico | 78 | 75 | 50 | 32 | 87 |
| 49 | Peru | 79 | 77 | 52 | 22 | 87 |
| 50 | Jamaica | 79 | 78 | 35 | 29 | 73 |
| 51 | Mongolia | 79 | 79 | 43 | 21 | 87 |
| 52 | Romania | 79 | 77 | 43 | 23 | 87 |
| 53 | Ghana | 79 | 83 | 50 | 20 | 73 |

| 54 | Hungary | 79 | 71 | 44 | 41 | 100 |
|---|---|---|---|---|---|---|
| 55 | Bangladesh | 79 | 87 | 56 | 26 | 60 |
| 56 | Tanzania | 80 | 84 | 52 | 21 | 73 |
| 57 | Sierra Leone | 80 | 84 | 52 | 24 | 73 |
| 58 | Chad | 80 | 89 | 58 | 24 | 60 |
| 59 | Croatia | 81 | 78 | 58 | 25 | 87 |
| 60 | Guyana | 81 | 80 | 58 | 35 | 73 |
| 61 | Malawi | 81 | 86 | 51 | 20 | 73 |
| 62 | Vietnam | 81 | 82 | 51 | 22 | 87 |
| 63 | Ecuador | 82 | 84 | 58 | 20 | 73 |
| 64 | Nepal | 82 | 85 | 78 | 21 | 87 |
| 65 | Nicaragua | 82 | 82 | 51 | 22 | 87 |
| 66 | Ethiopia | 82 | 84 | 49 | 20 | 100 |
| 67 | Egypt | 83 | 80 | 52 | 26 | 100 |
| 68 | Uganda | 83 | 85 | 47 | 22 | 87 |
| 69 | Colombia | 83 | 79 | 71 | 40 | 87 |
| 70 | Nigeria | 83 | 83 | 57 | 21 | 100 |
| 71 | Ukraine | 84 | 86 | 57 | 36 | 47 |
| 72 | Iran | 84 | 84 | 51 | 41 | 73 |
| 73 | Yemen | 84 | 90 | 48 | 36 | 47 |
| 74 | Angola | 85 | 88 | 61 | 29 | 73 |
| 75 | Mozambique | 86 | 84 | 57 | 49 | 100 |
| 76 | Syrian Arab Republic | 87 | 86 | 53 | 28 | 87 |
| 77 | Myanmar | 88 | 89 | 58 | 21 | 100 |
| 78 | Bolivia | 90 | 88 | 63 | 25 | 100 |
| 79 | Argentina | 92 | 88 | 75 | 27 | 100 |
| 80 | Serbia | 95 | 82 | 80 | 100 | 87 |
| 81 | Venezuela | 100 | 100 | 55 | 25 | 87 |

# 5 Challenging Issues in China's Mining Industry

## Human Resources and Others

*Ying Zhu*

## 1. Introduction

China has one of the world's largest mining industries, producing coal, gold and most rare earth minerals. In addition, China is also one of the world's leading consumers of most mining products, particularly for commodities like thermal coal and iron ore, approximately 49% and 58% of global total, respectively (HIN 2016). Currently, there are more than 10,000 (mostly coal) mines in China, producing a large amount of the world's supply. However, the mining industry in China is a fragmented one with many companies operating in the same area. The top is represented by large state-owned enterprises (SOEs) that extract and process resources on a provincial or regional scale. Most of the companies are also involved in various other business activities related to their mining operations with increasing involvement of local officials and private owners.

However, in recent years, due to the slowdown of overall national economic development, as well as the concern over serious air pollution in China, the central government has been targeting the mining sector in general, and coal mines in particular to reduce their capacity by closing certain mines. For example, China recently announced that it would shut down more than 1,000 coal mines, with a total production of 60 million tones in Guizhou, Yunnan, Heilongjiang and Jiangxi provinces; this is part of efforts to trim production capacity (HIN 2016). By the end of 2015, China reached its target by limiting the total number of coal mines below 10,000, and it will continue its efforts to reduce outdated capacity in the following years. In addition, according to Yin Weimin, the PRC minister for human resources and social security, 1.3 million job cuts will affect coal workers (Jamasmie 2016). In addition to closing mines, China plans to stop approving new coal mines for the next three years. As a part of new national thirteenth five-year plan, the development of the mining industry will facilitate various agendas such as developing western regions, protecting the environment and improving energy efficiency (Jamasmie 2016). The reduction of energy dependence on fossil fuels could be a key challenge for the mining sector. China plans to increase the use of non-fossil fuels from 11.4% in 2015 to 15% in 2020 of the country's total energy usage (HIN 2016).

So far, the key focus of the mining industry in China has been on its production capacity, its contribution to the national economy and on reports of accidents in the media. However, key challenges regarding human resource issues in the mining sector, including employment entitlements and working conditions, migrant workers and their treatment, safety issues and injury, and other related tensions, need to be discussed. Therefore, this chapter is designed to address these issues by using the recent statistical data and the author's previous fieldwork research in China. The structure of this chapter includes the following sections: Section 2 provides an underpinning theoretical framework based on the institutional theory and duty of care, at both macro and micro levels; it seeks to illustrate the role of key actors in the process of mining industry reform and development in general and by reference to work conditions and workers compensation (e.g. for injury) in particular. Section 3 illustrates key human resource challenges facing the mining industry in China. Section 4 discusses the relevant issues by responding to challenges from an institutional perspective as well as considering corporate management and human resource policies and practices. Finally, Section 5 concludes the chapter by highlighting the dilemma and on-going human resources challenges facing the mining industry in China and its possible future development directions.

## 2. Underpinning Theoretical Framework

Regarding the challenges facing the mining sector in China, analysis can be made at two levels, namely the macro and micro levels. At the macro level, an institutional approach can be used in order to identify the role and function of key players and their responsibilities within the Chinese society; at the micro-level, organisational and individual duty of care issues; consideration can also be given to deviant behaviour and compassionate responses towards work conditions; migrant workers and injured workers are discussed in order to see whether organisations and individuals, who are in the position to decide or assist workers to overcome bureaucratic barriers, influence the process to achieve positive outcome. By taking combined macro- and micro-level approaches, we can build a comprehensive understanding as suggested by Turner and Gray (2009) to investigate these issues through the social constructionist lens. In addition, a critical view of policy development, the role of government, trade unions, employers and other group and individual stakeholders, and future improvement in this regard could be generated.

### 2.1. Institutional Approach

Significant theoretical development in institutional theory has occurred since the second half of the twentieth century. The massive flow of interests from different schools of thought shows how institutions universally matter. Institutions are defined as "rules of the game in a society or, more formally, are the humanly devised constraints that shape human interaction" (North 1990: 3). Formal rules are, for example, legislation and constitutions, whereas informal rules are norms of behaviour, conventions and self-imposed codes of conduct (North 1994).

The institutional theory suggests that there are three components of institutions—namely formal rules, informal rules and the characteristics of their enforcement; each of these are of equal importance (North 1990). It also highlights the importance of embedded relationships and the power of informal rules. The theory claims that social actors are not entirely independent and certainly are not always rational. In relation to institutional change, the roles of informal rules should not be taken as given. Not only they could constrain institutional change, informal rules are also capable of instigating institutional change (Nee 1998). Indeed, as shown by more recent research, institutional changes may stem from changes in the path-dependent environment (Nee and Swedberg 2005).

However, in its early stage, institutional theory was silent in elucidating institutional change and gave relatively little attention to the role of strategic actors. In the early 1990s, a study of deinstitutionalisation (Oliver 1992) paved the ground for examining institutional change and theoretical advancement in response to the drawbacks that were identified. Institutional change is defined as "fundamental and comprehensive changes introduced to the formal and informal rules of the game that affect organisations as players" (Peng 2003). Further, Greenwood and Hinings (1996) highlight the role of different strategic actors, such as the government agents and company management, who act and interact with particular interests, and the relative permeability of organisations that are believed to drive institutional change.

In addition to the government and management, trade unions and other social groups such as NGOs could also be regarded as strategic actors. Strategic actors not only respond well to institutional change (Reay and Hinings 2005) but also initiate such change (Szelenyi and Kostello 1996; Dorado 2005). Hence, the theoretical focus has shifted to the phenomenon of institutional change and how the formal and informal rules of institutions interact. According to Nee and Swedberg (2005), the relationship between the formal and informal rules can be classified as 'close coupling', 'decoupling' and 'informal become opposition norms'. If an economy or organisation is to perform, it seems to be imperative for it to reach the state of 'coupling' within institutions. Nevertheless, 'decoupling' or 'oppositional informal rules' could be natural outcomes depending on the stage of institutional change. Yet, arriving at this idealistic point is extremely challenging. Given that behaviours are also path dependent, there is always temptation to sustain the status quo. In other words, the emergence of 'decoupling' has always been a real possibility.

Exposed to any institutional change, strategic actors are rarely silent. They could project themselves as being assets as well as liabilities to the initiators of changes. Inconsistency between their preferences or interests with the newly introduced formal rules could increase the possibility of their becoming liabilities. In order to secure their position, strategic actors could adopt a position of pragmatic legitimacy seeking, although this may not necessarily coincide with efficiency-seeking motives. This situation could not only block new initiatives, but may also jeopardise an organisation's performance (Nee and Ingram 1998) and its transformation process. Given that actors have the ability to respond to and initiate institutional change, there is a possibility that power could frequently shift between institutions and strategic actors.

Institutional change is particularly prevalent in an emerging economy such as China whose move toward a more open market with the 'new' concept of 'user pay' and profit-driven business decision-making rationale, which stands in contrast to the old central planning economy. Under such changes, workers who (in theory at least) were previously regarded as masters in the socialist society, become powerless groups. Mining workers, particularly those who are migrant workers or injured workers, become even more vulnerable given the reality of a lack of protection and inadequate compensation from employers whose only goal is to maximise profits as well as a lack of law enforcement and protection from the governments. Therefore, the institutional approach could guide us to investigate the role and interaction among the key strategic actors regarding such employment conditions and the treatment of mining workers in general; this is especially important for migrant workers and injured workers. It is also important to analyse whether current regulations and law enforcement are adequate to protect vulnerable working people in society. More detailed elaboration of this is presented in the discussion and conclusion sections of this chapter.

### 2.2. *Duty of Care and Positive Deviance: Compassion Towards Victims*

At a micro level, a key element that leads to positive outcomes regarding workers' well-being is the duty of care and compassion demonstrated by organisations and individuals who are in a position to manage workers. Such behaviour as 'positive deviance' could be defined as pro-social rule-breaking behaviour whereby acts are performed with the intention of promoting the welfare of another individual, group or organisation (Morrison 2006). This is constructive behaviour based on voluntary action that violates significant norms so as to enhance the well-being of the organisation or its stakeholders. To some degree, persons who display such behaviour could be seen as principled dissenter who refuse to behave as instructed due to their perception that policy is wrong (Morrison 2006). Waldman et al. (2011) examine the perception of victim and the way that organisations and individual officials react and respond to their needs after an abuse or injury has occurred. They note that victims expect government agents to provide them with a humane response for their mental and physical circumstance. Financial aid, physical, emotional and mental assistances are all important—an impact that necessitates compassionate responses. Given the reality that most government agents and service providers (e.g. insurance companies) are bureaucratic and ineffective in responding to both material and psychological needs of victims, if individuals working in these organisation could take a set of compassionate responses towards victims and push for changes, then the outcomes not only help victims to alleviate suffering and give meaning to their survival but also enable the government agents and other institutions to gain legitimacy and enhance their reputation; this will improve social stability in the long term (Waldman et al. 2011).

Furthermore, the handling of mistreatment towards workers is not only relevant to the government agents and other social institutions but also influences the legitimacy of an individual company's business; this satisfies the requirement for meeting the need to maintain the well-being and quality of life of their stakeholders, particularly their employees (Doh and Guay 2006). Managers must be made aware of the importance of social issues and maintain a focus on the interests of stakeholders who affect, or in turn are affected by, the company (Freeman 1984). If managers can behave in a socially responsible manner with a humane and compassionate attitude to the handling of mistreatment, then it would enhance the ability of their company to gain legitimacy in the wider society (Mitchell et al. 1997). This action could be seen as a means whereby companies take social responsibility seriously so that decision making is consistent with current social and cultural norms (i.e. developing social harmony) that emphasise desirable, proper or appropriate corporate behaviour within socially constructed systems (Mitchell et al. 1997).

Hence, this literature illustrates some of the key issues in this chapter, particularly whether individuals and organisations in both public and private sectors adopt certain positive and constructive actions to help workers, especially vulnerable migrant and injured workers so as to foster the well-being of multiple individuals, companies and institutions as well as the entire society. More detailed elaboration of these issues will be discussed in the later part of this chapter.

## 3. Challenges in the Mining Industry

### 3.1. *General Background to the Mining Industry*

According to China's 2003 Policy on Mineral Resources, the country has identified reserves of 10 energy-related mineral resources (including oil, natural gas, coal and uranium) and 54 types of metallic mineral resources (including iron, manganese, copper, bauxite, lead and zinc). Additionally, there are reserves of 91 varieties of non-metallic resources (including graphite, phosphorus and sulphur) (Greenovation Hub 2014). These resources are spread across the country, such as in the western and central regions (including the provinces of Xinjiang, Gansu, Shaanxi, Shanxi, and Inner Mongolia) which are known to have the most extensive resources (Greenovation Hub 2014). According to the National Bureau of Statistics, mining has directly contributed around 5% of China's total GDP (NBSC 2016). This figure is significantly higher if downstream industries and revenues are taken into account.

Traditionally, China was seen as a rich country in coal, but poor in other forms of resources. To ensure a reliable energy supply, China had relied largely on domestic energy resources to develop its economy. Under this policy, coal had provided the dominant component of China's primary energy needs and now accounts for more than 70% of the primary energy consumption, carrying the load for sustaining China's high GDP growth for the past three decades with the rate of self-sufficiency above 90% (Peng 2010). Moreover, coal provides 77% of the energy for power generation, 65% of chemical raw material and more than 50% of commercial civilian energy. The coal industry and related sectors offer many job opportunities. The economic development and social life of China are heavily based on domestic energy production and coal provides more than 90% of proven reserves of nationally available conventional energy (SETC) (Wang 2015).

However, the mining sector varies greatly considering its scale, geology, production technology and safety performance. The available statistics related to coal mining vary; formal large mines have more reliable data collection systems and production technology compared with small mines.

Although China has total proven coal reserves of 997 billion tones, they are located mainly in the west and northeast, very remote regions without sufficient population to support and an overwhelming majority of these reserves are only accessible by way of underground mining. This adds more difficulties to commercializing these mines and impose high cost in regard to building facilities and transportation.

Since 2000, China's coal industry has been progressively reorganised. Coal production has been controlled and production distribution is being reorganised. Larger coal production groups have been formed and small and medium coal mines are being consolidated. Township mines in particular were consolidated with larger national strategic mines under government guidance. Meanwhile, a Chinese-styled market economy was applied to the coal industry. Currently, China has about 15,000 mines; of these, 12,000 produced less than 300,000 tones annually (Wang, 2015). The latest policy is to build larger group companies with sufficient resources to manage and operate larger state-of-the-art mines.

Mines in China are traditionally grouped into three types: national, provincial national and township mines. National strategic mines are mines developed and operated directly by the central government under the original planned economy. In recent years, consolidated small mines have been included. There are a total of 268 national mines located in 22 provinces with production accounting for 50.7% of the national production (Wang 2015). Provincial national mines are mines developed and operated directly by the 26 provincial governments in which the mines are located, and their production accounts for 12.7% of the national total (Wang 2015). In recent years, consolidation of small mines has also occurred. Township mines are those developed after coal markets opened in 1980 and operated by county and city governments in which the mines are located or by private citizens. They are located in 26 provinces with production accounting for 36.6% of national output (Wang 2015). In addition, a majority mines in China are underground mines, accounting for 85.9% of total production, and open-pit mining only comprises 6% with other types of mining comprising 8.1%. There are more than 20 different underground coal mining methods used in China, but longwall methods predominate (Wang 2015).

### 3.2. Changing Government Administration on Mine Safety

In the process of changing administrative control over national industries in 1997, the central government decided to abolish the freestanding ministries of several industries including coal. More than 800 employees of the Ministry of Coal Industry in Beijing were going to be laid off, but after more than a decade's evolution, the State Administration of Coal Mine Safety (SACMS) was formally established. Today, SACMS has 26 provincial branch offices in coal-producing provinces with a total of 73 district offices (Wang 2015).

Mining accident rates vary widely for different mining groups. There are many safe mines, but many mines adopt unsafe mining practices. Accident rates, such as the fatality rate, are defined by number of fatalities per 1 million tons of coal produced. The fatality rate has been decreasing steadily for the past 30 years. However, the imbalance between areas of production and demand provides the opportunity for the unsafe small township mines to continue to contribute to fatality numbers. Township mines have been the major problem areas producing 37% of the total coal but accounting for 73% of fatalities (Wang 2015).

The major categories of accidents consist of gas, flooding, roof fall, fire and haulage problems. Gas accidents included primarily coal and gas outbursts, followed by methane explosions. They occurred more at the underground roadway development and in the township mines. The causes of methane gas explosions included either a lack of a methane monitoring system or improperly installed or insufficient sensors, improper local ventilation or mine ventilation systems, and illegal blasting and faulty electric equipment.

Under the pressure from social media, governments have been working to reduce accident and fatality rates. In addition to strengthening the enforcement of safety supervision of coal mines, and guiding local governments and enterprises to intensify efforts in technological upgrading for coal mine safety, the construction of safety facilities and shutting down the illegally operated small township mines, the most effective means of reducing fatalities has been the closure of small township mines.

### 3.3. Negative Environmental Impact

In recent years, both governments and citizens have paid much attention to the risk of serious environmental and social impact due to the development of the mining industry. The most obvious and immediate impact is generally on the environment in the immediate vicinity of the mine. Mining can be extremely intensive in terms of resource consumption, and large amounts of water and electricity are often required during various stages of mining and processing. For example, the mining, washing and processing of coal are all extremely water intensive. However, 70% of China's 15,000 coal mines are located in water-scarce regions, and inefficient mining operations in these areas threaten to exacerbate drought by over-exploiting groundwater (Greenovation Hub 2014).

Mining and processing also produce large amounts of solid and liquid waste, much of this is highly toxic. Waste that is not properly disposed of can become a serious environmental hazard. Chemicals used in mining may also run off and poison drinking water and land, rivers and lakes. In recent years, a number of serious water pollution cases have made headlines, and government studies have confirmed the existence of 'cancer villages' emerging in areas affected by heavy pollution (Greenovation Hub 2014).

### 3.4. Human Resources Challenges in Mining Industry

There are a number of human resources challenges currently facing China's mining industry. One of the most significant of these challenges is the need to reduce the workforce in the mining sector, especially in coal mines due to government policy to reduce pollution. The most recent data shows that the mining sector reached the peak employment level of 11.46 million in 2012 (CLSY, 2013) with 6.6 million in the coalmining sector (Wang, 2015); since then, the number of employed in this sector has declined gradually. In the coal mining sector, the total number of employees was reduced by a total of 1.3 million jobs in 2016 (The Guardian, 2016). Therefore, managing retrenched workers and retraining these workers has become a very serious challenge for the industry given that most mines are located in the relatively remove regions and far away from major industrial centres.

Another very challenging issue is the frequently reported problem of mine safety. The long-term health of workers is an issue, especially in coal mines, where they may fall victim to pneumoconiosis or 'black lung disease' after years spent working in mines with inadequate safety equipment. Although the overall death toll in China's coal mines has declined from 5,543 in 2000 to 1,973 in 2011 (Greenovation Hub 2014), this number is still high.

Serious problems are not only related to accidents, but the impact on family members as well as the need to pay compensation for dead and injured workers and their families.

Among the workforce in the mining industry, migrant workers (the so-called mingong) account for 56% of the total workforce (*China Daily*, 28/11/2006). Many migrant workers shift back and forth between mines and the family farm or constantly move between different mines. The working and living conditions of the mingong in the mining industry are poor and dangerous. They often obtain work in the industry through introduction by people from their village. For most mingong, earning more money is the main purpose for their leaving home where they earn less by doing agricultural work. They normally work through different shifts day and night with more than 10 to 12 hours work per day. Piece rates and hourly rate pays are normal and their income level depends on how much they produce. Therefore, many workers work tirelessly in long hours in order to get more income over a short period of time. This also increases the frequency of injury or other accident due to fatigue. Generally speaking, small mines have problems such as long working hours, many sanctions, a lack of labour contracts and violations of the Chinese Labour Law. However, in most cases, the local administrations do not act to correct these problems, not wanting to upset potential investors or endanger the bosses' profits. The gruelling work pace, the lack of breaks, lack of sleep and outdated and defective machines, missing or lacking instructions and maintenance or simple disregard of safety measures to reach production goals explain the high number of accidents leading to personal injuries. The high death toll in mines is well known and most of these death due to poor safety standards. Besides overt injuries and casualties, there are also 'hidden' problems such as workers who constantly faint or face mental health problems because they cannot stand the stress of mining work (Libcom 2010).

Pervious research shows that the major cause of 'black lung disease' is attributed to breathing dust in the workplace, mainly in coal mining (Zhu et al. 2014). The cause of other injuries include long working hours and heavy workloads that lead to injury as well as unsafe work or machinery design and no protection from poisoning (as result of gas and other chemicals being used in mines). Several key elements lead to the widespread presence black lung among workers working in those sectors, including a lack of protective equipment, a lack of regular physical examination of workers' health and a paucity of inspections by local government health and labour authorities. One mining worker claimed,

> I found my lung problem in 1997 after 7 years working in the coal mine. There was not any protection from getting dust arranged by the company. Actually, I brought my own mask to protect myself but others were laughing at me at that time. Eventually, workers without mask became ill earlier and their situation is worse than mine.

As for other injuries, they are mainly due to long working hours and heavy workload. As another worker complained,

> We have to work from 6am to 11pm. After lunch, we have to start work immediately. Other companies may have a 30 minutes break but we do not have any break. Workers fell so tired so that accidents happen from time to time.

Lack of regular health checks is a serious problem, and when workers found out they had lung disease, the employers would not want to pay the bill for treatment, as one worker explained,

> We don't have regular health checking, but when the people from the health bureau came to check, there were six workers with lung disease and I was one of them. We need to get immediate medical treatment in the hospital but the employer did not want to pay the bill and the treatment was delayed for another six months.

In fact, the cost of medical treatment and relevant compensation are the major concerns among injured workers, including issues such as who covers the treatment cost at the hospital and the continuation of medication after the hospital treatment, as well as who covers the compensation for the injury and loss of working capability, and determining how much compensation injured workers should get?

The entire process is very complicated, and in practice, it is difficult for injured workers to get adequate compensation. The first step is to get official certificate to prove the industrial injury. In order to get this done, workers need to get all the documents from their employers to demonstrate that they have an employment relationship and then they could take health checks at the local official hospital and obtain approval from the local health bureau with a certificate of industrial injury. However, there are cases of employers who have denied the employment relationship by not signing labour contracts and paying insurance coverage; some even lie to workers about no need for insurance coverage. Some employers even do not register the business and do not take out insurance coverage. Other extreme cases include employers terminating employment contract when a worker is found to be ill.

Two major issues concern injured workers during the post-injury process—namely, the cost of hospital treatment and related costs and the payment of final compensation to them. In my previous research, some workers have to cover their own treatment by borrowing money as they could not prove the existence of an employment relationship with the employers or because their employment contract was terminated. Others who have a clear employment relationship with their employers, the employers would cover the cost of hospital treatment, but workers do not dare raise the issue of the compensation during the period of their treatment due to their concern that they may lose financial support as a result. In addition, a number of cases did not receive any compensation for reasons presented earlier. Whilst some injured workers received compensation, most were not satisfied with the amount of compensation received.

## 3.5. Institutional Support for Injured Workers

Injured workers have mixed views about the support of relevant government agencies, trade union branches, NGOs and other supporting groups and individuals. There are both positive and negative reactions, but there is a great need for further improvement.

The major criticism of government agencies was that they did not take their duty of care seriously but play 'ping-pong' between each other as one worker claimed:

> The health bureau and labour bureau always tried to tell you that our problems did not belong to their agencies. We did not know every much about their duty and responsibility. Many injured workers could not wait for the final solution being made by the government agencies and eventually gave up.

Another worker explained the confusion among injured workers:

> Different government agencies did not work together, for instance, health inspection found the problem in the workplace, then we could have an opportunity to get a health check at the hospital. The health bureau issued an industrial injury certificate, then the labour bureau made judgement on the level of injury and relevant compensation. But if there was a disagreement between employer and employee on the amount of compensation, then they would go to labour arbitration. If this could still not lead to an agreement, they could go to court. You can see how many agencies get involved and what a complicated procedure there is for workers to understand. I have learnt all of these after being injured, otherwise I would not know at all.

Most injured workers also criticize the process of labour arbitration and note that legal procedures at court could drag on for a very long period; but injured workers could not afford this in terms of financial difficulty and time (i.e. workers with black lung problem could not live longer). Two workers had a similar experience and claimed,

> The law enforcement agents adopted a 'selective' approval that was not very good for workers. If the injury was not very serious, they would just pretend to care about it by making a phone call. But if the injury

was a serious one, then all the procedures could drag on for years from the initial health check to the end of getting compensation. Many workers even got an arbitration result or court judgement to obtain compensation, but the employers would not pay it. Lack of law enforcement has been a serious problem.

Another worker inquired about his black lung problem in April 2003: "I used legal aid and a lawyer has been helping me since then and the legal procedure has been dragging on till now (June 2010) and there has been no final result".

Most workers did not trust trade unions and thought trade unions were useless organisation. Some even criticised the unions taking sides with employers as one worker claimed, "The union leader at my company was a relative of the boss. He did not help workers at all". Another worker commented, "When we have troubles, we do not go to the unions for help because they are useless".

However, many injured workers had very positive comments about NGOs, legal aid professionals and others, they claimed, "People from labour protection NGOs were very helpful. They came to hospital to explain the compensation procedures, the relevant regulations and help us getting legal aid". "NGO groups came to look after us and explained the law and regulation to us so we understand how to protect ourselves". Some individual professional people such as labour lawyers and local People's Congress members also played an important role to help injured workers obtain justice; as one worker explained,

> I asked the labour bureau and health bureau to help me but they did not care about my case. I contacted a local People's Congress member and he helped me get a legal aid lawyer to submit my case to the court. Although my case has been dragging on for many years, both of them have been supporting me all the time.

Many injured workers were also grateful for the care and support obtained from their local hospital, in particular doctors and nurses.

## 4. Discussion

As an emerging economy, China has experienced rapid economic growth in the past three decades, but the areas of workers' rights, social justice and the 'rule of law' are still at a very backward stage. This chapter has discussed challenges in the mining industry in general, and human resources and work conditions in particular, and identified multiple causes of the social injustice outcome. In this chapter, two theoretical approaches have been adopted: at the macro level, the institutional theory provides the underpinning for the argument that social actors are not entirely independent and their interaction under the influence of formal and informal rules could lead to institutional change. The evidence demonstrates that formal rules, such as government laws and regulations have been developed in recent years, but the problems are more often associated with the lack of implementation and enforcement. This is more related to the informal rules being more important, such as officials taking a more favourable attitude towards investors and business in order to promote local economic development, but with less concern for the workers' rights and well-being. A feudalist tradition also influences the relationship between the official as 'guan' and ordinary people as 'xiaomin', namely little people (i.e. especially in regard to mingong), and with such a hierarchical social relationship, little people are left to beg officials to protect them. Among the injured workers, many felt the same way towards the government and experienced many difficulties in getting things done by the government agencies.

Another important phenomenon is related to the relationships between the formal and informal rules as 'decoupling' and 'oppositional informal rules'. From the evidence, people can observe the pattern of 'decoupling' between the formal laws and regulations on the one hand, but different responses by companies and different practices by law enforcement agencies (i.e. labour arbitration and people's court) on the other. Sometimes, there are even strong 'oppositional informal rules' occurring due to illegal and irregular behaviour among different actors, such as unregistered business without legitimacy, registered companies not paying social insurance contributions, the absence of labour contracts, nepotism between officials and business people; these problems are the major causes for social injustice and could also eventually lead to social conflict as we observed in recent years. Social groups, such as NGOs, are very helpful but at an infant stage in China and other groups, such as trade union branches, do not protect workers in a sufficient way. Therefore, these phenomena could be seen as some of the key characteristics of a society in transition, but there is no blueprint and clear eventual goal. Without careful guidance and management from above, the society could shift to chaos and upheaval, and 'transition to where' is a serious question for everyone.

At the micro level, individual behaviour of those people with the power and position that influences the well-being of workers through the application of a duty of care and positive deviance. Based on the comments made by some of the injured workers, they have had some positive experiences when dealing with officials, NGOs and other professional individuals (e.g. health officials, local People's Congress member, legal aid people and doctors and nurses in the hospital) who have done their best to help them. These people's actions, as Waldman et al. (2011) claim, are all important—an impact that necessitates compassionate responses. However, there are also many cases of bureaucracy and ineffective responses from the government agents as well as injustice caused by illegitimate and unethical behaviour of company owners, managers and other individuals holding political and economic power.

## 5. Conclusion

The evidence and considerations presented here lead us to develop a diagram of workers as victims under the process of social and economic transformation in China (see Figure 5.1). China's society is in transformation with 'social stability' as a top priority; this requires the support of 'social harmony' that is one of the core values and ideologies under the current leadership pushing for the socialist market economy. However, there are undermining phenomena which limit achieving such goals—namely, the continued existence of social injustice and unfairness, and these have been exemplified by the problem of injured workers without appropriate compensation. Within the new market-oriented economic environment, two aspects influence the outcomes of the transformation: economic competition and profitability for economic growth on the one hand, and social justice, ethics and the rule of law on the other. These elements influence organisational behaviour between economic-gain driven versus positive deviance behaviours. They also impact on the individual well-being; as for those cases, the injured workers being treated unfairly versus being treated fairly. Both negative and positive elements do exist in the society, but if negative elements dominate in society and then individual and society's well-being would be damaged and, consequently, there would be social conflict and chaos. As a result, the realisation of the eventual goal of creating a better society through economic development could be undermined.

Hence, this conceptualisation has some practical implications. The government agents and other social groups including trade unions need to act to protect vulnerable individuals in society so that social progression can be achieved along the way of economic development. In addition, business legitimacy requires mining industry owners and managers to behave like corporate citizens with social responsibility rather than as just profit makers. Business reputation building relies on fair treatment of their fellow workers. Otherwise, China can never become a true civilised society with social consciousness. These elements shed light on the future research direction by focusing on social justice and organisational safety and health issues, especially related to the policy on prevention, actual investment in safety facilities and maintenance, safety training, social insurance coverage and medical treatment and compensation procedures. A large scale of survey among different industry sectors and locations would enable a better understanding of safety and health policy and practices at the organisational level in China. In addition, better policy initiatives at the mining industry level, as well as at the individual mine level, could also be developed.

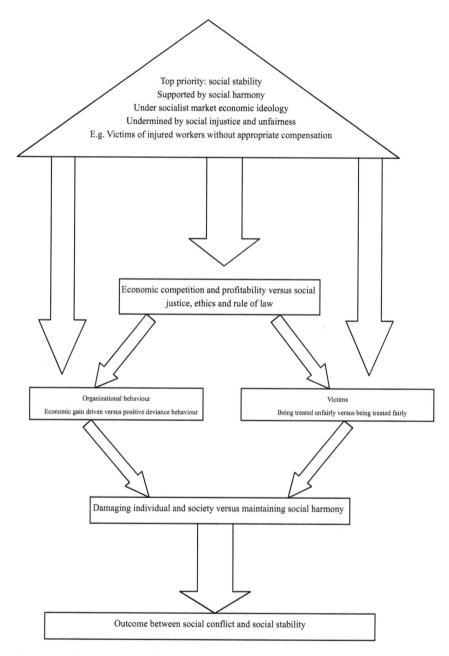

Top priority: social stability
Supported by social harmony
Under socialist market economic ideology
Undermined by social injustice and unfairness
E.g. Victims of injured workers without appropriate compensation

Economic competition and profitability versus social justice, ethics and rule of law

Organizational behaviour
Economic gain driven versus positive deviance behaviour

Victims
Being treated unfairly versus being treated fairly

Damaging individual and society versus maintaining social harmony

Outcome between social conflict and social stability

*Figure 5.1* The Diagram of Workers as Victims Under the Process of Social and Economic Transformation in China

# References

CLSY 2013, *China labour statistical yearbook*, China Statistics Press, Beijing.

Doh, J. P. and Guay, T. R. 2006, "Corporate social responsibility, public policy, and NGO activism in Europe and the United States: An institutional-stakeholder perspective", *Journal of Management Studies*, vol. 43, pp. 47–73.

Dorado, S. 2005, "Institutional entrepreneurship, partaking, and convening", *Organization Studies*, vol. 26, no. 3, 383–413.

Freeman, R. E. 1984, *Strategic management: A stakeholder approach*, Pitman, Boston, MA.

Greenovation Hub. 2014, "China's mining industry at home and overseas: Development, impacts and regulation", *Greenovation Hub*, available: www.ghub.org/.../China-Mining-at-Home-and-Overseas_Main-report2, accessed: 1 December 2016.

Greenwood, R. and Hinings, C. R. 1996, "Understanding radical organizational change: Bringing together the old and the new institutionalism", *Academy of Management Review*, vol. 21, no. 4, 1022–1054.

The Guardian 2016, "China to cut 1.8m jobs in coal and steel sectors", *The Guardian*, available: www.theguardian.com/business/2016/feb/29/china-to-cut-jobs-in-coal-and-steel-sectors, accessed 2 December 2016.

HIN 2016, "Mining industry in China", *Holland Innovation Network*, available: http://news.nost.org.cn/mining-industry-in-china/, accessed 2 December 2016.

Jamasmie, C. 2016, "China to Axe 1.8 million coal, steel jobs", *Mining Com*, available: www.mining.com/china-to-axe-1-8-million-coal-steel-jobs/, accessed 2 December 2016.

Libcom. 2010, "China's migrant workers", *Libcom.org*, available: https://libcom.org/history/chinas-migrant-workers, accessed 3 December 2016.

Mitchell, R. K., Agle, B. R. and Wood, D. J. 1997, "Toward a theory of stakeholder identification and salience: Defining the principle of who and what really counts", *Academy of Management Review*, vol. 22, pp. 853–886.

Morrison, E. W. 2006, "Doing the job well: An investigation of pro-social rule breaking", *Journal of Management*, vol. 32, pp. 5–28.

NBSC 2016, *National bureau of statistics of China*, available: http://stats.gov.cn/fjsj/jdsj/, accessed 1 December 2012.

Nee, V. 1998, "Norms and networks in economic and organizational performance", *American Economic Review*, vol. 87, no. 4, pp. 85–89.

Nee, V. and Ingram, P. 1998, "Embeddedness and beyond: Institutions, exchange and social structure", in I. M. Brinton and V. Nee (eds.) *The new institutionalism in sociology*, Russell Sage Foundation, New York, pp. 19–45.

Nee, V. and Swedberg, R. 2005, *The economic sociology of capitalism*, Princeton University Press, Princeton.

North, D. C. 1990, *Institutions, institutional change and economic performance*, Cambridge University Press, Cambridge.

North, D. C. 1994, "Economic performance through time", *The American Economic Review*, vol. 84, no. 3, pp. 359–368.

Oliver, C. 1992, "The antecedents of deinstitutionalization", *Organization Studies*, vol. 13, no. 4, 563–588.

Peng, M. W. 2003, "Institutional transitions and strategic choices", *Academy of Management Review*, vol. 28, 275–296.

Peng, S. S. 2010, *Understanding the Chinese coal industry*, available: www.coalage. com/features/593-understanding-the-chinese-coal- industry.html#.WGs0ytK7r48, accessed: 3 December 2016.

Reay, T. and Hinings, C. R. 2005, "The re-composition of an organizational field: Health care in Alberta", *Organization Studies*, vol. 26, no. 3, pp. 351–384.

Szelenyi, I. and Kostello, E. 1996, "The market transition debate", *American Journal of Sociology*, vol. 101, no. 4, 1082–1096.

Turner, N. and Gray, G. C. 2009, "Socially constructing safety", *Human Relations*, vol. 62, pp. 1259–1266.

Waldman, D. A., Carmeli, A. and Halevi, M. Y. 2011, "Beyond the red tape: How victims of terrorism perceive and react to organizational responses to their suffering", *Journal of Organizational Behavior*, vol. 32, 938–954.

Wang, Q. I. 2015, *Coal industry in China—Nautilus institute for security and sustainability*, available: www.nautilus.org/wp-content/uploads/2015/04/C5_final. pdf, accessed: 3 December 2016.

Zhu, Y., Chen, P. and Zhao, W. 2014, "Injured workers in China: Injustice, conflict and social instability", *International Labour Review*, vol. 153, no. 4, pp. 635–647.

# 6　China's Rising Online Food Trading

## Its Implications for the Rest of the World

*Pinghui Xiao*

## 1. Introduction: Emerging Online Food Trading in China

On April 20, 1994, Mainland China got access to the Internet on a permanent basis, marking China's entering an Internet era (Yiguan International 2016:6). Chen and Li put forward the three stages of China's Internet development: Introduction Period, Commercialisation Period and Social Embracing (Chen and Li 2014:6–14). However, it is widely recognised that the year of 1995 is the beginning of China's Internet commercialisation, as the year saw Jack Ma made an epoch by creating a Chinese yellow page portal. Since 1995, there has been dramatic development throughout China's Internet commercialisation. From 2000, online media companies like Sina, Sohu and Netease grow their popularity and become iconic online news providers in China. The period between 2003 and 2007 marked an entertainment and online shopping era. The outbreak of SARS (severe acute respiratory syndrome) in China in 2002 gave an unexpected boost to China's nascent e-commerce. Those confined to their dormitories or homes for days or weeks, began Internet surfing for information, entertainment and shopping.[1] In 2007, China's Ministry of Commerce released the first e-commerce development government blueprint, the eleventh five-year plan for e-commerce. The plan established the development strategy of e-commerce and roadmap to make it happen. The same year also witnessed the formation of a unified national e-government network framework (Jiang 2015; China Internet Information Center 2017; Huang 2016). Since then, China's online shopping has gained more momentum. Baidu, Alibaba, Tencent (so-called BAT elite group) and Jingdong (JD) grow to become top-ten world's largest Internet companies, making China a world player in this area (He 2015).

The Internet has a huge social influence and really changed how food businesses are conducted in China. It has created a new genre of food business running, called online food trading, which is somehow interchangeable with food e-commerce in relevant laws.[2] There are 32.1 billion Internet users in the world in 2015, and the number is expected to grow to 4.17 billion by 2020, meaning that more than half of the world's population is going surfing. At the same time, the mobile Internet is projected to experience a rapid growth. The year of 2015 saw that global smartphone users reached 1.86 billion and the number is expected to reach 2.87 billion in 2020. That means that more than half of the global mobile phone users are those using smartphones (Yiguan International 2016:5–6). China's Internet development exceeds the world average. In June 2016, the number of Internet users in China reached 700 million people, with the Internet penetration rate of 51.7%, well above global average (Yiguan International 2016:5–6). The Internet provides a virtual space and tool for communication and trading. Its merits lie in its convenience and ease to reach customers. Before the Internet, other means such as telephone also served for similar purposes. But the arrival of the Internet has made possible quicker and more interactive communications and trading with a full range of services, and gradually it grows to replace the traditional distance selling via phone call. According to the China Cuisine Association, its survey reports conducted in 2013 and 2014 show that telephone bookings have a substantial decline from 52.8% in 2013 to 40% in 2014, while at the same time Internet bookings (via third-party online platforms, App, corporate official website) are gradually climbing up to 39.8%.

The same period saw the ratio of cash payment declined from 39.3% to 20.3%. In 2014, payment via third party online platforms for catering services (including prepaid and on-site pay) climbed up to 30.3% (Jiang 2016:170–173). There is an ever-increasing boom in e-commerce including food e-commerce. In 2014, trade volume of e-commerce in China already recorded more than two trillion US dollars, which is around one-fifth of China's GDP in the same year and revenue by Alibaba Group alone is projected to overtake that of Walmart in 2015.[3] There are 45 million people regularly purchasing foods over the Internet in China, and the sales volume is projected to reach around 20 billion US dollars in 2018 (Xiao 2015).

Overall, China's online commodity and food trading presents the following characteristics.

First, scale is large. From 2012 to 2013, China's Internet industry put forward the concept of 'Internet Plus'. In the second session of the Twelfth National People's Congress in 2015, Premier Li Keqiang echoed on this notion and proposed the "Internet Plus" Action Plan in his work report. First-tier cities such as Beijing, Shanghai, Guangzhou and Shenzhen are the leading players in terms of the Internet development index (Yiguan International 2016:7). Within the 'Internet Plus" initiative in China, e-commerce plays a big role due to its huge market volume. Total turnover in 2015 amounted to 18.3 trillion yuan (2.66 trillion US dollar), an increase of 36.5%; of which Business-to-business (B2B) business accounting adding up to 19.3 trillion yuan (2.79 trillion US dollar) and online retailing reached 3.88 trillion yuan (562.3 billion US dollar) (Yiguan International 2016:8).

Second, the proportion of online food within the retailing sector is relatively small but online foods have an unprecedented growth potential. Food is also an important commodity category within online platforms (Zheng 2015). The Internet becomes an influential tool to facilitate food business operations. Consumers and food business operators use the Internet to communicate and pay, which makes transactions possible and efficient. As of 2014, there are online shops selling agricultural products as many as 750,000 within Alibaba (Ali Research Center 2015:153). Statistics show that China has 45 million people regularly purchasing foods through the Internet. The total online food trading accounts for about 2.5% of the total retail sales in China, with the total of the year 2013 reaching 32.4 billion yuan, 47.9% growth than 2012. In other words, there is a huge potential for growth (Food Industry Asia 2014).

Third, online food trading greatly grows in popularity. A research report by Nielson in 2015 shows that 46% of Chinese have done online food and grocery shopping. That is to say, almost one-half of the Chinese population has experienced online food trading (The Nielsen Company 2015:9).

Online food trading has many advantages. First, it is easy to transact online. The Internet provides a large amount of information and also makes communication easy. Secondly, there are a full range of all kinds of food products available for shopping. In particular, the third party online platform that is comparable to a wet market in the real world can accommodate infinite varieties of food ranging from specialty to normal foods, whether from domestic and foreign origins. Consumers can choose what to purchase from online shops with more ease and convenience than offline ones. What's more, the fact that online communication is virtual and cheap makes online food trading more efficient and effective. Thirdly, online food trading is never restricted by space and time. As long as there is an Internet connection, in theory, you can purchase foods from every corner of the world. In other words, it eliminates the space and time barriers to trade in foods and roughly offers 24-hour service all year round. Finally, there is a price advantage. For food products in online shops, the price is relatively transparent and price comparison is more ready than in offline shops. Different from offline shops, online food operators do not pay rent and can save on operating costs, so the price of their food products is relatively cheaper than that of those offline shops (Dai. 2014).

## 2. China's Online Food Trading: A New Food Business Landscape

### 2.1. Modes of Online Food Trading

China's online food trading has a variety of modes and can be classified into four categories by the nature of either business operators or customers. First, business-to-business (B2B) mode refers to a situation where one food business, which normally occurs in the case of wholesales. Secondly, in contrast with B2C, B2B includes various forms of offline and online retailing. Within B2C arena, no-shop retailing is often widely discussed. In Western countries, no-shop retailing includes but is not limited to mail order and online retailing; retailing is a more predominant form than mail order. Thirdly, consumer to consumer (or C2C) mode refers to a situation where transactions between consumers through a third party occur in most cases electronically. A typical example is the online auction in which a consumer posts an item for sale and others bid to purchase it. The third party generally charges a flat fee or commission. The third party normally runs sites as platforms, which only play the role of intermediaries to match consumers. In practice, these platforms do not have to check quality of the products being offered. However, C2C in China is less focused on online auction but more on retailing. Taking Taobao as an example, people can purchase food products easily from this platform, which is characterised as a C2C one. Food products offered by Taobao are run by all kinds of food business operators, who normally are food small and medium enterprises (SMEs). In the past, it was the case that officially these food business operators were required to apply for licenses before selling food products through Taobao, but in reality, most of them did not apply. Fourthly, it is the online-to-offline (O2O) mode. O2O may be defined as anything digital which attracts people to shop in real-world shops. Well-known O2O in the West include Groupon, OpenTable and Uber. Food businesses are operated in O2O mode in China too.

In B2B mode it is quite often the case that the two trading sides have comparable negotiating power, and each side typically involves professional staff or legal counsel, while within B2C and C2C modes, the trading relationship is shaped to a far greater degree by information asymmetry (Liu. 2015).

## 2.2. Business Model of Online Food Trading

According to China's legislation, online food trading are categorised by checking if foods are online traded via self-built websites or third party platform websites. The former refers to self-built model and the latter platform model (Li, 2014). While the former is comparable to traditional food business operators, the latter does not sell foods *per se* but serves as a matchmaker and meeting point for food business operators to sell foods to consumers.

Food safety appears to be safety across food supply chains taking into account time and space, and the chain consists of several components including agricultural production, food processing and production, food circulation and catering services. Foods can be imported from other countries and areas through import. Safety across the food chain is presented in Chart 5.1.

By applying the food safety chain to online foods, we can see that across circulation, catering services, import and export within the food chain, the Internet offers an effective and efficient communication and payment tool to make running of food businesses possible. In other words, by applying the Internet to the food safety chain, online food trading can be further classified into several sub-sectors: online retailing, online catering and cross-border food e-commerce. Finally, by applying two business models of online food trading to the aforementioned sub-sectors, online food trading in China can be categorised as follows (Chart 5.2).

For instance, the Internet plus catering has become the so-called online catering. Consumers can now order and pay for meals online and then they can either request a delivery to a requested location or go to restaurants for the meals themselves (Xiao 2015). In addition, due to the emergence of smartphones, the aforementioned food business formats, which usually occur in the era of desktops, are now more and more managed by using mobile handsets. Because the relatively small size of these handsets, food businesses run through apps within the handsets are called 'micro

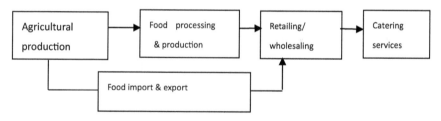

*Chart 5.1* Food Safety Chain

| Categories | Sub-categories | Examples |
|---|---|---|
| Online Retailing (including agri-foods, packaged foods) | Self-built | COFFCO's Womai, SF-Best, etc. |
| | Platform | Taobao etc. |
| | Mixed | Tmall, JD.com etc. |
| Online Catering | Online Delivery | KFC Delivery, Pizza Hut Delivery, etc. (self-built) |
| | | Ele.me, Baidu's Wamai etc. (platform) |
| | O2O | Baidu's Nuomi |
| | Mixed | Meida |
| Cross-Border Food E-commerce | Self-built | NetEase's Kaola, VIP etc. |
| | Platform | Amazon etc. |
| | Mixed | Tmall.hk, JD.hk etc. |

*Chart 5.2* Categorizing Chinese Online Food Trading

businesses'. Quite often, micro businesses conducted via mobile phones are preferred by small and boutique food businesses. Some are even operated predominantly by mobile devices. Within the micro business module, the so-called social networking platforms play an important role. WeChat, created by Tencent, is comparable to WhatsApp, Facebook or Twitter and is a free, cross-platform and instant messaging application. It becomes one of the largest social media platforms in China. WeChat supports users to post image and text, and people can pay via WeChat Pay, so quite often it is being used for food trading. It works in the following way: WeChat users create their own accounts, and once they have the accounts, they can post advertising information about food products through Moment Wall. Friends from the user's contact list are able to view each other's Moments' contents and comments. If they like, they can connect with relevant contacts and do payment through WeChat Pay to purchase food products. However, WeChat is not meant to be an e-commerce platform, though people using WeChat tend to treat it as an alternative to e-shopping. Nevertheless, WeChat is both a social media tool and an important part of the e-commerce platform, as it creates a hybrid version of online food trading—social media e-commerce.

### 2.3. Challenges for Regulation

With 1.3 billion population, the scale of China's food businesses is enormous. But when the Internet came at the beginning, food SMEs felt left out because they had no knowledge of what it was. That then creates huge opportunities for Jack Ma and his Alibaba platforms. Taobao from Alibaba then came into being to provide a solution for food SMEs. Previously, it was modelled on US eBay to provide second-hand products. Since China is the manufacture hub in the world and according to the Chinese culture, people do not like the idea of buying second-hand merchandises, so in the beginning, the SMEs chose Taobao to sell first-hand products and foods to consumers. Gradually, Taobao becomes probably the world's biggest C2C platform, selling all kinds products ranging from clothes, home appliances, to foods. In order to diversify its business models, Alibaba developed a Tmall platform. Tmall only allows bigger players with a good reputation to sell goods using its platform. Product ranges available on Tmall are almost the same as on Taobao. Foods are a growing phenomenon on Tmall. So it can be concluded that this platform is a dominant business model in China's online food trading arena in particular as far as food SMEs are concerned. For online food trading players of a large scale, quite often the boundary between self-built and platform models becomes blurred. For instance, Tmall as a platform operates its own online shop called Tmall Supermarket ("Tianmao Chaoshi" in Chinese Pinyin). In other words, Tmall, when accommodating many food business operators selling foods through its platform, operates itself as a food retailer. In comparison, JD, in a self-built model when acting as an online food retailer, gradually serves as a platform to attract lots of food business operators to sell products through it as well. So we can see that most influential online food trading players are using different platform models.

All the aforementioned situations make regulation of China's online food trading a complex one. And, indeed, online food trading can create market failure. There are situations where the quality of food products traded in a market can be compromised due to information asymmetry between buyers and sellers. Consumer rights are not guaranteed (Feng 2016). At present, these are the challenges: First, there are fake and inferior products. Although such problems appear both online and offline, consumer rights protection as applied to online food trading is less achievable than offline trading due to online foods are usually traded via distance selling, which makes it difficult to protect consumer rights. Food counterfeiting can also be an issue. Secondly, false information is an issue. This is particularly true as far as health foods are concerned. Traditionally, health claims related to health foods are an issue—e.g., false medicinal claims. The Internet makes it easier to create false claims and other improper information. The rise of WeChat and Webo particularly pose challenges for regulators (Lu 2015). Thirdly, unlicensed operation remains to be an issue. It is found that offline food businesses that should operate with licenses, actually do business without licenses; this is common as far as SMEs are concerned. The Internet provides an excellent shelter for online food operators to run businesses without licenses due to its virtuality (Wu and Chen 2016). Fourthly, the virtuality of the Internet creates a situation where everyone from every corner of the world can trade in foods without necessarily revealing their true identity. That makes concealment possible. Within a global Internet arena, online food trading involves many stakeholders and participants including buyer, sellers, logistics operators, payment platforms, advertisers, e-commerce platform, etc., posing a big challenge for regulators (Meng 2015). Nowadays, among the top 10 world's Internet companies, four are from China. They are Baidu, Alibaba, Tencent and JD. All these big four involve food products in a way, creating a unique landmark for the Internet sector (Lu 2016).

The Internet brings convenience to people's lives, but meanwhile government regulation faces new challenges. The popularity of all kinds of Internet tools and applications facilitates sales of fake and shoddy food products which pose threats to health of the public. From 2009 to date, crimes associated with online sales of fake and shoddy food and drugs are rising sharply. Online food trading modes are virtually behind the scene without constraint of time and space, which results in difficulty in investigating and collecting evidence (Li and Ren 2014).

## 3. Regulating China's Online Food Trading Under New Legal Order

### 3.1. *Changed Ecosystem of Chinese Food Governance*

On 28 February 2009, China's National People's Congress (NPC) Standing Committee passed the first comprehensive Food Safety Law in 2009 (hereinafter referred to as 2009 FSL). Six years later, on 24 April 2015, NPC Standing Committee adopted an amendment to the Food Safety Law (hereinafter referred to as the 2015 FSL Amendment), which is considered as the "toughest food safety law" in China's history. With additional 50 articles, the 2015 FSL Amendment which took effect on 1 October 2015, has brought significant changes to the law. This is a sign of the Chinese government's determination to further strengthen food safety governance. Following the amendment, several principles (i.e. Prevention First, Risk Management, Whole Food Chain Control and Social Co-regulation) are established. It is unclear as to how these principles will be substantialised since there are no further provisions elaborating on their relevant application. However, there is an overhaul of the existing food safety regulatory regime in China and major changes can be seen, in particular in the following aspects: demarcation of regulatory responsibilities among food agencies, food recall and Internet foods. More significantly, the inclusion of online foods marks that China's food regulation enters into a new era. With the booming of e-commerce globally, there will be considerable impacts on both China and the outside world.

After the release of the 2015 FSL Amendment, Chinese food safety regulatory landscape has changed significantly. In particular, it marks the arrival of China's online food trading regulations.

Firstly, there is further consolidation of China's food safety regulatory system. Prior to the Food Safety Law, food regulatory system was frequently criticised for inconsistency and inefficiency due to a large number of agencies involving in food regulation. Since the promulgation of the Food Safety Law, China has conducted a series of reforms (Xiao 2013; Xiao 2011). In 2013, an institutional reform package was approved by the NPC on 14 March 2013. In the same year, a new China Food and Drug Administration (hereinafter referred to as CFDA) was established as a ministry affiliated to the State Council rather than to the Ministry of Health. The 2013 reform consolidated CFDA's responsibilities for food safety, which include food production, food distribution and catering services (Huang 2013:216–217). This shows that the amendment to the Food Safety Law further consolidates China's food safety regulatory system by adding more responsibilities to the CFDA, which were either previously ignored within the Food Safety Law or fell under auspices of other ministries. For instance, now medical foods, which are specially formulated and intended for the dietary management of a disease that has distinctive nutritional needs, are to be regulated by the CFDA. In addition, previously, genetically modified (GM) crops and foods were almost exclusively regulated by Ministry of Agriculture (Xiao 2012: 507–520). With the amendments, now the CFDA has regulatory power over the GM foods as far as food labelling is concerned. For those GM food producers, who fail to label the foods as such, their production license maybe suspended or revoked according to Articles 69 and 125 of FSL. Similarly, the CFDA's regulatory responsibilities have expanded to include regulation on alcoholic beverages including wine products, which were previously regulated by the Ministry of Commerce (MOFCOM). This means for now both, manufacturing and retailing of alcoholic beverages are administered by the CFDA.

## 3.2. *The Evolution of Online Food Trading Regulation in China*

China's State Council in 2013 announced to change China's food regulatory agency, SFDA (State Food and Drug Administration) from a vice-ministry into a ministry (and renamed as CFDA). This change gives CFDA more power to enact rules relating to food safety. Administrative measures relating to food e-commerce since then has also become one of the emerging priorities for CFDA. In addition, the same year saw draft *Measures on Supervision and Administration of Online Food and Drug Trading* (hereinafter referred to as Measures I) was released for public opinion.[4] In 2015, draft *Measures on Supervision and Administration of Online Food Trading* (hereinafter referred to as Measures II) came into being following Article 131.[5] Under the leadership of Minister Bi Jingquan (for CFDA), Measures I was split into two pieces of legislation with the aim of trailing on rules for online food at first. In Minister Bi's opinion, food and drugs are totally different categories.

The 2015 FSL Amendment stipulates that platform operators need to (i) register the real contact information of its online food business operators, (ii) check the food business licenses of its online food business operators, (iii) report illegal activities and (iv) terminate services for food business operators who commit serious offences. According to the 2015 FSL Amendment, third-party platforms have quasi-regulatory responsibilities for the food business operators using their platforms. For instances, the platforms need to conduct real-name registration of the business operators as well as to check if business operators have obtained relevant licenses for food business operation according to Article 62. These are the legal obligations that platforms will have to fulfill. Most importantly, the 2015 FSL Amendment establishes a joint liability mechanism in case of any non-compliance from platform operators or food business operators. For instance, consumers whose legitimate rights or interests are infringed by purchasing foods through the third-party platforms can claim compensation from platform operators if the platform operator failed to identify the relevant food business operator who sold the foods in question according to Article 131 of FSL.

However, it was not until the Ele.me food scandal in 2016 that triggered CFDA to promulgate detailed rules relating online food trading. Ele.me, one of the, Chinese online catering service providing platforms was reported to have accommodated many unlicensed canteens. The scandal attracted lots of public attention. CFDA is pressured to improve regulations on online food trading. So, finally, in July 2016, a few months after the scandal that CFDA enacted *Measures for Investigation and Punishment of Unlawful Acts Concerning Online Food Safety* (hereinafter referred to as Measures III).[6] From Measures I to Measures II and Measures III, it shows that CFDA is determined to tighten its regulatory policy to ever-booming e-commerce.

Measures III, was established to implement the 2015 FSL Amendment by substantialising obligations imposed upon both third-party online platforms and online food business operators.

Under Measures III, online food trading sites can be run either on the self-built basis or in the form of platform. As far as the self-built site is concerned, the owner of the site is also the food business operator within the site. In comparison, the owner of the platform are not normally directly involved in online food trading but just provides matching services to the online food business operators within the platform.

Illegal activities as covered by Measures III can be conducted by three types of market participants, namely, platform provider, online food business operators through the self-built site and online food business operators through the third party platform (the latter two collectively referred to as online food business operators). Measures III creates common legal obligations for both platform providers and online food business operators. For example, online food trading occurs on a virtual basis, and the digital information becomes the heart of the transaction. Therefore, to ensure integrity and accuracy, information is shared amongst all the aforementioned participants. Participants who do not observe the regulation will be punished accordingly. However, in many circumstances, their responsibilities are distinguished from each other. For instance, though both platform providers and online food business operators through self-built websites will have to file registration on their sites, respectively, to relevant authorities, the specific filing procedures are different for different types of participants. The former needs to file with the provincial food and drug agency, whereas the latter files with the prefectural or county level one.

As mentioned in Article 62 of the 2015 FSL Amendment, the platform provider will have to terminate services for food operators in case of serious offences. Measures III move on to substantialise the 'serious offences' as stated below: (i) food operators are under investigation in relation to a court case, or are being publicly sued for an alleged food safety crime,

(ii) have had a penalty imposed for crimes involving food safety, (iii) have been detained for illegal conducts concerning food safety, or (iv) have otherwise been punished by Chinese food safety authorities (e.g. revoking licenses, ordering to suspend business).

Article 131 of the 2015 FSL Amendment articulates how the online platform will be punished in principle upon its violation. When serious consequences are caused, CFDA will 'order the suspension of operations for rectification and revocation of its license by the original issuer'. The Measures III again substantialise what can be 'serious consequences'.

More importantly, Measures III also articulates that the platform providers, apart from filing, will have to fulfil the following obligations among others,

- Ensuring that adequate technology is provided. Platform providers must maintain adequate technology—e.g., data backup and restoration technology to ensure the security of trading data.
- There shall be management systems to be established. Platform providers must establish various systems, including for (i) the registration of food traders, (ii) the self-inspection of food traders' operations and information disclosure, (iii) the prevention and reporting of illegal activities, (iv) the termination of services for food traders who violate laws and (v) customer food safety complaints.
- Conducting license inspections. Platform providers must examine the relevant food operation licenses and registration of food traders on the Platforms.
- Archiving. Online platforms must establish archiving systems for registered food traders to record their basic information and management team information.
- Trading records. Platform providers must retain trading records for at least six months after the expiration date of any product, or for at least two years if no expiration date is specified in the product in question.

## 4. Implications for the World

### 4.1. *Jack Ma and His Vision of E-WTP*

Alibaba Group, China's biggest online platform, raised $25 billion through its Initial Public Offering (IPO) in 2014. However, according to Jack Ma, the founder of Alibaba, his company is still in its early stage of development. Ma's ambition is to enhance its platform reach to serve two billion consumers all over the world. This means, ultimately, Ma will be building an "E-WTO", which is able to sell goods including food products from all over the world (Mathuros 2015).[7] Currently, there are around 400,000 business operators on his platforms to sell edible agricultural products.

Despite his success, Ma has decided to make his platforms more global by attracting customers from around the world and helping ten million small businesses outside of China to sell into global markets (Cookson 2014). In an interview with Charlie Rose, Ma mentioned that he can make a platform for global small businesses. The platform can then help Norwegian small businesses sell things to Argentina, and Argentina consumers can purchase things online from Switzerland. Finally, this platform will grow and expand into what he calls as the 'E-WTO', a network sharing the commonality of e-commerce platforms and the World Trade Organization (WTO) (Cookson 2014).

Later during the 2016 G20 meeting in Hangzhou, China, Ma changed the concept of E-WTO into E-WTP with the P representing platform (Allison 2016). What he envisioned indicates that China is a lead player in terms of world trade, including that of food and is now reshaping global business rules to some extent.

The 2015 FSL Amendment and relevant measures pose both opportunities and challenges for the world. As for opportunities, that regulation of online food trading has for the first time been introduced into the China's food legislation indicates that it has become an economy of scale in China. Online food trading has also been translated into a magnificent opportunity for other jurisdictions in the world with a significant food economy. Cross-border e-commerce has also dramatically reshaped trade and commerce between China and the outside world. For instance, through Tmall, operated by Alibaba Group, consumers in some tier-one Chinese cities such as Beijing can receive cherries just two days after they are picked by producers in the United States. This is made possible through cross-border e-commerce arrangements, i.e. a partnership between the US Department of Agriculture (USDA) and Tmall.com. For example, Tmall receives pre-orders from consumers and then cherries picked by US growers will be sent to China for Tmall to deliver directly to consumers. According to Chinese media, when products are purchased through cross-border e-commerce, the price is competitive. For instance, the price for a 2-kilogram box of US cherries is 22% less than that of the cherries sold in brick-and-mortar stores in China. Australia follows suit by engaging with JD, another e-commerce giant in China, in establishing similar partnership. However, when Chinese consumers are buying goods through cross-border e-commerce, packages for customs clearance are treated either as personal goods or general trade; if considered as the latter, packages will normally face delay in delivery and customs duty will be much higher (Li 2014).

In other words, there is a legal uncertainty for goods traded through cross-border e-commerce. The 2015 FSL Amendment, does not address cross-border e-commerce given the fact that cross-border e-commerce is still a pilot scheme. Now CFDA plays a principal role for food administration in terms of food recall, food labelling for most food products including high market margin foods like wine and high-quality edible agricultural products, the improved regulation will be of great interest to the outside world. The Chinese food sector has been long criticised for safety concerns. Coupled with the issue are counterfeit products and violation of Intellectual Property Rights (IPRs), when it comes to e-commerce (Xiao 2015). It remains to be seen how Chinese food regulation will embrace Chinese e-commerce giants' ambition towards an 'E-WTP'.

Defining e-commerce is never an easy task given the ever-increasing technologies to be used. It has been referred to as commercial transactions occurring over open networks like the Internet. Both B2B and B2C transactions are included by the OECD, whereas WTO considers it as "the production, distribution, marketing, sale or delivery of goods and services by electronic means" (Herman 2010; World Trade Organization 1998). In real business scenarios, however, e-commerce is even defined in a case-by-case way to serve specific audiences; for instance, a 2014 survey report of European e-commerce treated e-commerce as "the purchase of physical products over the Internet", with online purchases of services like travel, hotels and tickets on one hand and downloads of music files, films and applications on the other are excluded (PostNord 2014). Obviously, the definitions applied to e-commerce vary.

Though WTO members have been discussing e-commerce since 1998, there is a lack of consensus on how to define e-commerce and what it constitutes. And this reflects the fact that "rulemaking and regulation governing e-commerce trade have taken a slower pace" (Herman 2010). However, that doesn't stop China's from embarking on a journey to engage with foreign partners on cross-border e-commerce. Chinese private sectors associated with e-commerce are the lead drivers of the cross-border e-commerce.

### 4.2. Online Food Trading in the International Arena

#### 4.2.1. Ever-Expanding International Online Food Trading

Alibaba and JD along with other similar e-commerce giants like SF Best and Cereals, Oils and Foodstuffs Corporation's (COFCO) Womai have been racing to engage with producers and wholesalers globally to sell food products through their sites to meet China's ever-increasing demand for foreign food products (Noble 2015;Li and Lu 2014; Zhang 2014). The two New York–listed companies, i.e., Alibaba and JD.com are in cooperation with foreign governments with a view to promoting foreign produce among Chinese consumers (Noble 2015). To this end, Alibaba started with the US government and JD with its Australian counterpart to nurture cross-border food e-commerce, and both companies are seeking to work with more international partners all over the world to expand food e-commerce (Oz 2013). The ambition of Chinese food e-commerce giants grows as they see that there is a great potential for the boom of online food shopping. COFCO's Womai, for instance, raised a $100 million from lead investor IDG Capital Partners, alongside SAIF Partners in 2014 (Cheung 2014).

China's high demand for online food shopping and consumer's preference for foreign foodstuffs are mainly driven by three factors—namely, cost, convenience and ever-increasing Chinese food safety scandals. Because of the coming age of food e-commerce, increasing food sales became the company's top priority in 2015 (Noble, 2015). Since 2008, China has been engulfed in notorious food safety scandals involving a large range of products such as baby formula, meat and cooking oil, to name a few (Xiao 2011; Foster 2011).

### 4.2.2. Rising Business Innovation and Its Conflicts with Traditional Rules

In 2014, trade volume of Chinese e-commerce recorded 12.3 trillion RMB (2 trillion US dollar), which is around one-fifth of China's GDP for the same year. Sales volume by Alibaba was projected to overtake that of Walmart in 2015. There are 630 million Internet users and 12 million mobile phone users in China who generate 20 billion massages each day. As mentioned earlier, among the top-ten global IT companies, there were four from China on par with the United States and they all are associated with food products and food businesses to some extent. Hence, China has become a leading nation for the Internet. In 2018, China's Internet coverage will reach 90%. Internet and mobile connections with the outside means online food trading has never been easy. China's rising innovation in the Internet is continuously changing how food businesses are conducted.

There were 45 million people regularly buying foods online in China. These kinds of businesses now attract lots of attention from younger generations and middle classes. The sales volume is projected to reach 140 billion RMB (around 20 billion US dollar) in 2018. Innovation comes with new business models and online food trading has expanded further. Online ordering and catering become more and more popular in particular in some tier one cities. People can now order and pay for food online. Then they can further either request a delivery to a requested place or go to the restaurant for the meal they have ordered. More and more players like Baidu, Meituan, etc., have joined the battle of online catering. More significantly, online food retailing begins to turn west. A handful of players like Alibaba, JD, Yihaodian or YHD, SF-Best, COFCO's Womai and the like have made China's online food trading international by embarking on so-called cross-border food e-commerce. This creates an extremely diverse and vibrant atmosphere for China's online food trading. To some extent, it also brings challenges to food regulation. When foods become international commodities, normally, WTO rules are applied. When WTO rules relating to food products are discussed, we are talking about SPS (Sanitary and Phytosanitary measures) and national food standards. As far as cross-border food e-commerce is concerned, there is very limited multilateral legal agreement. In most cases, it is food products of foreign origins that come into China through e-commerce, but we seldom see Chinese food products sell to other countries via e-commerce. From time to time, infant formulas are the typical example in which milk products from Australia, Europe and other developed countries are extremely popular due to low confidence in China's domestic products. Young mothers like to purchase baby foods and other similar products online. Both the 2009 Food Safety Law and the 2015 FSL Amendment require that food products from other countries will have to be in conformity with China's national food safety standards. However, food products via cross-border e-commerce channels are those produced and targeted at local markets of foreign origins. In other words, it is quite often the case that those products are produced by complying with standards of countries of origin other than that of China.

### 4.3. Public and Private Co-regulation: A Solution for Online Food Trading Governance

In China, the development of Internet is now being promoted as a national strategy and priority. In line with this, the National Reform and Development Commission has commissioned the Alibaba Research Center to lay down a blueprint for China moving into the next stage of an into an Internet-based economy. The Chinese government realises that it alone cannot regulate food safety, therefore social co-regulation is mentioned first as a principle. By way of definition, 'social co-regulation' means food regulation is a shared responsibility among a range of social stakeholders such as food producers, public agencies, consumers, media and so on, to name a few.

The regulatory environment, which the Chinese government intends to create, is to mandate third-party platforms as co-regulators of online foods. Platform providers need to share co-responsibilities for any damage caused to consumers due to food incidents. This literally means that when consumers purchase food from a certain platform, they can go directly to the platform operator for concerns regarding the food quality instead of reaching out to the food business operators, with the assumption that the platform has the ultimate responsibility for food safety.

In addition, the government regulation is likely to be tightened in China. With the booming of food e-commerce in China and the food scandals associated with it, the Chinese government is very concerned about food safety.

Hence, relevant Chinese food regulators are now thinking to take the initiative to tighten regulations.[8]

When it comes to online food trading, private regulation put together by platform operators serves as an alternative for public regulation. Though private regulation is not intended to replace public regulation, in some cases, it actually plays a more important role than the public one. As mentioned before, there are around 400,000 business operators selling edible agricultural products through the Alibaba platform, most of which are SMEs spreading over more than 30 provinces across China. Food products as sold through the Alibaba platform could be produced in Province A and be delivered to a warehouse located in Province B for redistribution to customers through food e-commerce systems. However, the actual food business operators may run their e-commerce businesses in Province C. To advertise, food business operators might go to social media companies registered and operating in Province D for advertising. And, finally, the server for Alibaba platform could be located in Province E. All these different locations are organised and connected through the virtual network—the Internet. Public regulators could find it is almost impossible to supervise these players in so many different locations in the sense that traditional public regulation is very much territorial jurisdiction based. The other problem for private regulation lies in the fact that the Chinese legal system is lagging behind industry development. So there is a private regulation movement in e-commerce and this is applied to food e-commerce as well. Alibaba for instance, has established a so-called Shield Department to crack down on counterfeit goods. There are around 2000 people working in this department, of which one-half are data engineers. This department in cooperation with other Alibaba's divisions create rules to guide business running in Alibaba platform. These rules are enforceable like government regulations. For instance, Alibaba can order an inspection of goods to be sold on its platform and decide what can be sold on its platform based on inspection results. To this end, the Shield Department heavily relies on big data. Private regulation as adopted by Alibaba makes a lot of sense, and it is complimentary to government regulation. This is the case that as for food e-commerce, there is a co-regulation between public and private stakeholders.

Regarding cross-border e-commerce, Europe has its advantage of producing high quality food. For instance, with good regulation in Europe, wine and milk produced in Europe need to be labeled following a system of geographical indicators. Most of these products are also produced in an organic way, making them highly desirable for consumers in China. European Union (EU) delegation in China is also trying its best to promote this image. Since 2004, EU has embarked on an EU-China Trade Project aiming at better mutual understanding of trade barriers such as food safety and agriculture as presented in these two different jurisdictions.

In terms of US companies and e-commerce in China, Amazon, for instance, has just celebrated its tenth anniversary in China. Its Chinese branch just signed a memorandum of understanding with the Shanghai Free Trade Zone and Shanghai Information Investment Limited for cross-border e-commerce. This has paved the way for Amazon to bring millions of its products, including foods from around the world, directly to Chinese customers. As a US company, Amazon has a better understanding of US products and commerce and therefore will bring good opportunities to US traders. Walmart, the world's biggest supermarket chain is one of the biggest shareholders of Yihaodian, China's e-supermarket giant, which again presents good opportunities for US products, including food.

## 5. Conclusion

Further development of China's online food trading is mainly driven by the growth of food SMEs and the Internet revolution. The "Internet Plus" strategy helps improve food safety across the chain of online food supply in China. This 'marriage' creates different online food trading modes and generates new business opportunities. Third-party online platforms in particular create an open environment for every business whether small or big to operate food businesses on the platforms. In China, now food products can be purchased from every corner of the world through cross-border food e-commerce platforms. However, cross-border e-commerce also poses a big challenge for the compliance with China's food safety standards and labelling rules, which is related to WTO legal regimes.

Co-regulation has helped improve the legal environment for online food trading in China. It is also used by the Chinese government to compensate its lack of regulatory capacity to deal with the booming online food trading. Online platform operators which by nature are private players are given authority by the government to manage food business operators running food businesses on the platforms. However, the uniqueness of that regulatory approach lies in the fact that the authority online platform operators has is also an obligation. This means, if food businesses operators conduct wrongdoings and the platform operators do not manage them to a satisfied degree as expected from the Chinese government, the platform operators will be punished. In that sense, an online platform operator is also deemed as a co-regulator.

Nevertheless, since the platforms have become influential players in food businesses, public and private co-regulation has also gained more and more recognition. It is popular for food SMEs to operate food businesses within platforms so that gradually platform operators could become co-regulators for food safety. Since the co-regulation as envisioned by the Chinese government, and the detailed roadmap to make it happen is still evolving, it remains to be seen how well China's co-regulation system can be applied to online platforms.

## Notes

1. The SARS outbreak from 2002 to 2003 that infected 8,096 worldwide and killed 744. Streets were empty as most people stayed home to prevent exposure to the killer virus (Ghosh 2016; Hunt 2013).
2. In 2015, China revised its Food Safety Law and introduced 'online food trading'. China is discussing its E-commerce Law, which is intended to cover food e-commerce. Although online food trading and food e-commerce are yet to be defined, they are interchangeable in the industry.
3. Alibaba Group, founded by Jack Ma, is China's biggest e-commerce platform (Xiao 2015).
4. 互联网食品药品经营监督管理办法 in Chinese.
5. 网络食品经营监督管理办法 in Chinese.
6. 网络食品安全违法行为查处办法 in Chinese.
7. Ma said this at the World Economic Forum in Davos, Switzerland, in 2015 (Mathuros 2015).
8. CFDA, which is developed partially based on US FDA model, is, as the name indicates, China's principal regulator for food and drug sectors. As a consolidated new Ministry affiliated to China's State Council, it is facing ever-increasing governance challenges as far as sound legislation and capacity building are concerned. To address these, the CFDA's Department of Legal Affairs and the CFDA's Institute of Executive Development are playing important roles: the former is in charge of law drafting and reviewing, and the latter is responsible for high-level training and research relating to law enforcement and industry compliance. The CFDA Department of Legal Affairs needs to convince online food businesses that third-party platforms will have to be co-regulators of online food trading. The CFDA's Institute of Executive Development will have to provide capacity building to empower CFDA law enforcers to supervise the platform operators and co-regulate online food trading.

## References

Allison, I. 2016, "Alibaba's Jack Ma promotes free trade for SMEs via electronic world trade platform", *International Business Times*, available: www.ibtimes.co.uk/alibabas-jack-ma-promotes-free-trade-smes-via-electronic-world-trade-platform-1579950.

Cheung, S. 2014, "Chinese online grocer Womai.com raises $100M, catering to consumers amid food scares", *Wall Street Journal*, available: https://blogs.wsj.com/venturecapital/2014/08/05/chinese-online-grocer-womai-com-raises-100m-catering-to-consumers-amid-food-scares/.

Cookson, R. 2014, "Jack Ma aims for 2bn Alibaba customers", *Financial Times*, available: www.ft.com/content/9149f71a-a307-11e4-9c06-00144feab7de.

Food Industry Asia 2014, "Food safety in China's e-commerce platforms", *Food Industry Asia*, available: https://foodindustry.asia/food-safety-in-china-s-e-commerce-platforms.

Foster, P. 2011, "Top 10 Chinese food scandals", *The Telegraph*, available: www.telegraph.co.uk/news/worldnews/asia/china/8476080/Top-10-Chinese-Food-Scandals.html.

Ghosh, B. 2016, "China's internet got a strange and lasting boost from the SARS epidemic", *Quartz*, available: https://qz.com/662110/chinas-internet-got-a-strange-and-lasting-boost-from-the-sars-epidemic/.

He, Y. 2015, "Top 10 Internet companies in the world", Beijing. *China Daily*, available: www.chinadaily.com.cn/business/2015-12/11/content_22686526.htm.

Herman, L. 2010, "Multilateralising regionalism: The case of e-commerce", OECD Trade Policy Papers, No. 99, OECD Publishing, Paris.

Huang, Q. 2013, "From fingers to fist—China's new food supervision regime", *European Food and Feed Law Review*, vol. 8, no. 3, 216–217.

Hunt, K. 2013, "Sars legacy still felt in Hong Kong, 10 years on", *BBC*, available: www.bbc.com/news/world-asia-china-21680682.

Li, W. 2014, "Guangzhou starts to expedite customs clearing", *China Daily*, available: http://english.gov.cn/policies/latest_releases/2014/09/25/content_281474989337740.htm.

Mathuros, F. 2015, *Jack Ma wants Alibaba to serve 2 billion consumers* [Online]. The World Economic Forum, available: www.weforum.org/news/jack-ma-wants-alibaba-serve-2-billion-consumers.

The Nielsen Company 2015, *The future of grocery: E-commerce, digital technology and changing shopping preferences around the world*, Nielson, available: https://www.nielsen.com/content/dam/nielsenglobal/vn/docs/Reports/2015/Nielsen%20Global%20E-Commerce%20and%20The%20New%20Retail%20Report%20APRIL%202015%20(Digital).pdf.

Noble, J. 2015, "Alibaba and JD online take fresh approach to China food shopping", *Financial Times*, available: www.ft.com/content/bfaa55da-be4d-11e4-a341-00144feab7de.

Oz, P. 2013, "Cherries on top: U.S., Tmall push American farm products in China", *Alizila*, available: www.alizila.com/cherries-top-us-tmall-push-american-farm-products-china.

PostNord, 2014, *E-commerce in Europe 2014*, available: http://www.postnord.fi/globalassets/suomi/raportit/e-commerce-in-europe-2014.pdf.

World Trade Organization 1998, Work Programme on Electronic Commerce, adopted by the General Council on 25 September 1998, available: www.wto.org/english/tratop_e/ecom_e/wkprog_e.htm.

Xiao, P. 2011, "China's milk scandals and its food risk assessment institutional framework", *European Journal of Risk Regulation*, vol. 2, no. 3, p. 397.

Xiao, P. 2012, "China's food standardization system, its reform and remaining challenges", *European Journal of Risk Regulation*, vol. 3, no. 4, pp. 507–520.

Xiao, P. 2013, *China's food safety regulation: Institutional diversity, fragmentation and efficacy*. PhD Thesis, University of South Australia.

Xiao, P. 2015, "Why you should think about Jack Ma when you think about food in China", *Selerant*, available: http://compliancecloud.selerant.com/latestnews/food-e-commerce.aspx.

中国互联网络信息中心[China Internet Information Center]. 2017, 中国互联网发展史（大事记）[China's Internet Development]. 北京: 中国互联网络信息中心, available: www.cnnic.net.cn/hlwfzyj/hlwdsj/.

代大鹏[Dai, D]. 2014, 经济法视野下的网络食品安全监管研究[Research on online food regulation under the economic law] 宁波大学.

刘媛媛[Liu, Y.]. 2015, 我国网络市场食品安全规制研究[Study on regulation of China's online food trading. 山西医科大学.

吴文治，陈克远[Wu, W. and Keyuan, C.] 2016, 外卖平台"无证餐厅"屡禁不止 [Unlicensed canteens emerge in the third party online platforms]. 北京商报网, available: www.bbtnews.com.cn/2016/0818/158332.shtml.

姜俊贤[Jiang, J]. 2015, 中国餐饮产业发展报告[China's catering industry development report], 北京, 中共中央党校出版社.

姜俊贤[Jiang, J]. 2016, *中国餐饮产业发展报告[China's catering industry development report]*, 北京, 中共中央党校出版社.

孟璇[Meng, X.] 2015, 对网络食品安全监管的探讨[Research on online food safety]. *法制与社会*.

封俊丽[Feng, J.] 2016, 网络食品市场中的柠檬问题探讨[Research on market failure in online food trading]. *商业经济研究*.

张文婧[Zhang, W]. 2014, *顺丰电商模式的逆袭者 出招做海外直采再冒新风险* [SF e-commerce is determined to be an ambitious player and is going abroad for more]. 大公网, available: http://finance.takungpao.com/gscy/q/2014/0126/2243715.html.

易观国际[Yiguan International] 2016, "互联网+"产业创新发展关键监管政策创新研究课题[A study on keynote industry development and regulatory innovations in the Internet plus]. 北京.

李方磊[Li, F.]. 2014, *网购食品安全监管问题探析[Research on regulation of online food trading]*. 陕西科技大学.

李春雷，任韧[Li, C. and Ren, R]. 2014, 我国互联网食品药品经营违法犯罪问题研究[Research on illegal and criminal activities of China's online food trading]. *中国人民公安大学学报 (社会科学版)*.

李铎，卢亦杉[Li, D. and Lu, Y.]. 2014, 获1亿美元巨额融资中粮我买网加码海外直采[COFCO Womai obains 100 milliom dollars for overseas direct purchase]. *北京商报[Beijing Business Today]*, 8月4日.

郑春晖[Zheng, C.] 2015, 食品电商未来发展趋势分析[Prospect on food e-commerce]. *中国食品*.

阿里研究院[Ali Research Center] 2015, *互联网+从IT到DT[Internet Plus from IT to DT]*, 北京, 机械工业出版社.

陆悦[Lu, Y.]. 2016, 第三方平台扎紧制度管理的笼子[Consolidating management from third party online platforms]. *中国医药报*, 8月4日.

陆永博[Lu, Y.] 2015, 浅议网络销售食品安全问题[A study on food safety arising from online food trading]. *法制与社会*.

陈建功 and 李晓东[Chen, J. and Li, X.] 2014, 中国互联网发展的历史阶段划分[China's Internet historical development], *互联网天地*, 6–14.

黄有璨[Huang, Y]. 2016, *运营简史：一文读懂互联网运营的20年发展与演变* [Concise history of operation: To see through the development and evolution of the Internet via one stop article]. 北京, available: www.huxiu.com/article/176091.html.

# 7 Enforcement of Food Standards in China—Impact of the State-Led Stakeholder Model of Corporate Governance

*Jenny Fu and Geoffrey Nicoll*

## 1. Introduction

Over the last 30 years, China's industrial capacity has grown enormously and the global reach of its capacity is becoming increasingly evident. This is now reflected in the marked presence of China's major firms in infrastructure construction and consumer manufacturing. In promoting China's presence internationally, the lead has generally been taken by a number of state-designated national 'champions'—usually central state-owned enterprises (SOEs) which now take their place among the largest and most influential corporations in the world. The potential impact of China's natural resources companies associated with food production and processing, among them some very large SOEs, has been less evident to date. Nevertheless, it might be anticipated that the significance of the commercial activities of these companies is likely to follow the path of China's construction and manufacturing industries abroad.

Because of their equivocal association with the state, Chinese SOEs operating abroad have often encountered resistance in developed, regulated markets to their government's view that they are competitive, commercial enterprises. In the case of food production and processing companies, the potential impact on consumers and public health also demands particular attention to the setting, regulating and enforcing of safety standards in China, as well as the responsibility of corporate agents in maintaining these standards in practice.

This chapter examines the impact of China's state-led stakeholder model of corporate governance on the enforcement of food safety standards. Elsewhere, one of the authors of this chapter has argued that China's corporate law reforms since 2005 have given rise to a new model of corporate governance, namely the state-led stakeholder model (Fu 2014). While the active involvement of the state in the affairs of large companies, primarily SOEs, remains a central feature of this model, legislative and regulatory reforms have been carried out to strengthen the monitoring of managers, the protection of minority shareholders and other non-shareholder stakeholders, such as employees, creditors and consumers. A highlight of these reforms has been state mandating corporate social responsibility (CSR) through the 2005 Company Law revision.[1]

Although difficult to reconcile with outsider models of corporate governance commonly found in the United States and the United Kingdom, this model seems to facilitate the maintenance of the Chinese form of state-led economic development while also responding to the diverse demands made on the state for protection by investors and other stakeholders with globalisation and the pluralisation of interests within the Chinese society. As such, this model forms an integral part of the policy tools of the state to promote economic development and the symbiotic social stability, amid rapidly changing international and domestic dynamics.

This new state-led stakeholder governance model appears to sit more comfortably within China's post-2005 regulatory framework for corporate governance, than the reality of the governance of SOEs. The lack of more substantive improvements in the latter aspect has been, in part, caused by the disadvantages of the state as essentially the sole guardian of this model. Despite the various plausible policy goals it serves, the long-term viability of this model is likely to hinge on the balance between the will and capacity of the state in coordinating and adjusting the diverse stakeholder interests that might be affected by the activities of SOEs and the risk associated with lax internal controls that persists at the company level.

China's regulation of food standards has improved significantly over the past ten years. However, food safety remains a highly contentious issue (Jensen and Zhou 2015: 167). Using the 2008 tainted milk scandal as a case study, this chapter explores the links between the lax enforcement of the food standards and the internal workings of the state-led stakeholder model of corporate governance in China. It argues that while the utility of the state-led stakeholder model in facilitating economic development and maintaining social stability is evident, it is likely to continue to contribute to the lack of substantive improvement in the enforcement of food standards in China. Thus, examining the power and autocracy of the Chinese state, evident in its utilitarian approach to resolving competing objectives in the 2008 tainted milk scandal, suggests some important limitations in the state-led model of corporate governance and flaws in the wider regulatory framework in China. Continuing to address these limitations will be most important to maintaining China's credibility internationally as a global food supplier.

This case study is particularly instructive for a number of reasons. Firstly, although a single case study often runs the risk of being unrepresentative, the scandal provides us with rare insights into state involvement in corporate governance within a particular Chinese industry, namely the dairy industry. Secondly, due to its large scale and profound social, economic and political implications, the scandal provides a useful platform from which to examine the interaction between the exercise of state power, the forces of globalisation and the representation of diverse interests within Chinese society in corporate activity. Thirdly, as Milhaupt and Pistor have pointed out, although a corporate scandal may not be representative of the everyday governance practices in Chinese companies, it may better expose the features and weaknesses of corporate governance than when the company functions smoothly (Milhaupt and Katharina Pistor 2008: 10–11). Finally, although the scandal occurred nearly eight years ago, a similar state-led approach has been adopted by the central government in handling some more recent corporate sandals, such as the ConocoPhillips (China) oil spill (2011), China Petro Chemical (Sinopec) Qingdao oil pipeline explosions (2013) and the capsize of the Oriental Star Cruise Ship on the Yangzi River (2015). As such, the ramifications of the scandal and the lessons it offered remain current to the enforcement of corporate responsibility in China.

## 2. Overview of the Scandal and Its Main Players

Food scandals are not new in China. None, however, has reached the degree of intensity and magnitude of the milk scandal. In September 2008, beginning with Sanlu, 22 companies, including almost all of the large and medium-sized producers in the Chinese dairy industry, were found by the State Administration of Quality Supervision, Inspection and Quarantine (SAQSIQ), China's food safety authority, to be using melamine at various levels in their products.[2] By December 2008, the scandal had led to 6 infant deaths and nearly 300,000 suffering from 'urinary problems' including kidney stones, according to the Chinese Ministry of Health.[3] Also known as 'protein powder', melamine is an industrial chemical used in producing plastics and fertilisers. Sustained consumption by human beings may cause kidney stones and kidney failure, particularly among infants for whom kidney stones are rare.[4]

It is instrumental to set out the four leading dairy groups implicated in the scandal at the outset. These were Sanlu (as mentioned earlier), Yili, Mengniu and Guangming Dairy. Most of the four corporate groups were essentially state-controlled enterprises but this high level of state ownership and control alone was unable to ensure the protection of consumer interests, or to prevent the corporate failures in the disaster. Sanlu was the group at the epicentre of the scandal. Most of the baby victims were fed Sanlu's lower-end infant formula by their generally middle-to-low income parents.[5] Headquartered in the northern city of Shijiazhuang, Hebei province, Sanlu used to be the largest infant formula producer in China, as well as one of China's top 500 enterprises ranked by revenue. The predecessor of Sanlu was a cooperative of local dairy farmers, which, under the Chinese Constitution, is a special form of state ownership.[6] The cooperative was then converted into a joint venture, but continued to be widely perceived as a SOE in the market. Immediately prior to the scandal, 56% of shares in the joint venture were held by its management and employees through a company called Sanlu Limited.[7] Another 43% were held by the New Zealand dairy giant Fonterra, which appointed three of the seven directors on Sanlu board.[8] The remaining 1% shares in Sanlu were held by several small shareholders.[9] Public listing of Sanlu was sought before the establishment of the joint venture. Commentators suggested that if not for the exposure of the scandal, Sanlu could have been listed on the Shanghai Stock Exchange by 2008.[10]

Yili was (and remains) a company based in Inner Mongolia and listed on the Shanghai Stock Exchange. Yili's largest shareholder, the Inner Mongolia Autonomous Region government, owned about 10% shares in the company in 2007. The balance was distributed among public investors including securities investment funds. Mengniu was another Inner Mongolia-based dairy giant and a Hong Kong-listed company. The ultimate controllers of Mengniu used to be its founders, primarily the chairman who was also the general manager. In the aftermath of the milk scandal, the group was taken over by COFCO, the state-owned largest food processer, manufacturer and trader in China. Guangming Dairy is a listed company controlled by the Shanghai municipal government through two local SOEs.[11]

Sanlu was placed into liquidation in December 2008, following failed negotiations for the group to be taken over by Sanyuan Foods Co., Ltd. The latter is a listed SOE controlled by the Beijing municipal government. By January 2009, a number of former Sanlu senior executives and other persons involved in the scandal had been convicted of different criminal offences. By this time also, the compensation for tort victims had been finalised, with most of the victims' families accepting a compensation scheme put forward by the dairy companies and backed by the central and local governments. In March 2009, the assets of the bankrupt Sanlu were purchased by Sanyuan Foods through public auction, with the bidding terms tailor-made to Sanyuan, who also took over responsibility for Sanlu's employees. The Sanlu bankruptcy case was concluded on 22 November 2009, 10 months following the issue of the bankruptcy order[12] and 13 months since the scandal erupted.

As illustrated next, the state-led stakeholder model of corporate governance was better reflected in the central and local governments' involvement in the handling of the aftermath of the milk scandal than in the lead up to the scandal. While close state-manager relations underpinned both stages, the central government took on a more inclusive approach in the protection of company stakeholders such as tort victims and trade creditors in the scandal aftermath. However, it is useful to briefly review the causes of the scandal which demonstrate some negative impact of close government-business association on the setting and enforcing of food safety standards.

## 3. State Involvement in the Lead Up to the Scandal

In its aftermath, the 2008 milk scandal has been widely attributed to a combination of the relentless self-interest of the milk station operators and poor internal controls of dairy companies in sourcing raw milk. However, at a deeper level, an important cause for the scandal was the extremely close state-manager relations in promoting business expansion. This obscures the distinct role of the government in safeguarding public health and, in Sanlu's case, led to unfortunate consequences.

The milk station operators added melamine to diluted raw milk to artificially raise its protein levels. Also, the self-seeking behaviour of the milk station operators could not be separated from lax internal controls of the dairy companies in sourcing raw milk. As a report provided by Xinhua News Agency stated,

> The testing and quality check personnel can't have been completely ignorant or innocent. An explanation is that the milk company's rapidly expanding business scales led to a shortage of milk sources, which forces them to collect milk loosely, turning a blind eye to poor quality raw milk.[13]

Indeed, the dairy companies' overreliance on milk station operators to collect raw milk in itself, suggests poor internal controls. Dairy companies in China used to run their own dairy farms, so that quality control over raw milk supply was less problematic. However, with the Chinese dairy industry growing at an annual rate of 23% since 2000,[14] fierce competition for raw milk became industry-wide. In a quest to expand milk sources in the most 'cost-effective' ways, most large dairy companies, including Sanlu, Mengnui and Yili, turned to privately-run milk stations to collect raw milk from small dairy farmers. However, with the poor quality controls of the dairy companies and the extremely low prices they set for raw milk, 'spiking raw milk with all sorts of additives, such as melamine' became a 'public secret' in the industry, at least within Hebei province.[15]

Poor internal controls aside, the Sanlu case presented an example of blatant disregard for corporate ethics and social responsibility. The company had received complaints about babies who became ill after drinking Sanlu's infant formula since December 2007. However, during the eight months that followed, the management of Sanlu took extensive measures to cover up the complaints, leaving the number of infant victims to continue to grow. This was until early August 2008, when tests reluctantly carried out by Sanlu with an outside agency confirmed melamine contamination in Sanlu's infant formula.[16]

The (possibly calculated) shifting of cost and risk to smaller agents by large dairy companies, while turning a blind eye to the difficulties those agents may face in meeting business and operational demands, finds many analogies in private companies operating in western market economies. In a western setting, similar corporate behaviour has also raised issues in corporate ethics and social responsibility. Despite these clear analogies, however, a strong desire of the municipal governments in China to maintaining strong levels of regional economic performance, and the concern of the central government stakeholder for ensuring national economic growth, tend to obscure the responsibilities of both the corporate enterprise and the state regulator.

In Sanlu's case, a close local government-business relationship was manifested in the former's extensive delay in reporting Sanlu's milk contamination incident to the Hebei provincial government. It took the Shijiazhuang government 38 days to forward Sanlu's report to the provincial government, rather than the two hours required by the relevant central government regulation.[17] This meant that the central government was not informed of the incident until September 9, nine months after the first sign of the melamine tainted milk.[18] When asked to explain the extensive delay, a spokesperson of the Shijiazhuang government referred to "support for local businesses" and cited a letter from Sanlu that pleaded the government to *increase control and coordination of the media, to create a good environment for the recall of the company's problem products . . . to avoid whipping up the issue and creating a negative influence in society*.[19] The relationship between Sanlu and the Shijiazhuang government was so close that it even 'convinced' Fonterra, the New Zealand joint-venture partner of Sanlu, to 'work within the system' to effect an official product recall. When informed of the milk contamination by its Chinese partner, Fonterra went public only after three failed meetings with the Shijiazhuang municipal authorities.[20]

In the case of the milk scandal, close state-business relations were not limited to the local government levels however. At the central level, public criticism focused on the extremely business-friendly approach the government had adopted in regulating a fundamental area of food safety. As early as 2000, SAQSIQ introduced a system of exemption for quality inspection to "ease the burden for companies that otherwise would undergo repeated inspections".[21] The system allowed many products, including food products, of well-known brands, such as 'Sanlu', to enjoy the quality inspection-free status. This was despite alarms on food safety in China repeatedly raised by a series of major scandals.[22] Once again, cases of 'regulatory capture' are common also in western market systems (Grabosky and Sutton 1989), but the greater the number of regulatory roles assumed by the state and the more dependent stakeholders become in relying upon the state to protect their interests, the greater the possibility that regulatory roles become less clear and the enforcement of breaches less likely to be reviewed.

The 2008 tainted milk scandal indeed revealed many of the dangers associated with close government-business relationship. As will be further discussed, once the association between the state and production companies for the purpose of promoting economic growth and business expansion becomes a top priority, other governance issues such as the monitoring of managers and protection of investor and other stakeholder interests may be ignored.

On the other hand, as the examination of the handling of the scandal aftermath that follows will suggest, while close state-manager relations continued to underpin this latter process, the central government took on a more proactive approach to the protection of various company stakeholder groups affected by the scandal. Nevertheless, while this all-encompassing approach was pivotal in bringing a major corporate scandal to a quick end, its effect on the governance practices within Chinese companies remains questionable.

## 4. The Handling of the Scandal Aftermath

The state-led stakeholder approach adopted by the central government in the scandal aftermath was obviously driven by multiple pressures. Apart from its effect on hundreds of thousands of infant victims, the exposure of the scandal threw the fast-growing dairy industry, accounting for about 30% of the food industry in China, into a major crisis. While the Sanlu group consisted of 30 subsidiaries, and other entities became hopelessly insolvent, other dairy groups, including Yili and Mengniu, were also deeply affected, as their sales plummeted with lost consumer confidence and worldwide bans on Chinese dairy products.[23] Furthermore, as state involvement in corporate affairs was an important cause of the scandal, the legitimacy of the Chinese form of state-led economic development was also at risk.

State involvement in corporate affairs to promote economic development and social stability was a major theme in the handling of the demise of Sanlu. Placing Sanlu into liquidation would be a good test case for the new Chinese *Enterprise Bankruptcy Law*.[24] Drawing heavily upon the US bankruptcy law regime, the new *Enterprise Bankruptcy Law* was introduced in August 2006 to replace an old piece of legislation that only applied to industrial SOEs.

Although Sanlu did not eventually escape a court-ordered liquidation, this fate was not intended by the government in the first place. This can be seen from the refusal of the Shijiazhuang Intermediate Court to hear an earlier bankruptcy application filed against Sanlu by one of Sanlu's sales agents. The refusal was given with no clear reason.[25] However, as discussed next, the same court subsequently heard Sanlu's bankruptcy case when all efforts to rescue Sanlu failed.

The idea of having Sanlu taken over by another company was preferred by the central and local governments for various reasons. The famous 'Sanlu' brand had become worthless. However, other 'intangible assets' accumulated by Sanlu (ranging from advanced production and marketing systems to extensive network for sourcing milk) through its 20 years of history could be better preserved through a takeover.[26] In addition, should Sanlu be allowed to stay in business, there would be a greater chance for Sanlu to repay its debts and retain its over 10,000 employees. All these liabilities posed a serious threat not only to the local Shijiazhuang government but also to economic development and social stability at the national level.

The takeover plan emerged on 26 September, when share trading in Sanyuan Foods, a listed company controlled by the Beijing municipal government, was suspended, and the company announced that it 'had received a notice from the government to consider a Sanlu merger plan'.[27] Industry experts suggested that Sanyuan was chosen to take over Sanlu for two main reasons: first, the company was the only relatively large Chinese dairy company that was not implicated by the scandal and, second, Sanyuan is a state-controlled company, which 'makes it easier for the government to manipulate'.[28]

The proposed Sanyuan takeover of Sanlu was widely considered 'an impossible mission'.[29] The differences in size and scale between Sanyuan and Sanlu were enormous. Sanlu was one of the leading Chinese dairy groups with businesses around the country. Sanyuan, with its annual sales amounting to only about 10% of Sanlu, was largely unknown to consumers outside Beijing. Sanyuan claimed that the acquisition would raise its market share by adding to its liquid milk operations an extra line of business in powdered milk. Industry experts, however, suggested that problems such as business integration and cash flow, particularly with the indeterminate amount of tort liabilities faced by Sanlu, could drag Sanyuan into insolvency. The Sanyuan takeover plan did not eventuate, and was followed by an order of the Shijiazhuang Intermediate Court placing Sanlu into liquidation (on the application of a local branch of a state-owned bank, a Sanlu creditor). However, with the backing of Beijing and Hebei governments, the takeover negotiations went on for months prior to the issue of the bankruptcy order.[30]

The Sanlu liquidation case turned out to be another politically manipulated process, due to similar considerations that had underpinned the government-backed takeover plan. Sanyuan became "perhaps the greatest winner" in Sanlu's demise (Katz 2010, 466). Sanlu was declared insolvent on 12 February 2009. On 4 March 2009, Sanyuan acquired Sanlu's assets in insolvency at a public auction with the bidder criteria tailor-made to Sanyuan: the auction was only open to Chinese domestic dairy producers that had not been implicated in the milk scandal.[31] As some core enterprises in the Sanlu group had already resumed production under lease agreements with Sanyuan before the auction, commentators said the 'government-led bankruptcy' of Sanlu probably worked even more favourably for Sanyuan. This is because, unlike a takeover, it provided the company with an opportunity to acquire Sanlu's assets without its liabilities.[32] The Sanlu bankruptcy case was concluded on 22 November 2009, within ten months following the issue of the bankruptcy order.[33]

On another note, the swift handling of the bankruptcy case could not have been achieved without Sanlu's out-of-court settlements with its tort victims and trade creditors. The carefully coordinated and government-backed settlement plans, particularly for the tort victims, not only played a crucial role in directing the tort claims away from the courts but also demonstrated the all-encompassing approach adopted in China's state-led stakeholder model of corporate governance. Here, once again, were blurred lines between the role of the state in apportioning responsibility and compensation for injuries to claimants and the role of the courts in assessing legal liabilities and damages for injuries suffered.

The compensation for the tort victims was one of the most contentious issues in the aftermath of the milk scandal. Had the scandal occurred in a western market economy such as Australia, one would expect a slew of lawsuits, or more likely, class actions being launched on behalf of the tort victims against the dairy companies, as well as the Shijiazhuang municipal government (should the government be found to have played a part in the loss or injury suffered by the victims). If such actions were permitted, the adverse publicity would not only lead the local and central governments into disgrace but also jeopardise economic development and social stability.

Curiously, in the aftermath of the scandal, no single tort claim against either Sanlu or any other dairy companies was reportedly heard in any Chinese court. It is not that the Chinese law failed to provide any redress for these victims. To the contrary, the 1986 *General Principles of Civil Law* (which sets out a basic framework for Chinese civil and commercial legislation) imposes on manufacturers, as well as sellers, the liability for economic loss and physical injury caused by defective goods.[34] This general provision has been reinforced by at least two pieces of legislation on consumer protection, namely the *Law on the Protection of Consumers' Rights and Interests* (the *Consumer Protection Law*) and the *Product Quality Law*.[35] Article 35 of the *Consumer Protection Law*, echoed in Article 31 of the *Product Quality Law*, allows a "consumer or other victim" who suffers economic loss or physical injury as a result of defective goods to claim compensation from both the seller and the manufacturer. The heads of damages include "medical expenses, nursing expenses during medical treatment, and the reduced income for loss of working time and other expenses".[36] Should a consumer or victim be 'disabled' by the defective product, the compensation should also include "the victims' expenses for self-help devices, living allowances, compensation for disability and the necessary living cost of the persons supported by the disabled". Further, should death be caused by defective goods, the defendant will also be liable for "funeral expenses, death compensation and the necessary living cost of the persons supported by the deceased during their lifetime" '.[37] Although Chinese legislation does not provide for compensation for pain and suffering ('mental loss' in Chinese terms) or exemplary damages, it is not rare for the court to award such compensation in practice, under either the heads of 'compensation for disability', 'compensation for death' or a judicial opinion issued by the Supreme People's Court (SPC) on 'mental and spiritual loss' in civil claims.[38]

In relation to the forms of litigation, the 1991 Chinese *Civil Procedure Law* provides for individual actions, 'representative suits with fixed number of litigants',[39] as well as 'representative suits where the number of litigants comprising one party is unfixed at the commencement of the action'.[40] The SPC disallowed the second type of collective action, which accords with the US-style class action, for securities-related civil claims. It, however, has not banned the action for other tort claims including consumer claims.

Nevertheless, despite availability of the legal remedies, the central government opted for extra-legal mechanisms to achieve 'better justice' to the tort victims, as well as for a quick resolution of the scandal. The compensation plan emerged on 30 December 2008, one week after Sanlu was issued the bankruptcy order. The state media *China Daily* announced that the 22 dairy companies implicated in the milk scandal, including Sanlu, had committed RMB900 million (US$131 million) as 'one-off compensation' to all tort victims. Hence, each victim family would receive an amount ranging from RMB2, 000 (US$292) to RMB30, 000 (US$4,400), depending on the degree of sickness of their babies, or a payment of RMB200, 000 (US$29,000) in case of death. In addition, a RMB200 million fund was to be established by the companies to 'cover medical bills for any lingering problems related to the tainted milk'.[41] The fund would also allow the tort victims to access insurance coverage with a leading state-controlled insurance company for the "full amount of medical bills related to the tainted milk incurred before they turn eighteen years of age".[42]

This arrangement was not, as it appeared to be, a purely voluntary act of the dairy companies. As early as 10 December 2008, following three months of contention surrounding the issue of victim compensation, the Ministry of Health issued a media release stating, "Relevant departments are now considering a compensation plan for the Sanlu infant milk powder incident", and "the Ministry was compiling information about the victims who may receive compensation".[43] No further details of the plan were subsequently released. As a corollary to the government's silence, there was, however, sporadic media exposure of victim claims being rejected by several Chinese courts, as the courts were waiting for "instructions from the government", or "a compensation plan to be released by the government".[44] News reports also suggested that the RMB902 million contributed by Sanlu to the compensation plan, one week before it was declared bankrupt, was raised "with the assistance" of the Shijiazhuang government.[45]

The implementation of the compensation plan has been generally considered a successful example of government-led resolution of mass dispute, despite controversies surrounding the inadequacy of the compensation proposed.[46] The extremely high acceptance rate by the tort victims' families was not surprising.[47] Firstly, for those victims who suffered minor injuries, free medical treatment and a small one-off compensation payment may be seen as adequate (Katz 2010, 466). Secondly, for the families of victims suffering major loss, there was no guarantee that they could receive more than the plan had offered. These families were ranked equally with other unsecured creditors at the bottom for distribution of the bankruptcy assets.[48] And, thirdly, given the background of the tort victims' families, for many with a low economic status, poor education and limited travel experience, the difficulties faced by them in bringing a complex law suit before the Shijiazhuang Court were insurmountable. As such, a government-coordinated compensation scheme is arguably a more effective means to "maximise substantive justice for the greatest number of victims in a practical manner" (Katz 2010, 466).

Indeed, in Sanlu's case, state coordination of company relations with their outsider stakeholders was not limited to dealing with tort victims. The swift conclusion of the Sanlu bankruptcy case was also facilitated by a government-backed debt repayment plan reached between Sanlu and its unsecured trade creditors. The agreement was signed by Sanlu Trading Company, a wholly owned subsidiary of Sanlu on its behalf.[49] It was finalised on 23 December, when the Shijiazhuang court's delivery of the bankruptcy order to Sanlu led over 300 Sanlu's sales agents, most unsecured creditors, to gather at the Sanlu headquarters and in front of Hebei Provincial government. On the same day, following a meeting between "the Hebei Provincial Communist Party Committee, the Provincial government, and the Shijiazhuang city Party Committee and the government", the Hebei and Shijiazhuang governments agreed to "guarantee the co-ordination of the full repayment should Sanlu have difficulties in repaying the debts".[50]

The validity of the separate debt repayment agreement is dubious. Under Article 16 of the Chinese *Bankruptcy Law*, once a court has accepted an application for bankruptcy, any repayment of debts by the debtor company to individual creditors should be void. However, in the Sanlu bankruptcy case, it appeared that neither the court nor the bankruptcy administrator (headed by an official of the Shijiazhuang State-Owned Assets Supervision Commission)[51] exercised their power to set aside the agreement. Furthermore, Sanlu Trading Company, the wholly owned subsidiary of Sanlu, which had signed the agreement on behalf of Sanlu with its trade creditors, was excluded from the liquidation process.[52]

The Chinese central and local governments' involvement in the handling of the aftermath of the 2008 milk scandal brought into sharper relief some basic flaws in the state-led stakeholder model of corporate governance and state involvement in the milk companies prior to the scandal breaking. Strong state involvement in corporate affairs to promote economic development and social stability was clearly an important priority, but the state arguably assumed a far too active role in coordinating the competing interests of different corporate stakeholder groups affected by the scandal. Government involvement in corporate failures with mass effects may occur in all systems. However, the manner and extent of state involvement in the milk scandal aftermath, for example, in the government's orchestration of the bankruptcy and the compensation scheme before the court became involved, would be exceptional in Anglo-American jurisdictions. As discussed next, this model has played an important role in maintaining China's rapid economic development and social stability. Nevertheless, the inherent disadvantages associated with this model also help to explain the limited success achieved by China's post-2005 legal and regulatory reforms to strengthen corporate governance.

## 5. The State-led Stakeholder Model of Corporate Governance and the Enforcement of Food Safety Standards

State-led corporate governance has both advantages and disadvantages. Focusing on CSR, Ho saw China's efforts in this regard as a state-centric or state-led model, and argued that one of the greatest advantages of this model is the strong capacity of the state to bring together a variety of formal and informal tools to promote corporate commitment to social responsibility (Ho 2013, 431–432). Some of these tools, such as the formulation and enforcement of law, regulation and other state-sponsored programs, are not commonly available to private sector organisations. Further to the resourcefulness of the state, another important advantage of this model lies in its "inherent communicative effect" (Ho 2013, 434). State-led or sponsored initiatives may send a strong signal to the business community about government's endorsement of CSR and may therefore play a major role in guiding the formation of norms about the importance of respect for law and social responsibility.

Nevertheless, the state-led model also harbours significant disadvantages. One of these is that where the state plays such a pervasive and comprehensive role in monitoring and disciplining CSR, the scope is narrowed for any role that might otherwise be played by legal regulation, social media and market-based mechanisms for example, through expressions of disapproval by social organisations and the wider community (Ho 2013, 437).

Further, where the state is the single most important determinant of the ultimate adjustments to be made in liabilities and compensation, as in this model, the advantages of such active state involvement may in fact become its disadvantages. Firstly, because the various state-led initiatives depend on the will and capacity of state agencies and government officials for implementation, the lack of will or capacity of either detracts from the effectiveness of the model (Ho 2013, 432). Secondly, although state-backed initiatives may send a strong signal about the importance of compliance with CSR, the formation of the relevant norms among business community, as well as the wider society, depends on the "consistency of the message and the legitimacy of the state itself as a CSR [corporate social responsibility] supporter" (Ho 2013, 434). A lack of consistency in the message, for example due to the conflicting goals of the state in promoting economic development, preserving social stability and maintaining good corporate governance, may lead to misconceptions among the business community about the standards and responsibilities expected of them by the state (Ho 2013, 435–436). This is particularly the case where the legitimacy of the state, as a supporter of CSR, is undermined by government, or government-endorsed corporate leaders who "[turned] out to be the culprits in a compliance-related scandal" (Ho 2013, 414). Although these advantages and disadvantages were propounded by Ho in relation to the state-led model of CSR, they may be applied equally to the state-led stakeholder model of corporate governance, given the blurred boundary between these two spheres at least in China.

China's new state-led stakeholder approach to corporate governance has reflected some of the positive aspects of the model articulated by Ho. Its capability to serve as an efficient and cost-effective conflict management tool was certainly manifested in the handling of the milk scandal. After the eruption of the scandal, the central government responded quickly by utilising a multitude of formal and informal tools to strengthen the monitoring of dairy companies and to enforce their 'social responsibilities' towards their injured stakeholders, including the tort victims and trade creditors. Indeed, apart from the measures discussed earlier, many other steps, ranging from frequent product quality inspections and swift criminal conviction of melamine producers, milk station operators and the Sanlu executives, were adopted for the same purposes.[53] Nor did the 10,000 Sanlu employees miss out. As the Party Secretary of Sanlu declared, "Whoever wants to buy Sanlu must also take Sanlu's employees".[54] Hence, with the comprehensive and decisive response of the state, social stability was maintained, and disruption to economic growth was kept to the minimum. Similar to the state-centric model of CSR as enunciated by Ho, the model also enabled the state to act promptly to bring some structural changes to the regulation of the milk industry. These include removing the system that granted certain products with quality inspection-free status and tightening up milk standards, which may be conducive to the long-term development of the industry.

However, the disadvantages inherent in this degree of state involvement were also evident in the central and local government's handling of the milk scandal. Firstly, as mentioned earlier, strong state involvement in corporate affairs may limit the role played by market forces, including expressions of disapproval by private sector organisations, in monitoring corporate governance. These forces had been introduced by the Chinese state to reform corporate governance, primarily governance of SOEs. Unfortunately, strong state intervention motivated by other higher-ranking policy goals in the handling of the scandal did not allow the benefits of these forces to be exploited. This was despite the extensive coverage of the scandal in the commercial media and social websites, which probably prompted the government's adoption of the compensation plan for tort victims. While the early response from Fonterra to Sanlu's contaminated milk incident was cooperative, the silence maintained by the Chinese semi-government, semi-not-for-profit organisations, such as the stock exchanges and consumer protection associations, was striking.

Secondly, juggling its competing policy goals in promoting economic development, while maintaining social stability and good corporate governance may render the state a less rigorous guardian of corporate governance. The Chinese state has for a long time played the roles of a controlling shareholder, corporate regulator, business and stock market promoter. Under the state-led stakeholder model of corporate governance, the state also took upon itself a greater role in monitoring corporate governance and promoting CSR. These overlapping and conflicting roles of the state had some unintended effects on corporate governance as evidenced in the milk scandal. In the aftermath of the scandal, the Chinese governments at both central and local levels were clearly mindful of their overriding roles in driving China's economic growth and social stability. They appeared to have been swayed by these considerations in dealing with issues of corporate governance and CSR. For this reason, many laws such as those relevant to consumer protection, enterprise bankruptcy, civil procedure and the company law were left unenforced, which inevitably reduced their rigour in deterring corporate misconduct.

Indeed, in relation to the executives of the dairy companies implicated in the scandal, only the chairwoman and several other executives of Sanlu were prosecuted. They were convicted for "producing and selling fake or defective products" (rather than the more serious offences of "producing and selling poisonous food products" for which the maximum penalty is death) under the PRC *Criminal Law*.[55] In this regard, the combination of strong state involvement in corporate affairs and the ease with which the state might adjust stakeholder claims while promoting economic objectives, have arguably obscured the difficult task of assigning fault within the company itself and enforcing failures to uphold expected standards. However, in the absence of a special public inquiry similar to an Australian style Royal Commission, questions concerning the adequacy of internal controls in the dairy companies and the attribution of criminal or civil fault to those involved will remain unanswered.

Finally, among all the disadvantages associated with the state-led model, the erosion of confidence in corporate governance and CSR, and of public trust in the independent rule of law, may be the most significant casualties. The mixed messages sent by the state in its administrative handling of the scandal contributed significantly to its reach. The expansive utilitarian adjustments made by the central and local governments in rescuing Sanlu and other dairy companies—ranging from the government-negotiated takeover of Sanlu to the state-sponsored media campaign to restore consumer confidence in domestic dairy products—do not necessarily encourage basic legal compliance, let alone corporate governance and CSR that often go beyond the limits of law.

The government's swift handling of the 2008 milk scandal has indeed not helped to reduce the number of food and other corporate scandals in China. Within the dairy industry, a series of other incidents (such as the 'leather milk scandal',[56] and the aflatoxin M1-tainted milk incident[57]) have since occurred, perpetuating the lack of consumer confidence in Chinese infant formula.[58] In the meantime, food safety outside dairy products has continued to be a chief concern of Chinese consumers.[59] With the frequent exposure of food and other types of corporate scandals, such as work safety and environmental pollution, corporate governance and CSR remain highly contentious in China (Chen *et al* 2012; Lu *et al* 2011). If allowed to grow, this lack of public trust in the rule of law is not conducive to sustainable economic development and social stability.

## 6. Conclusion

Despite extensive reforms in China's post-2005 regulatory framework for the governance of listed SOEs, changes to the underlying practices in these companies have been more limited. One important factor which may have reduced the positive effect of these reforms has been the role assumed by the state in the new state-led stakeholder model of corporate governance. Clearly, this model has two obvious and attractive strengths. First, it enables the state to bring rapid formal or structural changes to Chinese corporate governance. Second, in times of major corporate crisis, it may serve as an extremely efficient and cost-effective conflict management tool supporting both economic growth and social stability. Nevertheless, these benefits are likely to be accompanied by more fundamental disadvantages which will tend to inhibit the continued development of good governance practices in China.

As explained in this chapter, these disadvantages include restrictions upon the role that might be played by both state and non-state institutions in disciplining corporate governance, erosion of the will and/or capacity of the state to maintain good corporate governance and the sending of mixed messages to both companies and society about the importance of compliance with the law and CSR. The supervening goals of the state in promoting economic development and preserving social stability while also attempting to maintain good corporate governance, lie behind most of the disadvantages and failings of the state-led stakeholder model evidenced in the milk scandal.

As this chapter highlights, the irony may be that the disadvantages inherent in the state-led stakeholder model of corporate governance may ultimately impede the achievement of China's global ambitions. Fundamental failures of corporate governance within China's major natural resource companies, particularly those responsible for food production and processing in which the potential injury to consumers is immediately significant, are sure to be relayed quickly to consumers in China's major markets around the world. There is no doubt that China has tightened food standards since the 2008 milk scandal and will continue to do so. It is, however, in this respect that corporate responsibility for maintaining food safety standards may yet have a way to go in China.

## Notes

1. 《中华人民共和国公司法》 [Company Law of the People's Republic of China] (People's Republic of China) National People's Congress Standing Committee, 27 October 2005, Art 5.
2. 'China Seizes 22 Companies with Contaminated Baby Milk Powder' *Xinhua Net* News Story (17 September 2008) <http://news.xinhuanet.com/english/2008-09/17/content_10046949.htm>.
3. 'Two Executed in China Over Tainted Milk Scandal' *Xinhua Net* News Story (24 November 2009) <http://news.xinhuanet.com/english/2009-11/24/content_12530798.htm>.
4. World Health Organisation, 'Melamine-Contaminated Powdered Infant Formula in China—Update 2' (29 September 2008) <www.who.int/csr/don/2008_09_29a/en/>.
5. 'Two Executed in China Over Tainted Milk Scandal', n 3.
6. 《中华人民共和国宪法》 [Constitution of the People's Republic of China] art 6.
7. 张旭 [Zhang Xu], '还原三鹿前世今身' [An Overview of Sanlu's History], *China Times* (online) (22 September 2008) <www.chinatimes.cc/huaxia/pages/159/moreInfo.htm>.
8. Richard Spencer and Peter Foster, 'China Milk Scandal Threatens Giant Dairy Firm', *The Telegraph* (online) (24 September 2008) <www.telegraph.co.uk/news/worldnews/asia/china/3073998/China-milk-scandal-threatens-giant-dairy-firm.html>.
9. The ownership of Sanlu became a controversial issue at the exposure of the scandal, as many people believed Sanlu was a state-owned enterprise. At a press conference held on 13 September 2008, Mr. Yang Chongyong, vice-governor of Hebei Province denied any government ownership in Sanlu. See '河北省副省长: 政府在三鹿集团有限公司中没有股份' [Hebei Vice-Governor: Government Does Not Own Shares in Sanlu], *China Central Television News* (online) (13 September 2008) <http://news.cctv.com/china/20080913/103040.shtml>.
10. 龙丽 [Long Li], '三鹿相关材料已报批有望2008年实现A股上市' [Application Submitted, Sanlu Hopeful of Getting Listed in A Share Market in 2008], *21 Century Economic Report* (online) (17 September 2008) <http://news.hexun.com/2008-09-17/108945053.html>.
11. The 2007 and 2008 Annual Reports of Yili Industrial Group Co Ltd, China Mengnui Dairy Co Ltd and Guangming (Bright) Dairy Shareholding Co., Ltd.
12. Yan Wang, 'Compensation Lawsuit Over Tainted Milk Postponed', *China Daily* (online) (9 December 2009) <www.chinadaily.com.cn/business/2009-12/09/content_9144184.htm>.
13. 'Survivor Leads China's Milk Industry', *Xinhua Net* News Story (15 November 2008) <http://news.xinhuanet.com/english/2008-11/15/content_10361534_3.htm>.
14. '乳制品工业产业政策发布' [Chinese Dairy Industry Policy Released], *China Economic Net* News Story (17 June 2008) <http://finance.ce.cn/macro/gdxw/200806/17/t20080617_13226765.shtml>.
15. 徐超 [Xu Chao], '三聚氰胺溯源' [Tracing the Source of Melamine], *Caijing Magazine* (online) (29 September 2008) <http://magazine.caijing.com.cn/20080928/77700.shtml>. The practice of spiking source milk with melamine was traced back to April 2005 by the Deputy Governor of Hebei Province. See '河北省副省长透露：不法份子2005年已开始向牛奶掺三聚氰胺' [Deputy-Governor of Hebei: Law Offenders Started to Add Melamine to Raw Milk from 2005], *21 Century Economy Reports* (online) (18 September 2008) <http://news.cnfol.com/080918/101,1280,4781164,00.shtml>.

16. Spencer and Foster, n. 8; '三鹿事件真相大暴光' [Truth of Sanlu Incident Revealed] *Xinhua Net* News Story (1 January 2009) <http://news.xinhuanet.com/politics/2009-01/01/content_10587575.htm>.
17. 《国家重大食品安全事故应急预案》 [National Emergency Plan for Handling Major Food Safety Accidents] (People's Republic of China) State Council (27 February 2006), s3.2.2.
18. '党中央国务院严肃处理三鹿奶粉事件相关责任人员' [Central Party Committee and State Council Dealing with Persons Involved in the Sanlu Milk Scandal Seriously] Chinese Central Government Website News Update, 22 September 2008 <www.gov.cn/jrzg/2008-09/22/content_1102256.htm>. There have been different explanations regarding how the scandal was exposed. Sanlu's New Zealand partner Fonterra claimed that it was informed by its Chinese partner of the milk contamination on 2 August, 2008, the same day on which the Shijiazhuang city government was informed. After three unsuccessful meetings with the Shijiazhuang health officials to raise the alarm, the company reported the incident to the New Zealand Foreign Affairs Department on 22 August, which led to the issue finally being brought to the attention of the Chinese central government by the former New Zealand Prime Minister on 9 September. See Spencer and Foster, n. Error! Bookmark not defined.
19. 王明皓 [Wang Minghao], '石家庄市政府新闻发言人:三鹿事件为何迟迟不报' [Spokesperson for Shijiazhuang Government: Why Report of Sanlu Incident Was Delayed], *People's Net* News Story (1 October 2008) <Http://paper.people.com.cn/rmrb/html/2008–2010/01/content_112000.htm>; 'China Dairy 'Asked for Cover-Up', *BBC News* (online) (1 October 2008) <http://news.bbc.co.uk/2/hi/asia-pacific/7646512.stm>.
20. Spencer and Foster, n. 8; Also see Shanshan Wang, 'Fonterra CEO Reflecting on Investing in China', *Caijing Magazine* (online) (5 December 2008) <www.caijing.com.cn/2008-12-05/110035012.html>.
21. Yang Binbin, 'Food Product Inspection Waivers Revoked' *Caijing Magazine* (online) (18 September 2008) <http://english.caijing.com.cn/2008-09-18/110013644.html>.
22. These included a separate incident in 2004 where about ten babies were reportedly killed by fake or defective infant formula sold in Anhui Province. See Di Fang 'Milk Powders Kill Babies in Anhui Province', *China Daily* (online) (20 April 2004) <www.chinadaily.com.cn/english/doc/2004-04/20/content_324727.htm>.
23. 王锦 [Wang Jin] '中国乳业危机行业洗牌不可避免' [Crisis of Chinese Dairy Industry: Restructure Inevitable], *China Securities Net* News Story (22 September 2008) <www.cs.com.cn/xwzx/05/200809/t20080922_1591661.htm>.
24. 《中华人民共和国企业破产法》 [The Enterprise Bankruptcy Law of the People's Republic of China] (People's Republic of China) National People's Congress Standing Committee, 27 August 2006.
25. '三鹿破产案：是消失还是涅磐' [Sanlu Bankruptcy Case, Demise or Rebirth?] *Xinhua Net* News Story (5 January 2009) <http://news.xinhuanet.com/fortune/2009-01/05/content_10604233.htm>.
26. Ibid.
27. '知情人士谈三元并购三鹿：三元身不由己 '[Insiders Comment on Sanyuan Sanlu Merger：not Sanyuan's Will], *Xinhua Net* News Story (4 January 2009) <http://news.xinhuanet.com/fortune//2009-01/04/content_10598930.htm>; Wang Qian, 'Sanyuan May Take Over Tainted Milk Brand Sanlu', *China Daily* (online) (27 September 2008) <www.chinadaily.com.cn/china/2008-09/27/content_7064279.htm>.
28. Ibid.

29. '三鹿：完达山旁观三元或孤独破局' [Wandashan Onlooking Sanlu Takeover: Sanyuan Likely to Struggle Alone', *Xinhua Net* News Story (5 November 2008) <http://cs.xinhuanet.com/cqzk/05/200811/t20081120_1659972.htm>.

30. '三元并购三鹿:关系敏感的局中局' [Sanyuan Taking Over Sanlu, a Sensitive Case] *Xinhua Net* News Story (2 January 2009) <http://news.xinhuanet.com/fortune/2009-01/02/content_10590487.htm>.

31. 'Sanyuan Buys Scandal-Hit Sanlu Dairy Company at Auction', *People's Daily* (online) (4 March 2009) <http://english.peopledaily.com.cn/90001/90783/91300/6606135.html>.

32. '三鹿将宣告破产传言利好三元收购' [Sanlu to be Declared Bankruptcy: Rumoured in Favour of Sanyuan Takeover] *Xinhua Net* News Story (23 December 2008) <http://news.xinhuanet.com/fortune/2008-12/23/content_10547631.htm>.

33. Yan Wang, n. 12.

34. 《中华人民共和国民事诉讼法》 [Civil Procedure Law of the People's Republic of China] (People's Republic of China) National People's Congress, 9 April 1991, art 122.

35. 《中华人民共和国消费者权益保护法》 [Law of the People's Republic of China on the Protection of Consumers' Rights and Interests], (People's Republic of China)National People's Congress Standing Committee, 31 October 1993; 《中华人民共和国产品质量法》 [Product Quality Law of the People's Republic of China (People's Republic of China) National People's Congress Standing Committee, 22 February 1993.

36. 《中华人民共和国消费者权益保护法》 [Law of the People's Republic of China on the Protection of Consumers' Rights and Interests], art 41; 《中华人民共和国产品质量法》 [Product Quality Law of the People's Republic of China], art 32.

37. 《中华人民共和国消费者权益保护法》 [Law of the People's Republic of China on the Protection of Consumers' Rights and Interests], art 42.

38. 《关于确定民事侵权精神损害赔偿责任若干问题的解释》 [Explanation of Several Issues Relating to The Assessment of Mental Losses in Civil Litigation] (People's Republic of China) Supreme People's Court, 8 March 2001.

39. 《中华人民共和国民事诉讼法》 [Civil Procedure Law of the People's Republic of China] (People's Republic of China) National People's Congress, n. 34, art 54.

40. Ibid art 55.

41. '22 Dairy Firms to Pay $160m in Compensation', *China Daily* (online) News Story (30 December 2008) <www.chinadaily.com.cn/cndy/2008-12/30/content_7351554.htm>.

42. '结石患儿民事赔偿案无一获受理 河北律协解释' [Why Tort Claims Associated with the Milk Scandal Refused to Be Heard by Courts? Explained by Hebei Lawyers Association] *Xinhua Net* News Story (7 January 2009) <http://news.xinhuanet.com/legal/2009-01/07/content_10615043.htm>.

43. '中国相关部门正在讨论问题奶粉时间赔偿方案' [Relevant Chinese Departments Considering a Compensation Plan for Problem Powdered Milk Victims], *Xinhua Net* News Story (10 December 2008) <http://news.xinhuanet.com/newscenter/2008-12/10/content_10484532_1.htm>.

44. '结石患儿民事赔偿案无一获受理 河北律协解释' [Why Tort Claims Associated with the Milk Scandal Refused to Be Heard by Courts? Explained by Hebei Lawyers Association], n. 42; '三鹿索赔暂不立案：谁来赔偿受害者' [Compensation Claims Against Sanlu Suspended: Who to Compensate the Victims?], *China News Net* News Story (11 November 2008) <www.chinanews.com.cn/cj/xfsh/news/2008/11-11/1445254.shtml>; 'Courts Compound Pain of Chinese Tainted Milk', *New York Times* (online) (17 October 2008) <www.nytimes.com/2008/10/17/world/asia/17milk.html?fta=y>.

45. '石家庄官方称抵押政府大院筹三鹿赔款子虚乌有' [Shijiazhuang Official Dismissed Alleged Government Assistance of Sanlu to Repay Debt by Mortgaging Government Office Buildings] *Xinhua Net* News Story (8 January 2009) <http://news.xinhuanet.com/politics/2009-01/08/content_10625612.htm>.

46. '22 Dairy Firms to Pay $160m in Compensation', n. 41. According to *Xinhua Net*, many parents found the 2000 yuan for 'minor kidney problems' is too inadequate to accept. Other criticisms on the inadequacy of compensation plan related to the scope and the period of the insurance coverage and the lack of involvement of the victims' families in the formulation of the scheme.

47. '超 90% 婴幼儿奶粉事件患儿家长已接受主动赔偿' [Over 90 Per Cent of Tort Victims of Tainted Milk Incident Have Accepted Compensation Voluntarily], *Xinhua Net* News Story (24 January 2009) <www.he.xinhuanet.com/news/2009-01/24/content_15543516.htm>.

48. The order of distribution of bankruptcy assets provided in Article 113 of the Enterprise Bankruptcy Law is as follows: (1) bankruptcy expenses and common benefits debts (certain debts incurred by the debtor company after the commencement of the bankruptcy proceedings such as those arising from agency by necessity or personal loss or injury caused by the company property; (2) unpaid wages and other welfare payments; (3) unpaid social insurance premiums and taxes; (4) unsecured claims; Where the insolvent assets are not enough to satisfy the debts in the same ranking, the *pari passu* rule will apply. 《中华人民共和国企业破产法》 [The Enterprise Bankruptcy Law of the People's Republic of China] (People's Republic of China) National People's Congress Standing Committee, 27 August 2006, art 113.

49. '三鹿破产拍卖还债估计三鹿总负债近20亿元' [Sanlu to be Sold Through Bankruptcy Auction: Total Debts Estimated Nearly RMB2 Billion] *Xinhua Net* News Story (25 December 2008) <http://news.xinhuanet.com/fortune/2008-12/25/content_10555709.htm>.

50. 石家庄市政府通报三鹿集团破产案情况(全文) [Shijiazhuang City Government Report on Sanlu Bankruptcy Case (full text)] *Xinhua Net* News Story (25 December 2008) <http://news.xinhuanet.com/fortune/2008-12/25/content_10557898.htm>.

51. '三鹿破产清算小组十四人组成' [Fourteen-Member Sanlu Bankruptcy Liquidation Team Formed], *Dongfang Daily* (online), 31 December 2008 <www.dfdaily.com/html/113/2008/12/31/351068.shtml>.

52. '三鹿破产拍卖还债估计三鹿总负债近20亿元' [Sanlu to Be Sold Through Bankruptcy Auction: Total Debts Estimated Nearly RMB2 Billion], n. 49.

53. '党中央国务院严肃处理三鹿奶粉事件相关责任人员' [Central Party Committee and State Council Dealing with Persons Involved in the Sanlu Milk Scandal Seriously], n. 18.

54. '三鹿党委书记：想买三鹿必须接受全部职工' [Sanlu Party Committee Secretary: Whoever Wants to Buy Sanlu Must Also Take Sanlu's Employees] *Xinhua Net* News Story (11 January 2009) <http://news.xinhuanet.com/local/2009-01/11/content_10638134.htm>.

55. '原三鹿集团董事长田文华一审被判处无期徒刑' [Former Sanlu Chairwoman Tian Wenhua Sentenced to Life Imprisonment], *Xinhua Net* News Story (22 January 2009) <http://news.xinhuanet.com/legal/2009-01/22/content_10701439.htm>; 《中华人民共和国刑法》 [Criminal Law of the People's Republic of China] (People's Republic of China) National People's Congress, 14 March 1997, arts 141, 144.

56. Peter Foster, 'Top 10 Chinese Food Scandals', *The Telegraph* (online), 27 April 2011 <www.telegraph.co.uk/news/worldnews/asia/china/8476080/Top-10-Chinese-Food-Scandals.html>. The scandal, exposed in February 2011,

involved dairy companies using leather-hydrolysed protein, which, like melamine, artificially boosts the protein-content of milk. The scandal led the
authority to close almost half of Chinese dairy companies in a bid to clean up
the industry.
57. 'Questions Remain over Mengniu Milk Scandal, Experts Say', *Caixin* (online)
(27 December 2011) <http://english.caixin.com/2011-12-27/100343210.html>.
On December 2011, Mengniu Dairy Company Ltd. issued an announcement
on its website, apologizing to consumers for aflatoxin M1- contaminated milk,
which was spotted by the General Administration of Quality Supervision,
Inspection and Quarantine in a sample survey of dairy products. Aflatoxin M1
is a liver cancer-causing agent.
58. Rahul Jacob, 'Hong Kong Arrests Baby Milk Smugglers', *Financial Times*
(online) (4 March 2013) <www.ft.com/cms/s/0/9d6a35a8-84bb-11e2-aaf1-
00144feabdc0.html#axzz2Nx0YnQgm>.
59. Foster, n. 56.

# Bibliography

Chen Jiagui et al. 陈佳贵等2012,《中国企业社会责任研究报告 (2012) 》 [Research
report on corporate social responsibility report of China (2012)] (社会科学文献出
版社 [Social Sciences Academic Press], Beijing.
Chinese Central Government Website 2008, "党中央国务院严肃处理三鹿奶粉事件
相关责任人员" [Central party committee and state council dealing with persons
involved in the Sanlu milk scandal seriously], 22 September, available: www.gov.
cn/jrzg/2008-09/22/content_1102256.htm.
Fu, J. 2014, "Governance of listed state-owned enterprises in China: The rise of a
new state-led model?" unpublished thesis, Australian National University.
Grabosky, P. and Sutton, A. (eds.) 1989, *Stains on a White Collar: Fourteen Studies
in Corporate Crime or Corporate Harm*, The Federation Press, Sydney.
Ho, V. H. 2013, "Beyond regulation: A comparative look at state-centric corporate
social responsibility and the law in China", *Vanderbilt Journal of Transnational
Law*, vol. 46, no. 2, pp. 375–442.
Jensen, H. and Zhou, J. 2015, "Food safety regulation and private standards in
China", in Hammoudi, A. et al. (eds.) *Food safety, market organisation, trade and
development*, Springer, Switzerland.
Katz, L. M. 2010, "Class action with Chinese characteristics: The role of procedural
due process in the Sanlu milk scandal", *Tsinghua China Law Review*, vol. 2,
no. 2, pp. 421–466.
Lu, F.卢福才 (ed.) 2011,《中央企业公司治理报告》(Report on corporate governance
of central state-owned enterprises] (中国经济出版社) (China Economic Publishing
House), Beijing.
Milhaupt, C. and Pistor, K. 2008, *Law and capitalism: What corporate crises reveal
about legal systems and economic development around the world*, University of
Chicago Press, Chicago.
Minghao, W. 王明皓 2008, "石家庄市政府新闻发言人：三鹿事件为何迟迟不报"
[Spokesperson for Shijiazhuang government: Why report of Sanlu incident was
delayed], *People's Net News Story*, 1 October, available: http://paper.people.com.
cn/rmrb/html/2008-10/01/content_112000.htm.

Qian, W. 2008, "Sanyuan may take over tainted milk brand Sanlu", *China Daily* (online), 27 September 2008, available: www.chinadaily.com.cn/china/2008-09/27/content_7064279.htm.

Shanshan, W. 2008, "Fonterra CEO reflecting on investing in China", *Caijing Magazine* (online), 5 December, available: www.caijing.com.cn/2008-12-05/110035012.html.

World Health Organisation 2008, "Melamine-contaminated powdered infant formula in China—update 2", 29 September, available: www.who.int/csr/don/2008_09_29a/en.

Xinhua Net 2008, "China seizes 22 companies with contaminated baby milk powder", 17 September, available: http://news.xinhuanet.com/english/2008-09/17/content_10046949.htm.

Xinhua Net 2008, "Survivor leads China's milk industry", 15 November, available: http://news.xinhuanet.com/english/2008-11/15/content_10361534_3.htm.

Xinhua Net 2008, "三鹿：完达山旁观三元或孤独破局" Wandashan onlooking Sanlu takeover: Sanyuan likely to struggle alone", 5 November, available: http://cs.xinhuanet.com/cqzk/05/200811/t20081120_1659972.htm.

Xinhua Net 2008, "三鹿将宣告破产传言利好三元收购" [Sanlu to be declared bankruptcy: Rumoured in favour of Sanyuan takeover], 23 December, available: http://news.xinhuanet.com/fortune/2008-12/23/content_10547631.htm.

Xinhua Net 2008, "三鹿破产拍卖还债估计三鹿总负债近20亿元" [Sanlu to be sold through bankruptcy auction: Total debts estimated nearly RMB2 billion], 25 December, available: http://news.xinhuanet.com/fortune/2008-12/25/content_10555709.htm.

Xinhua Net 2008, "中国相关部门正在讨论问题奶粉时间赔偿方案" [Relevant Chinese departments considering a compensation plan for problem powdered milk victims], 10 December, available: http://news.xinhuanet.com/newscenter/2008-12/10/content_10484532_1.htm.

Xinhua Net 2008, "石家庄市政府通报三鹿集团破产案情况 (全文)" [Shijiazhuang city government report on Sanlu bankruptcy case (full text)], 25 December, available: http://news.xinhuanet.com/fortune/2008-12/25/content_10557898.htm.

Xinhua Net 2009, "三鹿事件真相大暴光" [Truth of Sanlu incident revealed], 1 January, available: http://news.xinhuanet.com/politics/2009-01/01/content_10587575.htm.

Xinhua Net 2009, "原三鹿集团董事长田文华一审被判处无期徒刑" [Former Sanlu Chairwoman Tian Wenhua sentenced to life imprisonment], 22 January, available: http://news.xinhuanet.com/legal/2009-01/22/content_10701439.htm.

Xinhua Net 2009, "三元并购三鹿:关系敏感的局中局" [Sanyuan taking over Sanlu, a sensitive case], 2 January, available: http://news.xinhuanet.com/fortune/2009-01/02/content_10590487.htm.

Xinhua Net 2009, "三鹿党委书记：想买三鹿必须接受全部职工." [Sanlu Party committee secretary: Whoever wants to buy Sanlu must also take Sanlu's employees], 11 January, available: http://news.xinhuanet.com/local/2009-01/11/content_10638134.htm.

Xinhua Net 2009, "三鹿破产案：是消失还是涅磐" [Sanlu bankruptcy case, demise or rebirth?], 5 January, available: http://news.xinhuanet.com/fortune/2009-01/05/content_10604233.htm.

Xinhua Net 2009, "知情人士谈三元并购三鹿：三元身不由己" [Insiders comment on Sanyuan Sanlu Merger：not Sanyuan's will], 4 January, available: http://news.xinhuanet.com/fortune//2009-01/04/content_10598930.htm.

Xinhua Net 2009, "石家庄官方称抵押政府大院筹三鹿赔款子虚乌有" [Shijiazhuang official dismissed alleged government assistance of Sanlu to repay debt by mortgaging government office buildings], 8 January, available: http://news.xinhuanet.com/politics/2009-01/08/content_10625612.htm.

Xinhua Net 2009, "结石患儿民事赔偿案无一获受理 河北律协解释" [Why tort claims associated with the milk scandal refused to be heard by courts? Explained by Hebei Lawyers Association], 7 January, available: http://news.xinhuanet.com/legal/2009-01/07/content_10615043.htm.

Xinhua Net 2009, "超 90% 婴幼儿奶粉事件患儿家长已接受主动赔偿" [Over 90 per cent of tort victims of tainted milk incident have accepted compensation voluntarily], 24 January, available: www.he.xinhuanet.com/news/2009-01/24/content_15543516.htm.

Xinhua Net 2009, "Two executed in China over tainted milk scandal", 24 November, available: http://news.xinhuanet.com/english/2009-11/24/content_12530798.htm.

Xu, C. 徐超 2008, "三聚氰胺溯源" [Tracing the source of melamine], *Caijing Magazine* (online), 29 September, available: http://magazine.caijing.com.cn/20080928/77700.shtml.

# 8 Water Security, Governance and Sustainable Development Goals in China—Radical Laws, Institutions and Courts

*Jennifer McKay[1] and Jin Zheng[2]*

> The way in which society is run remains inadequate to afford effective protection to water ecology and environment.
>
> (PRC Ministry of Water Resources (MRC), Highlights
> of Water Resources Development Legislation, 2017)

> The pursuit of economic growth has been the priority overshadowing the vital issues of water resources and ecological balance.
>
> (*China Daily*, official Chinese Media outlet report, 2017)

## 1. The Concept of Water Security and the UN's Sustainable Development Goals

Water security is a concept that has been increasingly used by governments and intergovernmental bodies such as Global Water Partnership, the World Economic Forum and academics, but, as yet, its definition remains unclear. One commentator has said that the definition depends on the disciplinary base of the people tasked with writing government policy (Cook and Bakker, 2012). In some ways, that is implicit in all paradigm shifts; a healthy debate can, however, create shared understandings. The modern world of water governance requires multi-disciplinarity, sound and ethical public consultation regarding the choices in using resources to achieve sustainable development.

In the last ten years, the scope of the term water security has widened to reflect the 2015 Rio principles so as to include human and ecological impacts of planned works; the first meeting using the term as a leading concept was the Asia Pacific Water Forum held in 2007. This event was focussed on "Water Security: Leadership and Commitment". So the term could be seen to embrace governance and has been applied over multiple domains, such as human use and ecological preservation. This ensured that the term embraces all the interconnected issues in water management. This interconnectedness makes water problems difficult in that the multiple dimensions of this problem mean that the existing forms of regulation and laws in this area have found it difficult to deal with this interconnectedness. Overall, this has been a problem in all legal systems as, historically, these evolved with a simplistic understanding of the environment and with a predominant view of enabling human use without an appreciation of the environmental consequences of such use. An example of this would be to point to the sources of pollution in the USA Love Canal and Australia in the 1960s prior to state-based environmental protection laws. China is now implementing these types of laws to redress many current issues, as we will see in the following discussion.

The modern regulatory question in relation to water (in all nations), is to identify democratic ways of achieving sustainable water use which include a consideration for the environment and for future generations, for issues of equity and for public participation in the processes. These concerns are embodied in the Sustainable Development Goals (SDGs) released by the UN in 2015 after a bottom-up consultation process. These SDGs are a new, universal set of goals, using targets and indicators that UN member states will be expected to use to frame their agendas and political policies over the next 15 years. China has agreed to implement the SDGs (SDG Knowledge Hub, 2016). On 12 October 2016, China released its national plan for implementing the 2030 Agenda for Sustainable Development; this plan translates each target of the SDGs into "action plans" for China. The plan was posted on the website of the Ministry of Foreign Affairs (MFA), following the announcement of the plan by China's Premier Li Keqiang during the Seventy-First UN General Assembly high-level week, held in New York in September 2016. An MFA press release highlighted China's overarching approach of seeking an "innovative, coordinated, green, open and shared development."

China held the Group of 20 (G-20) presidency until 2017, and has previously called on the G-20 to formulate its own action plan on the 2030 Agenda. At a special briefing for UN member states in April 2016, Li Baodong, China's Vice Foreign Minister and G20 Sherpa, highlighted China's position paper on the 2030 Agenda and the establishment of a domestic inter-agency mechanism to coordinate implementation of the Agenda. Achieving this goal will require further changes to existing rules and laws in China.

---

**Box 8.1　The Sustainable Development Goals
Are 17 Steps to a Better World (UN 2015)**

1. End poverty in all its forms everywhere
2. End hunger, achieve food security and improved nutrition and promote sustainable agriculture

3. Ensure healthy lives and promote well-being for all at all ages
4. Ensure inclusive and equitable quality education and promote lifelong learning opportunities for all
5. Achieve gender equality and empower all women and girls
6. Ensure availability and sustainable management of water and sanitation for all
7. Ensure access to affordable, reliable, sustainable and modern energy for all
8. Promote sustained, inclusive and sustainable economic growth, full and productive employment and decent work for all
9. Build resilient infrastructure, promote inclusive and sustainable industrialisation and foster innovation
10. Reduce inequality within and among countries
11. Make cities and human settlements inclusive, safe, resilient and sustainable
12. Ensure sustainable consumption and production patterns
13. Take urgent action to combat climate change and its impacts
14. Conserve and sustainably use the oceans, seas and marine resources for sustainable development
15. Protect, restore and promote sustainable use of terrestrial ecosystems, sustainably manage forests, combat desertification and halt and reverse land degradation and halt biodiversity loss
16. Promote peaceful and inclusive societies for sustainable development, provide access to justice for all and build effective, accountable and inclusive institutions at all levels
17. Strengthen the means of implementation and revitalise the global partnership for sustainable development.

China has also been making huge changes to its system of financing water resources development and, in the area of water pollution, has introduced three legal innovations; these are the Captain of the River concepts, green courts and new ways of regulating pollution. These will be discussed further in section 4. Also, section 3 will outline the water security issues for urban and agricultural China and explain the background to the decision to de-emphasise public-private partnerships (PPPs) in urban water supply, whilst section 2 will describe the legal system's approach to water issues.

On climate (SDG 13), China's nationally determined contributions will be integrated into national strategies, and climate mitigation actions will be leveraged in the shift to a new model of economic growth that advances environmental protection. China will urge developed countries to formulate a road map and timetable for mobilizing the international community's commitment of US$100 billion annually by 2020 to address the climate-related needs of developing countries and to fully operationalise the Green Climate Fund. Actions on SDG 6 (water supply and sanitation) include plans released by the Ministry of Water Resources (MWR) to monitor rivers and pollution. As is evident from the quote at the head of this chapter, the MWR acknowledges that business as usual will not protect China's ecology.

## 2. China Water Security Issues

Water is essential for life and for economic growth; but in China, the problems of pollution, overdrawing and mismanagement have created grave problems (Wang et al., 2002). Such problems have been exacerbated by the crippling weakness of the State Environmental Protection Administration (SEPA) (Turner, 2006), which was replaced in 2008 by the new Ministry of Environmental Protection (MEP). Poor distribution and pollution has been coupled with rapid economic growth and this has damaged many water resources in China (Wang et al., 2002). Another factor contributing to water degradation has been that Local Governments in China prefer to promote economic growth and seek to protect local jobs; this is aggravated by acute corruption in government (Gleick, 2009).

Measures to address these problems have been in place since the early 1990 and the twelfth five-year plan of 2011 served as a watershed moment in China's call for 'quality growth'. This plan was adopted on 14 March 2011 and promised to shift China's focus from unbridled economic expansion, which has delivered annual GDP growth rates of up to 10% on average for the last three decades, to a model which delivers green growth and social stability but which slows down the GDP growth rate to a target 7%. Water issues in China, as in every nation, have specific sectoral aspects and these will be discussed next (China Daily 2007).

### 2.1. Urban Water Supply

Sixteen Chinese cities are considered to be in the top 20 of most polluted cities in the world (Asia Pacific Water Forum 2007); the industrial and populous north is considered to be highly water insecure (Xia et al., 2007). A major north south diversion supplies water to 53 million people in China and has benefited more people in the cities of Beijing, Tianjin, and Hebei and Henan provinces (Xinhuanet, 2017). However, China still has huge urbanisation targets and seeks to achieve an urban population of 70% by 2030. This will lead to 100 million new urban residents (Taylor, 2015).

### 2.2. Agricultural Water Use

It has been reported that since the 1970s, eutrophication of major Chinese lakes by nitrogen and phosphorous has increased; this has come from non-point source pollution from agricultural land use such as cropping and animal husbandry. Since the 1980s, China has multiplied its land under agriculture by 4.4 times and has allowed very high uses of fertilisers; the Ministry of Agriculture has stated that this is unsustainable Zhang Wei et al (2002) and Reuters (2016)).

Much of China's agricultural expansion has resulted from the use of local and internationally created Living Modified Organisms (LMOs). China has however acceded to the *Cartegena Protocol on Bio-safety*, which is based on Article 19 of the *Convention on Biological Diversity*; this was signed in May 1992 and entered into force in December 1993. This will require China to formulate a protocol regulating the transportation, handling and use of (LMOs) that might have adverse effects on biodiversity and its components. There are more than 30 approved applications relating to genetically modified (GM) cotton, with a planting area that reached 1,500,000 hectares in 2001, 70% of which belong to the United States company Monsanto (Wang Xi et al, 2004).

China has formulated the *China Framework on Biosafety*. This document provides important guidance on national policy and regulation formulation, and strengthens biosafety capacity building. Moreover, China has also developed public education and training on biosafety issues through holding international conferences and workshops and provides a remedy for incorrect labelling (to be discussed next). Biosafety legislation in China reflects the following principles: the precautionary principle, the scientific management principle, and the principle of strengthening international cooperation. The precautionary principle is also a very important principle of international law.

Principle 15 of the Rio Declaration states that in order to protect the environment, the precautionary approach shall be widely applied by states according to their capabilities. The principle states that where there are threats of serious or irreversible damage, lack of scientific certainty must not be used as a reason for postponing cost-effective measures seeking to prevent environmental degradation. However, the real issue is the standard to be used. The following *Nestlé* case illustrates this point.

Nestlé was involved in *Yanling Zhu v Nestlé (China) Co Ltd*; this was the first GM labelling case in China. In 2003, Ms Yanling Zhu sued Nestlé for not labelling GM ingredients in its cocoa powder product "Qiaobanban", Zhu claimed compensation of the product price and sought an order for Nestle to label GM ingredients on its packaging. The court appointed the Shanghai Academy of Agricultural Science to test the cocoa product for GM ingredients. The result was negative when using the Protocol of the Quantitative PCR Analysis included in the recommended industrial standards issued by the Ministry of Agriculture. However, the sample tested positive on GM glyphosate-resistance soybean with the Nested PCR analysis provided by international standards. The GeneScan Analytics GmbH also confirmed the existence of a GM ingredient. The court ruled in favour of Nestlé and, as a result, no GM labelling was required. The case shows that Chinese courts will rule on the basis of domestic standards (HIL, 2015).

In northern China, another consequence of excessive withdrawals of surface and groundwater is the problem of desertification (Feng, 2007). The twelfth five-year plan (FYP), aims to reduce water intensity consumed, per unit value added of industrial output, to 30% from 37%; however, it also anticipates record levels of water usage, rising to 620 billion cubic meters by 2015—up from 599 billion cubic meters in 2010. The plan also aims to reduce emissions of sulphur dioxide, chemical oxygen demand, ammonium nitrate, nitrogen oxide reduction and five heavy metals reduction (lead, mercury, chromium, cadmium and arsenic). These measures will have a positive impact on water resources in rivers and aquifers. These energy intensity and carbon emission reduction targets have significant implications for water use as well. Circle of Blue (2016) has calculated that if carbon emissions are cut by 17% and energy consumption by 16% unit of GDP, then water use would decline by nearly a fifth for each new dollar of economic growth.

With 'scientific development' at its core, the twelfth FYP calls for a total transformation of China's economic structure which incorporates new limits on energy consumption and introduces targets for reducing pollution. This is a complicated matter as multiple provincial, sectoral and special plans require careful and coordinated implementation. Yet, little detail was provided regarding implementation, as is usual in these FYPs (World Bank, 2006).

Recent plans released by the Ministry of Agriculture 2016 state, "The State Council advised local governments to reduce the areas of crops with high water consumption and promote the planting of drought-tolerant crops if the underground and surface water in the region has been overexploited." It also highlighted the use of pipe irrigation and drip irrigation to conserve water (Ministry of Agriculture, 2016). Other policy and legal reforms were also on the table. China plans to make the water use in agriculture more efficient by use of measures such as tiered pricing, wider use of drought-tolerant crops, and provision of rewards for water conservation (Ministry of Agriculture, 2016). The Ministry of Agriculture's guideline specifically mentions that groundwater will be closely monitored as well. Finally, it does mention that the PPP model will be used. "The government will also encourage private investment to contribute to the building and maintenance of irrigation and water conservation facilities through business models such as public-private-partnerships". It is be important to see how this will be used (see 3.1 in the next section) where issues with urban PPP have seen a retreat from the model.

To achieve the target of a 'Beautiful China', the Chinese government in 2016 issued a series of regulations and standards, such as, the 'Environmental Protection Tax' (released on 25 December 2016, to commence on 1 January 2018) and the 'Measures for Soil Environment Management for Polluted Land (Consultation Paper)' (released on 31 December 2016) (China Water Risk (2017a)). Whilst there is much action taking place, there is as yet little information on enforcement. In the 13FYP on the Water Conservation Reform and Development, subsidies for agricultural water conservation were to be provided (China Water Risk, 2017b).

### 3. Water Law of the People's Republic of China and Its Experimentation With Public-Private Partnerships in the Urban Sector

The Constitution of the People's Republic of China clearly provides that water resources shall be owned by the state. In addition, it requires that the means of production must remain in public ownership. Article 6 states: *The basis of the socialist economic system of the People's Republic of China is socialist public ownership of the means of production, namely, ownership by the whole people and collective ownership by the working people.* With regard to water, Article 9 of the Constitution of the PRC states that mineral resources, waters, forests, mountains, grassland, unreclaimed land, beaches and other natural resources are owned by the state—that is, by the whole people.

The water law of the People's Republic of China is the first basic law on water to be promulgated in China (this occurred in 1988 and revised in 2002). The law states that water resources shall be owned by the state. The water law deals with general principles, planning, utilisation, protection of water resources and water projects, water resources allocation and conservation, water dispute settlement and law enforcement, supervision and inspection, legal liability and supplementary regulations. The State Council is required to exercise ownership of water resources on behalf of the state. The only exception to this relates to water held in the ponds of rural collective economic organisations and in the reservoirs constructed and managed by rural collective economic organisations shall be used by those organisations.

The state applies a system of water licencing (Article 7) and requires payment for use except in collective economic organisations. The department of water administration under the State Council is responsible for organising the implementation of the water license system as well as the nationwide system for payment.

Water policy and regulation is primarily created and implemented by the MWR, under which there are several agencies including Water Resource Bureaus (WRBs) that operate at provincial, prefectural and county levels, as well as River Basin Commissions in each of China's main river basins. The WRBs serve to implement water policy and regulations at a local level and the River Basin Commissions were established to provide some oversight and authority over the local Water Bureaus. How much power they actually have at the local level would, however, appears to be debatable.

In addition to MWR, there are several ministries that have some influence (to a lesser or greater extent) over different aspects of the management of China's water resources. Foremost amongst these, is the MEP which was created in 2008 to replace the SEPA; the MEP has substantive responsibilities regarding urban and industrial water pollution, through its role in formulating environmental protection policies and regulations as well as in the implementation and enforcement of environmental laws. In addition to these two ministries, at least seven other ministries and agencies have a role in water resource management. As a result, there exist notable overlapping functions in planning, standard setting and monitoring that lead to conflicts of interest and inefficiencies in policy implementation, as well as in legal enforcement. To further complicate matters, the WRBs at the local level also create and execute water policy and regulations based on jurisdictional needs (World Bank, 2006).

The MWR published *Highlights of Achievements in Developing Water Policies and Regulations* in 2017. The highlights included legislative and policy making initiatives codifying the central government's guiding policy on water management and the philosophy of sustainable development, thus laying a solid institutional foundation for reform and development of the water sector (MRW 2017 viewed 21 June 2017). Another highlight was that the MRW promulgated the *Implementation Opinions on All-round*

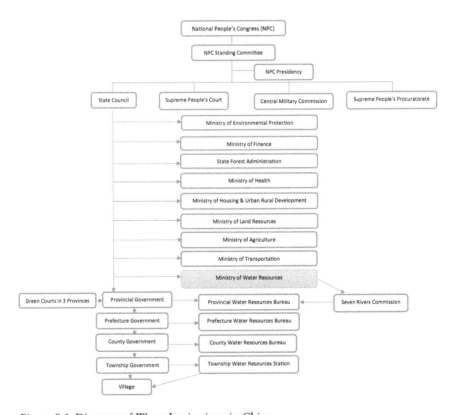

*Figure 8.1* Diagram of Water Institutions in China

Source: Adapted from (i) Economic Research Services/USDA, "China's Agricultural Water Policy Reforms/AIB-782" and (ii) WEPA web site. NB: The new green court (see later) is to be located at the provincial level, but only in some provinces.

---

**Box 8.2 Implementation Plan for Comprehensive Water Law System 2017 by Ministry Water Resources**

First, it is imperative to improve the approach to legislation. The quality of preparatory work prior to legislation will be enhanced. Vigorous efforts will be made to identify future legislative items.

Accountability will be enforced against the failure to meeting the target in enacting water legislation. A scientifically sound approach will be taken to develop a water legislative program and annual work plan. These documents will become more instrumental in giving practical guidance and assume more binding force. The drafters of water-related regulations should undertake legislative fact-finding trips by immersing themselves in communities and seeing first-hand how things are going on the ground. It is desirable to enhance appraisal and examination of the necessity, legality and merit of proposed laws with a view to rendering them more targeted, coherent, effective and. . . .

Legislative procedures should be improved with broader public participation. A system featuring post-legislation assessment will be put in place so as to keep track of the implementation of water-related regulations. A holistic approach should be taken in the enactment, amendment and abolition of water-themed legislation

Source: MRW www.mwr.gov.cn/english/mainsubjects/201604/P020160406508815936 744.pdf viewed 21 June 2017

---

*Enhancement of Rule-of-Law Water Governance and Management*; these explicitly provided for the need to construct a sound regulatory framework for water resources, which would include a comprehensive water law system, an effective enforcement system based on rule of law, a stringent supervision system for rule-of-law water management, and a strong assurance system for rule of law in the water sector. This framework mentions plans to implement.

### 3.1. Financing of Urban Water Infrastructure With Moves to and From Public-Private Partnerships

This section will discuss the changes to the financing approaches to water governance from 1980 to present.

### 3.1.1. Before 1980s: Loan Systems

The water supply and drainage system in China were seen as a matter of public welfare, and water plants and sewage treatment plan were state-owned enterprises (SOEs) and entities controlled by the government. The emergence of foreign participation in funds and capital in China started after 1980. China built water projects in major cities through direct or indirect guarantees of loans from inter-governments and international financial organisations. The World Bank, the Asian Development Bank and other international financial organisations, as well as from Japan, France and other foreign governments which provided long-term preferential loans for China's urban water supply industry. In 1986, under the joint efforts of the Governments of China and Japan, the Changchun City Second Water Purification plant renovation project was provided with 3.913 billion Yen from the Japanese government and 135 million RMB Yuan from the Chinese government and was officially named the Chinese-Japanese People Friendly Water Plant (China Water Network, (2003). Following the Changchun water plant construction project, inter-governments fund had become an important channel for Chinese water supply enterprises to raise funds in the mid-1980s.

### 3.1.2. 1990–2002: BOT Fixed Return

China has rapidly urbanised from 1990, but the state did not have sufficient capital to build large-scale infrastructure. The State Planning Commission began to advance the reform of the investment and financing system, with the policy of encouraging foreign investment in the construction of public utilities, foreign water companies began to invest directly in China. World water giant French Suez group invested in the Guangdong, Zhongshan, Tanzhou Water Plant in 1992. This was seen as the first water plant in China to be built and operated wholly through foreign investment (China Water Network, 2016)) In 1994, the state announced policies encouraging private and foreign investment in the urban water industry, and began to introduce the BOT (Build-Operate-Transfer) model. In 1994, the Chengdu Sixth Water Plant was selected as a pilot water project, and French Veolia undertook this BOT project. Starting from Veolia's Chengdu project, large-scale foreign investors (such as Sino-French Water, Berlin Water Affairs, Taysons and other multinational water companies), successively entered China's water industry. Accompanied by the implementation of the reform of China's tax system, local governments have launched a number of pilot BOT projects, such as the Beijing Tenth Water Plant, the Beijing Xiaojiahe sewage projects and others. Foreign investments became the main force regarding private participation in China's water industry in 1990s, but they were still confined to sewage treatment at that time, but under Chinese law and policy, no foreign capital could be provided to build pipe networks.

Under Article 55 of the Water Law of the People's Republic of China, (Constitution of PRC 2004) a user of water is required to pay to the water supply unit an amount set in accordance with state regulations; the price of water supply is required to be determined in accordance with the following principles: compensation of cost, reasonable profit, high price of water depending on excellent quality of supplied water, reasonable price and equitable commitment. The 1994 City Water Supply Ordinance has allowed water prices to be adjusted reasonably. China reserves the government's right to set pricing in five public utilities areas, including water pricing, as provided in annex 4 of China's Accession to the WTO Protocol. Article 26 of Urban Water Supply Ordinance (1994) provides that the price of urban water supply should be formulated in accordance with the principle of reasonable cost and small profit for the use of water.

Article 11 of Measures of Urban Water Supply Price Management (Revised 2004) provides that the average level of reasonable profit of water supply enterprises should be the 8%–10% of net asset profit: (a) Under these measures, the net assets profit margin of a water supply enterprise mainly relying on government investment should be less than 6%. (b) In regard to water supply enterprises that have been funded mainly by loans, the introduction of foreign capital, the issue of bonds or stocks and other ways of financing the construction of water supply facilities, the profit margin of these net assets should not exceed 12%. After a water company proposes an increase in water price, the local government is required to convene a public hearing, and then make its decision.

As can be seen from the aforementioned, the price of city water cannot be as easily raised as investors might wish. In addition, water prices will be counted in China's Consumer Price index (CPI) statistics, and the CPI of local government will be related to their performance, as appraised by central government; consequently, local governments dare not increase water price too much. On the other hand, the number of foreign investments in local government areas has also been an important index for their performance appraised by the central government. In order to attract more foreign investments, local governments had promised to pay fixed return to investors (*People's Daily* 2002b).

The fixed rate of return for foreign investment in water construction promised by local governments was usually around 15%–18%. But such projected fixed returns in a joint-venture contract had no legal basis, and were contrary to Chinese law and regulation. However, as some commentator have noted, "The reality is that there is a decoupling of between central government and local governments, and each has a set of practices of its own in China" (China Water Network (2004).

In 1998, the central government (through the State Council) promulgated the Notice on the Proper Handling of the Existing Fixed Return Items of Foreign Investment, and clearly pointed out that the guarantee of foreign investment with fixed returns was not in line with the cooperation principle of profit-sharing and risk-sharing between Chinese and foreign investors, prohibiting "constant earnings promise and the profit promise by damaging Chinese national interests". However, some local governments continued to offer the promise of investors fixed returns to attract foreign investments, notwithstanding that at the beginning these fixed rate were too high (for instance, 18.2%-21% in the case of Shenyang Eighth Water Plant for Sino-French Water) to be considered to be fair, and as time passed, such fixed returns would increasingly burden city finances, notwithstanding their lack of a proper legal basis (*People's Daily* 2002a).

One might wonder what would happen if a local government could not afford to carry out such a fixed rate of return as promised to investors in their joint-venture contracts. Local governments tended to focus on the effects of attracting foreign direct investment (FDI) upon the evaluation on their own performance, and underestimated the subsequent burden that would be placed upon public finances after the project had been implemented. At the same time, due to the lack of supervisory mechanisms, no one was held responsibility for the enormous loss that would be incurred by the country and the people, as in all such cases, no relevant official was ever called to account for its act. Elsewhere, the inconsistency in policy enforcement in this area could become the biggest risk and problem for a foreign investor, but this was not the case in China. On the contrary, it was the local government that in the end had to learn quite expensive lessons, as shown by the following case of Shanghai Dachang Water Management Project discussed next.

In 1996, Thames Water, the former British Bovis Company and Shanghai North Tap Water Company jointly operated the Shanghai Dachang Water Management Project. The entire 20-year project comprised three phases, namely building, operation, and transfer. Thames Water acquired the former British Bovis Company's share, making the projects wholly owned by Thames Water in 2001. In the franchise agreement with the Thames Water Company, Shanghai government promised to pay Thames Water 15% fixed returns. In September 2002, State Council issued its No. 43rd Notice—the "Notice on the Issue of Proper Handling of the Existing Promise of Foreign Investment in Fixed-Return Project," which clearly stated that the promise to foreign investment of fixed returns was in violation of Chinese law and regulations. On 20 June 2004, the UK Thames Water Company announced that it would withdraw from the Shanghai sewage treatment plants because the Shanghai government withdrew its policy of guaranteeing 15% of the fixed investment returns. Thames Water and Shanghai North Tap Water Company signed the equity transfer contract, and thus Shanghai Dachang Water Plant was repurchased by Shanghai Water Assets Management Company (Zhao Yang 2016).

Statistical data for 2000 from the National Bureau of Statistics has shown that the highest profitable industry for foreign investment in China was not oil, chemical, mobile phone, home appliances, automobiles or any other prominent enterprises in China in 1999, but the tap water industry, with its annual profit margin reaching to 24.48% (China Water Network, (2004)).

Another example of a poorly structured investment project, from the Chinese viewpoint, is the Shenyang Eighth Water Plant; this was terminated in 1999; after only two years of operation, Sino-French Water (French

Suez group) received back twice what it had invested (China Construction News(2002)).

### 3.1.3. *After 2002: Acquisition of Equity-High Premium*

With China's efforts to obtain access to the WTO, the original prohibition on foreign investment in the city pipe network for the first time was relaxed and China began to be open to foreign capital under Article 9 (1) of the revised MFA "Foreign Investment Industry Guidance." Thus, foreign companies such as French Suez, Veolia, UK Thames entered into the field of city water supply networks in China through mergers and acquisitions. After China's successful accession to the WTO, the level of Chinese domestic water market opening has accelerated significantly. The Chinese Ministry of Construction promulgated *Views on Accelerating the Marketization Process of Municipal Public Sector* by the end of 2002, together with the 2004 Municipal Services Public Utilities Franchise Management Method; this provided the legal basis for private entity entering into public utilities. Foreign capital streamed into China's water market, and there was a surge of acquisitions by international companies with the payment of high premiums (Ministry of Finance 2015).

The marketisation of water supply in China entered into the phase of equity transfer with the payment of high premiums (Ministry of Foreign Affairs 2017). Veolia, Sino-French Water and other foreign water giants, began to purchase equity from domestic state water plants. Many water projects deviated from their previous BOT mode of participation in franchising in China. As Professor Fu Tao observed, the reform and marketisation of China's urban water supply industry was supposed to advance the franchise policy rather than the selling of equity—essentially the reform of a property right; this led to the problem of the disposition of the city water industry assets (Fu et al., 2007)

French Veolia bought a 50% stake in Shanghai Pudong Water Plant with a premium of 2.6 times value. Veolia Water adopted aggressive bidding tactics in China: first, it set a high premium to obtain franchising, and then through the second negotiations with the government, it sought to increase the price of services so as to make up the cost of bidding and create a more profitable outcome. Consumers were the ones who were ultimately injured by this strategy. Furthermore, Veolia demanded additional projects through connected transactions aimed at benefiting its affiliated enterprises. When Shanghai Pudong Veolia Tap Water Company purchased key equipment for 17 million euros to expand its water plant, the foreign investor, French Veolia, ignored Chinese law and the Shanghai government's requirements, and designated its affiliated Veolia enterprises to provide all the equipment at higher prices, for example, the price of the water meters bought from an affiliated French Veolia company in France was ten times than that of water meter made in China. This kind of behaviour of extracting getting higher returns is contrary to the requirement of the tender and the price competition mechanism under law. It was also a deliberate evasion or even violation of the Law of the People's Republic of China on Tenders and Bids (Li Hui, 2014). Large-scale acquisitions with high premiums began to appear nationwide, from the East (Shanghai, Tianjin) to the West (Lanzhou, Zunyi, Baoji); this wave of takeovers peaked in 2007.

The aforementioned events and the prices charged for water were in conflict with the legal nature of water as public interest property. According to the China Water Network Report 2015, from 2002 to 2009, the average annual growth rate of drinking water prices of China's 36 key cities was 4.69%, and annual growth rate of sewage treatment fees was 11.9% (Cai Xin, 2015). In the green city of Tianjin, Veolia started a project in 1997 and the price of water increased five times in the ten years to 2007 (Chinese Business Journal, 2007).

But not every city is as developed as Shanghai or Tianjin in East China, especially those in less developed cities, such as Zunyi, or Baoji, in the west of China. Zunyi City sold its two water plants in 2004 at a premium of 24.59%, but three years later, it had to buy them back at twice this price. This was because the plants could not produce the volume of water that was required. Since the introduction of foreign investment of 130 million yuan in 2003, the annual losses experienced by the Baoji Tap Water Company were 30 million yuan, and its net assets were close to zero in 2008, Baoji municipal government was also forced to buy these back from investors in 2010.

Water quality was also an issue in China under the foreign companies. The Veolia Water alone produced 13 water pollution incidents in China up to 2014 (Beijing Youth Daily, 2014). The Lanzhou Veolia Incident of water pollution on 11 April 2014 particularly brought public attention to this issue. In this incident, benzene escaped into the aquifer due to the seepage prevention material cracking. The local community asked, "Why not invest in the transformation of pipe network?" Veolia Water Company responded: "Water price has not risen for 4 years, the company therefore had a financial deficit and was unable to invest in the transformation pipe network" (Zhou Wei; Boulanger Mathieu; Adel Ben Youssef; Grazia Cecere, 2016). In December 2016, the High Court of Gansu Province dismissed a petition brought by three citizens of Lanzhou for a retrial application. Veolia Water withstood the lawsuit against it finally, but it has seems to have lost the trust of the local people, and may not regain this very soon (China Environmental News, 2017).

In 2008, due to the rise of various water costs, the return rate of domestic water enterprises had been close to negative, but the profit of Veolia in China was still 12% to 18% (Li Hui, 2014). In the face of the global financial crisis in 2008, the Chinese government launched its four trillion plan to stimulate the economy. Consequently, SOEs also became increasingly active in water projects. French Veolia's takeover project in City Xi'an failed in 2008. The

Xi'an City Tap Water Company cancelled the former plan of "Lanzhou model" foreign investment and instead relied on Xi'an City Water Company itself, and restructured the state-owned water company's affairs. Since then, the takeovers by foreign water companies in China has slowed down. In terms of the participation of private enterprise, local Chinese companies began to emerge and have risen in Chinese water market since this time.

In November 2013, the Third Plenum of the Eighteenth Communist Party of China emphasised the decisive role that market forces play and that PPPs should have a place in the Chinese economy. The year 2014, therefore, became an important year in the development of private participation in public utilities in China. To advance the PPP initiative, in February 2015, the Ministry of Finance Ministry Housing and Urban Construction jointly issued a Notice on the Promotion of Government and Private Capital Cooperation Projects in Municipal Public Utility Areas, particularly emphasising the PPP projects of the urban water plant and pipe network and their integration. This notice provided that franchise agreements should not commit to fixed investment returns and other matters prohibited by laws or by administrative regulations (Measures of Management on Franchising, 2015).

On December 31, 2016, the Ministry of Residence and the NDRC issued the "thirteenth FYP" on national urban sewage treatment and recycling facilities construction plan. It encourages private participation in the construction and operation of sewage treatment facilities, and the state will continue to provide appropriate support to the facilities construction according to the planning tasks and construction priorities, and gradually tilted to the less developed and poorer areas. It also encourages cross-regional and cross-sectoral cooperation, with the purpose of establishing a unified national market, and further promote the PPP mode in the field of urban sewage treatment with the integrated operation of water plant and pipe network.

On October 11, 2016, the government issued a Notice on the In-depth Promotion of Government and Private Capital Cooperation in the field of public services, noting that the state support for the new pilot projects financially in the public services sector such as garbage disposal, sewage treatment, should explore PPP model 'mandatorily', and that the central government will gradually reduce and finally abolish the special construction fund subsidy for this sector.

On 2016 October 20, the government issued a booklet called "Further Encouragement and Guidance of Private Capital into Urban Water Supply", which provided encouragement, guidance and convenience for the entry of private capital into the city water supply, gas, heating, sewage and garbage treatment industry. It aims to mobilise the enthusiasm of private capital's participation and strive to create a fair and open competitive environment for the entry of private capital, and promote the healthy development of municipal public utilities.

On 2017 February 6, State Council Office issued the Guiding Opinion on the System of Innovating Mechanism of Investment and Financing of Rural

Infrastructure, clarifying that in regard to the investment in basic facilities with certain profits, such as the rural water supply and sewage disposal, should mainly occur by way of the PPP mode (Ministry of Finance 2015).

An example of this approach is to be found in regard to the Shantou City Sewage Plant which is the first sewage treatment facility PPP project of Guangdong province. In June 2015, after a number of rounds of the government procurement process, Beijing Origin Water Technology Co Ltd (BOW) won the first project package (three sewage plants in the Chaonan), with the price of the total annual fee of 54,8961 million yuan. During the franchise period of 30 years, private capital would be responsible for completing the design, investment, construction, operation and maintenance of the project facilities (including the plant and pipe network), providing sewage treatment and network operation services, and charging the government for sewage treatment and network operation maintenance. The government is responsible for supervising and managing the services provided by private capital, and paying the sewage treatment fee and the network operation maintenance fee according to the project agreement (Shantou City Sewage Plant 2015).

China is now actively seeking PPPs and is regulating them and allowing government subsidies. In the '13FYP on the Construction of Water Saving Society', water saving facilities are able to apply for subsidies. In the '13FYP on the Construction of Urban Wastewater Treatment and Recycling Facilities' (released on 31 December 2016), water treatment and recycling facilities which are not open to capital markets can apply for policy and financial support for construction and operation (China Water Risk, 2017b).

## 4. Three Innovative Instruments for Urban Water Quality/ Pollution Issues

In addition to financing and the general legal framework, China is experimenting with instruments to overcome pollution problems in urban areas. These new measures will now be described and evaluated.

### 4.1. Captain of the River

The Captain of the River concept was created by Wuxi City in Jiangsu province, a city with acute water quality problems, where an algal bloom in 2007 meant that two million residents could not access clean tap water for five days (Dai, 2015). The Wuxi communist party committee and the Wuxi city government then created the Captain of the River concept. This imposed a contractual obligation on party heads in that city and upon government officials (at all administrative levels) to be captains of 64 rivers. The results from water quality monitoring are now used to assess the achievements of the river captains. The government employing the Captain of the River is required to deposit 8% of the annual disposal income in

2013 into an account at the beginning of each year and the fund is used to reward or punish the captain. The results of this innovation have been stated as being 'amazing' with over three-quarters of captains achieving the required water standard in Wuxi Province with huge reductions in pollution. The veto system was the main driver under this system, called *yipiao foujue*, failure to attain an assigned target will result in failure of the official to gain promotion. Eight other provinces have been using this system and the MWR reports that it is particularly valuable where large rivers and lakes span multiple regions. This system has improved administrative efficiency, and as Dia says, has overcome fragmentation which is the primary weak point in China's institutional arrangements and legal frameworks in this area.

Details on how this scheme actually works are hard to find but it would seem that there are some human rights and rule-of-law issues in SDGs and many other official statement by the PRC in relation to water. Another issue, as illustrated in the *Nestlé* case, concerns the determination of which standards are being used to assess the reduction in pollution. China Water Risk 2017 reported, "Conferences and information sharing scheme will be established to report the management and protection of rivers and lakes."

## 4.2. Green Courts

This parallels the Australian experience in the 1970s when laws creating criminal and civil offences for 'point source pollution' were enacted. Each state eventually established specialist courts at the District Court level (comparable to intermediate courts in China) and three Chinese Provinces have done likewise; the Guiyang green court was established in 2007, the Wuxi Jiangsu green court in 2008 and those in Kumming and Yuxi in Yunnan province were established in 2008. These courts are called environmental courts and have jurisdiction over civil, administrative and criminal cases relating to all environmental issues; they have power to enforce their decisions. The Guizhuo Provincial High Court and the Yunnan Provincial High Court have suggested that they would like to expand the jurisdiction for these courts in cases that involve water pollution and give these laws an extraterritorial effect. This has huge potential to have a massive positive impact on the environment. It is also possible for many parties to bring actions in the public interest, for example, this includes relevant government departments, environmental NGOs and the Procuratorate. The Procuratorate is the highest agency at the national level responsible for both prosecution and investigation in the PRC. The standing rules are much wider than those in Australia which is still struggling with notions around standing and public interest. These new courts will enable individuals to stop pollution (rather like our *qui timet* injunction system) rather than only seeking compensation after the event. The main issue for them to resolve will be finding evidence of the pollution.

There are reports of several cases where injunctions have been granted to stop pollution in China. For example, the Qingzhen Environmental Court in December 2007 ruled that the Trustee of two lakes had a right to obtain an injunction to stop the Tienfeng Chemical company from dumping phosphorous waste into Hongfeng Lake that would have exceeded the permitted standard. The court supervised the termination of discharge and stopped the production line of phosphorous gypsum (China Water Risk, 2009).

Of late, more powers have been provided to the highest courts, the Supreme People's Courts and the Supreme People's Procuratorate) Two leading institutions have also issued wider interpretations the law on issues concerning environmental pollution crimes (released on 27 December 2016). They categorise 18 scenarios as "severely polluting the environment" and 14 scenarios as "resulting in severe consequences", as well as identifying corresponding criminal penalties. The 'Measures for the Connection of Environmental Protection Administrative Enforcement and the Criminal Enforcement' (released on 25 January 2017) provides guidance on the transfer of criminal cases from environmental protection administrations to public security organs, as well as collaboration schemes among environmental protection administrations, public security organs and people's Procuratorate, such as those concerning information sharing (China Water Risk, 2017a).

China Water Risk interviewed Hyeon-Ju Rho on Feb 8 2010 (China Water Risk, 2010) and at this early stage a key problem that was identified was a lack of certified forensic assessment agencies dealing with pollution issues; as a result, the courts were experimenting with different types of expert testimony in cases of pollution.

### 4.3. *Other Enforcement Mechanism for Water Protection Laws*

The MEP has become a stronger regulatory body over the decade since 2007, but the enforcement of environmental standards remains limited by inconsistent, overlapping and fragmented regulatory requirements and complex jurisdictional authority (Economic Research Services, 2017). For example, although regulatory enforcement is effective in areas that have received significant foreign investment, such as in Shanghai, Beijing and Tianjin municipalities and in Guangdong, Zhejiang, and Jiangsu Provinces, outside of these developed areas, regulatory enforcement is often inconsistent (ERM, 2017). The burden of enforcing anti-pollution laws falls to local environmental protection bureaus that are hampered by insufficient resources, a lack of training and conflicts of interest. This parallels the experience of other countries such as Australia in the 1970s when laws creating criminal and civil offences for point source pollution were passed.

China has environmental and water quality standards which apply to surface water, groundwater and irrigation water quality and to fisheries. The law of the PRC on the prevention and control of water pollution was passed in 2008 and adapted from earlier laws of 1984 and 1996 (Winalski, 2009). Authorities are now obliged to make plans to maintain proper river flows of water, levels of lakes and proper groundwater levels, to protect urban water sources preventing and controlling urban water pollution, controlling the placement of industry, designating protection zones and controlling direct and indirect discharge of pollutants into water bodies.

Under the *13th Five-Year Plan Work Plan on Energy Saving & Pollution Reduction* (released on 5 January 2017) and the *13th Five Year Plan on the Construction of Water Saving Society* (released on 17 January 2017), the names of companies placed on blacklists for pollution, will be published on the national information platform (China Water Risk, 2017b).

Complete and accurate disclosure can also be a useful resource for business. In the *13th Five Year Plan on Development of National Strategic Emerging Industries* (released on 29 November 2016), environmental protection equipment/service trading and bidding platforms are encouraged; these can take advantage of the pollution data disclosures made in different sectors. In the *13th Five Year Plan on Water Conservation Reform and Development* (released on 27 December 2016), water conservation technology sharing platforms are also encouraged (China Water Risk, 2017a). These statements seem to demonstrate a general trend towards greater openness.

In the *Guiding Opinions on Establishing a Green Finance System* (released on 31 August 2016), a green finance system was first initiated (Ministry of Foreign Affairs 2017). Subsequently, different financial institutions have been involved in the provision of green finance, including the Bank of China, which issued a green bond of USD 3 billion in July 2016, thereby breaking the record of international green bond issuance. Under the *13th Five Year Plan Work Plan on Energy Saving & Pollution Reduction* banks are encouraged to provide different kinds of financial support to key pollution reduction projects, financial institutions are encouraged to perfect the green credit scheme, mandatory insurance is suggested in fields with high environmental risk and private capital is to be encouraged to establish a fund for energy saving investments (China Water Risk, 2017b).

## 4. Summary and Conclusions

Water in China is often referred to as a multi-headed dragon (Dai, 2015) since so many government departments are involved. However, this is a common problem in all legal systems once the nettle of sustainable development has been grasped.

China is taking massive strides to improve its water management laws and governance policies toward the goals of water security and to achieve the Sustainable Development Goals. Water management presents what political scientists describe as a 'wicked' problem in balancing competing objectives of the SDGs. One reason for this is that China has significant legacy issues with regard to water depletion and pollution. The governance mechanisms that have been selected to deal with this include financing with green priorities; also, PPPs are still on the agenda with regard to dealing with sewerage and agriculture problems. However, the future for PPPs will involve more of a domestic interplay, and where foreign companies are involved, the lessons from the past have seen a heavy handed regulation of industry profits. This may be attributed to the aim of maintaining constitutional values around the public ownership of water.

Other notable instruments include the green courts that have been established in some provinces. These courts have wide standing rules and generally provide a right to consumers to enforce relevant environmental laws. These courts presently operate differently and it will be important that such a court is established in every province so as to ensure that forum shopping does not lead to some provinces enacting weaker laws. The interplay between the green courts and the superior courts will play out over time and this will be a huge issue in achieving water security in China. The *Nestlé* case illustrated that the real issue here will be the standard to be applied, so that more uniform national standards will need to be developed. These will then add to the international catalogue of such standards. Finally, imposing a strict personal role of the Captain of the River will cut through the legal fragmentation that is to be found in this area, but it is unclear how this will work and whether the rule of law will always applied to achieve the outcomes reported.

## Notes

1. Correspondence author Professor Jennifer McKay, professor of business law, UniSA, School of Law and part-time commissioner in the Environment, Resources and Development Court South Australia.
2. Dr Jin Zheng, lecturer, School of Law, South China Normal University, Guangzhou; Dr Zheng wrote some of part 3 after reading Chinese texts and translating them into English.

## Bibliography

Asia Pacific Water Forum 2007, "Asia pacific challenges on water security", available: www.apwf.org/event/, viewed 24 June 2017.

Beijing Youth Daily 2014, "Veolia, infiltrating Chinese water pipes", 21 April 2014, available: http://epaper.ynet.com/html/2014-04/21/content_53349.htm?div=-1, viewed 4 July 2017.

Caixin 2015, http://www.marketwatch.com/story/inside-chinas-grand-plan-for-water-pollution-2015-05-04.

China Construction News 2002, "Shenyang Eighth water plant returns", 28 November 2002), available: www.chinajsb.cn/gb/content/2002-11/28/content_18521.htm, viewed 4 July 2017.

China Daily 2007, "Before We Run Dry", 28 February 2007, available: www.mwr.gov.cn/english1/, viewed 21 June 2017.

China Environmental News 2017, "Why did 'Foreign Water Company' Ebb in the PPP Boom?", 28 February 2017, available: www.cenews.com.cn/syyw/201702/t20170228_823092.html,Viewed 4 July 2017.

China Water Network 2004, "Taysons encounters 'Policy Gate' and 'Hit the Rocks' in Shanghai", 14 June 2016, available: www.h2o-china.com/news/28391.html, viewed 4 July 2017.

China Water Network 2004, "Is it really a 24% windfall? —discussion on the profit of water market", available: www.h2o-china.com/news/28849.html, viewed 4 July 2017.

China Water Network 2016, "27 years of Thames water's entrance into China's water service", 14 June 2016, available: www.h2o-china.com/news/241617.html, viewed 4 July 2017.

China Water Network Report 2003, "Changchun Chinese-Japanese people friendly water plant renovation project completed", 22 October 2003, available: www.h2o-china.com/news/22303.html, viewed 4 July 2017.

China Water Network Report 2015, available: http://opinion.caixin.com/2015-08-11/100838384.html, viewed 5 June 2017.

ChinaWaterRisk 2009, "Law of the people's republic of China on prevention and control of water", available: Pollutionchinawaterrisk.org/regulations/water-regulation, viewed 15 June 2017.

ChinaWaterRisk 2010, "Interview with Hyeon-Ju Rho", http://chinawaterrisk.org/interviews/china's-green-courts/, viewed on 24 June 2017.

ChinaWaterRisk 2017a, "Five regulatory trends from enforcement to finance", available: http://chinawaterrisk.org/resources/analysis-reviews/5-regulatory-trends-from-enforcement-to-finance/, viewed 24 June 2017.

ChinaWaterRisk 2017b, "Are corporates and government acting on water risk?", available: http://chinawaterrisk.org/regulations/water-regulation/, viewed 20 June 2017.

*Chinese Business Journal* 2007, "Foreign capital muddied China's water supply", 4 November, available: www.h2o-china.com/news/63761.html, viewed 4 July 2017.

Circle of Blue 2016, "Water security hot spots", available: www.circleofblue.org/2016/water-climate/infographic-water-and-security-hot-spots-2016/, viewed 10 June 2017.

Constitution of PRC 2004, available: http://en.people.cn/constitution/constitution.html, viewed 21 June 2017.

Cook, C. and Bakker, K. 2012, "Water security: Debating an emerging paradigm", *Global Environmental Change*, vol. 22, pp. 94–102.

Dai, L. 2015, "A new perspective on water governance in China Captain of the River", *Water International*, vol. 40, no. 1, pp. 34–56.

ERM 2017, "China's history of Environmental Protection", available: www.erm.com/en/insights/publications/archived-publications-2009–2010/chinas-history-of-environmental-protection/

Feng, Z. 2007, "More deserts, less water could sink rising China", 20 March 2007, available: www.mwr.gov.cn/english/20070320/82887.asp.

Fu, T., Chang, M. and Zhong, L. 2007, *Reform of China's urban water sector*, IWA Publishing, The Netherlands.

Gleick, P. 2009, "Three Gorges dam project, Yangtze River, China", available: http://worldwater.org/wp-content/uploads/2013/07/ch05.pdf, viewed 21 June 2017.

HIL 2015, "Global agriculture law 2015", HIL International Lawyers and Advisers, General Editor: Jan VM Holthuis, available: www.hil-law.com/wp-content/uploads/2015/05/Global_Agriculture_China.pdf, viewed 24 June 2017.

Huang, C. 2014, "Proposal for circuit courts a step forward for greater judicial independence in China", *South China Morning Post*, 25 November 2014, available: www.scmp.com/news/china/ article/1648537/proposal-circuit-courts-step-forward-greater-judicial-independence.

Li, H. 2014, "The review on foreign capital in water industry of ten-year", *Oriental Outlook Weekly*, no. 16, available: http://china.findlaw.cn/wstz/wstzdt/1098462.html, viewed 4 July 2017.

Measures of Management on Franchising of Infrastructure and Public Utilities 2015, available at: (www.ndrc.gov.cn/zcfb/zcfbl/201504/t20150427_689396.html).

Ministry of Agriculture 2016, "China works for more efficient water use in agriculture", available: http://english.agri.gov.cn/news/dqnf/201602/t20160202_164989.htm, viewed 24 June 2017.Ministry of Finance 2015, "Finance system for water",(In Chinese) available at: http://nys.mof.gov.cn/zhengfuxinxi/czpjZheng CeFaBu_2_2/201104/t20110408_534242.html.

Ministry of Finance 2015, "Finance system for water", (In Chinese) available: http://nys.mof.gov.cn/zhengfuxinxi/czpjZhengCeFaBu_2_2/201104/t20110408_534242.html.

Ministry of Foreign Affairs 2017, "Foreign Investment Industry Guidance", available at: www.fmprc.gov.cn/ce/cgsf/chn/kj/zyxx/t38777.htm, Viewed 2 April 2017.

Ministry of Water Resources China 2017, "China laws about Water", available at: www.mwr.gov.cn/english/laws.html *viewed 21 June 2017.*

*People's Daily* 2002a, "Inadequacy of Total Volume, Unreasonable Distribution and Serious Pollution: The Three Problems Perplex China-On how to Utilize Water Resources", *The People's Daily*, 22 April 2002.

*People's Daily* 2002b, "Perplex China- On how to Utilize Water Resources", *The People's Daily*, 22 April 2002.

PRC Ministry of Water Resources (MRC) 2017, *Highlights of Water Resources Development Legislation*, Beijing, booklet.

*Reuters* 2016, "China farm pollution worsens, despite moves to curb excessive fertilisers and, pesticides", available at: www.reuters.com/article/china-agriculture-pollution-idUSL4N0XA3CO20150414, *viewed 23 June 2017.*

Shantou City Sewage Plant 2015, *Project plan*, available: http://huanbao.bjx.com.cn/news/20160126/704708.shtml.

Sustainable Development Hub of International Institute for Sustainable Development, McGill University Canada 2016, *SDG's China releases national plan to implement*, available: http://sdg.iisd.org/news/china-releases-national-plan-to-implement-sdgs/.

Taylor, J. R. 2015, "The China dream is an urban dream: Assessing the CPC's national new-type urbanization plan", *Journal of Chinese Political Science*, vol. 20, no. 2, pp. 107–120.

Turner, J. L. 2006, "New Ripples and Responses to China's Water Woes", *China Brief*, Woodrow Wilson International Center for Scholars, Volume 6, (Issue 25), 112–114.

Wang, X. I., Tianbao, Q. and Lu, F. 2004, "Cartagena protocol on biosafety and China's practice", *Asia Pacific Journal of Environmental Law*, vol. 8, nos. 3–4, p. 14.

Wang, X. I., Zhang, X., Li, W., Gu, D. and Zhou, Y. 2002, "Managing water resources for a sustainable future: Law, policy and methodology of China", *Asia Pacific Journal of Environmental Law*, vol. 7, pp. 3–5.

Wei, Z., Mathieu, B., Youssef, A. B. and Cecere, G. 2016, "On foreign direct investment of foreign water enterprises in China", *Journal of Economics of Water Resources*, vol. 34, p. 4.

Winalski, D. 2009, *Cleaner water in China? Implications of the Amendments to China's law on prevention and control of water pollution*, University of Oregon Law School.

World Bank 2006, *China water quality: Policy and institutional considerations*.

Xia, J., Zhang, L., Liu, C. and Yu, J. 2007, *Towards better water security in North China, integrated assessment of water resources and global change—a North-South analysis* (1st ed.), Kluwer Academic Publishers, Netherlands.

Xinhuanet 2017, *China's water diversion benefits 53 mln residents*, available: http://news.xinhuanet.com/english/2017-05/26/c_136317375.htm, viewed April 12 2017.

Yang, Z. 2016, "The analysis on the issue of public private partnerships in China", *The Times Finance*, vol. 2, no. 2, Cumulatively No. 616.

Zhang, W., Zhang, W., Wu, S., Ji, H. and Kolbe, H. 2002, "Estimation of agricultural non-point source pollution in China and the alleviating strategies", Estimation of Agricultural Non-Point Source Pollution in China in Early 21 Century, available: http://en.cnki.com.cn/Article_en/CJFDTOTAL-ZNYK200407011.htm, viewed 24 June 2017.

# Index

agricultural water use 168–170
Alibaba Group 133, 136
Amazon.com, Inc. 138–139
Anglo American plc 68–70
annual reports 42–43
Asian Development Bank 174
Ausgrid 12
Australia 27–29, 30–32

Beijing Origin Water Technology Co Ltd (BOW) 180
Beijing Tenth Water Plant 174
Beijing Xiaojiahe sewage projects 174
BHP Billiton Limited 67–68
biosafety legislation 169
Build-Operate-Transfer (BOT) model 174–177
business-to-business (B2B) mode 125
business-to-consumer (B2C) mode 126, 135

Captain of the River concept 180–181
centrally controlled state-owned enterprises (CSOEs) 4, 9, 10
Cereals, Oils and Foodstuffs Corporation (COFCO) 135, 136
Changchun City Second Water Purification plant renovation project 174
ChemChina 4
China Chamber of Commerce of Metals, Minerals and Chemicals Importers and Exporters (CCCMC) 40–41
China Coal Energy Co., Ltd. 42
China Food and Drug Administration (CFDA) 131–133, 134
China International Contractors Association (CICA) 40
China International Telecommunication Construction Corporation (CITCC) 44

Chinalco 12
China Machinery Engineering Corporation (CMEC) 44
China Merchant Bank 11
China Minmetals Corporation (CMC) 45
China National Offshore Oil Corporation (CNOOC) 12, 42, 44
China National Petroleum Corporation (CNPC) 2, 44, 70–71
China Nonferrous Metal Mining (Group) Co., Ltd. (CNMC) 44–45
China Securities Regulatory Commission (CSRC) 3, 38
Chinese-Japanese People Friendly Water Plant 174
CITIC Construction Co., Ltd. 31, 42–44
Communist Party of China (CPC) 3, 4–6, 29
community-related social issues 61–63
community resettlement 61–63
Confucianism 36
Constitution of the People's Republic of China 171
consumer protection legislation 151
consumer to consumer (C2C) mode 126, 128
contract disputes 30–32
corporate governance 9–10, 28, 34, 143–157
corporate social responsibility (CSR): benefits of 35; case cameos 43–45; development of 36–37; dimensions of the CSR-related risk space 86–87; emergence of 33–34, 35–36; extractive sector 57–59; focal issues and foreign direct investment 84–86; government policies and guidelines 38–39, 45, 65–66; impact of state-led stakeholder model of corporate

governance on enforcement of food safety standards 143–157; implementation by government 38–40; implementation of norms 37–49; implementation problems 34; implementation through industry associations in natural resources sector 40–41, 45; industry association guidelines 40–41; key policies and regulations regarding sustainable overseas development 46–49; mining companies 70–74; responses to 34–37; risk management 83–97; SOEs in natural resources sector implementing codes abroad 41–49; as soft law 33–34, 36–37; theories 34–35

Country Responsibility Risk Index: change of government (governance system) component 96–97; for Chinese overseas investment 100–103; components of 94–97; country assessment indices 87–88; development of 87–97; dimensionality of index space 89–92; distance measures and effectiveness 88–89; environmental ecosystem component 96; general FDI environment component 94–96; index scores 97; screening and verification 92–94; unemployment (focal social issue) component 96

Democratic Republic of Congo 73
duty of care 108–109, 117–118

e-commerce 123–125, 136–137, 138–139
economic development 1, 2–4, 13–14, 118
economic/enterprise reform 2–3, 10
energy security 13
environmental issues 13–14, 61–63, 112
Environmental Performance Index (EPI) 88
'Environmental Protection Tax' 170
E-WTO 134
E-WTP 135
Extractive Industry Transparency Initiative (EITI) 65
extractive sector: case of Anglo American plc 68–70; case of BHP

Billiton Limited 67–68; community-related social issues 61–63; CSR 57–59; environmental and social management of global extractive companies 66–69; environmental issues 61–63; global principles and voluntary standards to help address social and environmental issues 63–65; governance of 59–61; government policy in CSR and responsible mining 65–66; guidelines for social responsibility 65–66; mining companies 70–74; role of government 59–60; role of major shareholders 60; role of NGOs and communities 60–61; *see also* mining industry

food governance 130–131, 134–135, 137–139
food safety: impact of state-led stakeholder model of corporate governance on enforcement of standards 143–157; milk scandal 145–154; online food trading 126–127, 140; resource governance and 13
Food Safety Law (2015 FSL Amendment) 130–133, 134
food security 13–14
foreign direct investment (FDI) 84–86, 176
Foreign Investment Review Board (FIRB) 12

General Administration of Quality Supervision, Inspection and Quarantine (AQSIQ) 38–39
genetically modified (GM) labeling case 169
Global Competitiveness Index (GCI) 88
Global Reporting Initiative (GRI) 42
'go global' strategy 3, 11, 28–30
'grasping the big, letting go of the small' (*zhua da fang xiao*) domestic strategy 2
green courts 181–182
green finance 183
Guangming Dairy 145–154

Hofstede Cultural Distance Index 88
Huawei Technologies Co., Ltd. 12

injured workers 113–116
'insider-based' model 9
institutional theory 106–108, 116–117
International Council on Mining and
    Metals (ICMM) 64
International Institute for Environment
    and Development (IIED) 64
Internet 123–125, 136
"Internet Plus" strategy 124, 139

JD.com 135

Kinsevere Mine 73

Lagos 73
land acquisition 61–63
Las Bambas mine 72–73
*lex mercatoria* 45
loan systems 173–174

Ma, Jack 133–135
Mengniu Dairy 145–154
migrant workers 113
milk scandal 145–154
mineral resource security 13
Minerals and Metals Group (MMG)
    45, 66, 71–74
mine safety 111–112
mining companies 31–32, 70–74
mining industry: challenges 109–116;
    changing government administration
    on mine safety 111–112; companies
    31–32, 70–74; efforts trimming
    production capacity 105–106;
    general background 109–111;
    government policy in CSR and
    responsible mining 65–66; health of
    workers 112–113; human resources
    challenges 112–115; institutional
    support for injured workers
    115–116; negative environmental
    impact 112; policy initiatives 118;
    underpinning theoretical framework
    106–109, 116–118; *see also*
    extractive sector
Mining, Minerals and Sustainable
    Development (MMSD) project 64
Ministry of Commerce (MOFCOM)
    38–39
Ministry of Environmental Protection
    (MEP) 38
Ministry of Water Resources (MWR)
    168, 170–171

national champions: governance of
    4–11; overseas expansion of 4,
    11–12, 28–32; promotion of 3–4
National People's Congress (NPC) 130
national security concerns 11–12
National Social Security Fund
    (NSSF) 11
Nestlé (China) Co Ltd 169
Nexen Inc. 12
non-governmental organizations
    (NGOs) 60–61, 74, 117

'One Belt, One Road' (OBOR) policy
    28, 30
online food trading: advantages
    125; business model of 126–128;
    categorisation 127–128; challenges
    for regulation 128–129; emerging
    practice of 123–125; evolution of
    regulation 131–133; food governance
    130–131, 137–139; in international
    arena 135–137; modes of 125–126;
    public/private co-regulation
    137–139; regulating under new
    legal order 130–133; rising business
    innovation and conflicts with
    traditional rules 136–137
'open door' policy 2
outbound foreign direct investment
    (OFDI) 11–12, 27
'outsider-based' model 10

People's Bank of China 38
Peru 72–73
PetroChina Company Limited 66, 70
pollution 14, 112, 170, 180–183
positive deviance 108–109, 117–118
Principles for Responsible Investment
    (PRI) 60–61
public/private co-regulation 137–139
public-private partnerships (PPPs) 167,
    170, 173–180, 284

real option model 84
resource governance 13–14
resource security 11–12
Rinehart, Gina 12
Rio Tinto plc 12

Sanlu Dairy 145–154
Sanyuan Foods Co., Ltd 146, 150
Sepon Mine 73
SF Express (Group) Co Ltd 135, 136

Shanghai CRED 12
Shanghai Free Trade Zone 139
Shanghai Information Investment
    Limited 139
Shanghai Pengxin 12
Shanghai Pudong Veolia Tap Water
    Company 177
Shanghai Stock Exchange 2, 146
shareholders 60
Shenzhen Stock Exchange 2
Sino Iron Pty Ltd 31–32
Sinopec (China Petroleum & Chemical
    Corporation) 2, 42, 44
S. Kidman & Co. Ltd. 12
soft law 33–34, 36–37
split-share structure 3–4
Standard & Poor's Global Rating
    (S&P) 88
Standardisation Administration of PRC
    (SAC) 38
State Administration of Quality
    Supervision, Inspection and
    Quarantine (SAQSIQ) 145
State Food and Drug Administration
    (SFDA) 131
State Grid Corporation of China 2, 12
state-led stakeholder governance
    model 144
State-Owned Assets Supervision and
    Administration Commission (SASAC)
    4, 9–10, 15–22, 38–39, 65, 70–71
state-owned enterprises (SOEs):
    contract disputes 30–32; under
    direct control of SASAC 15–22;
    governance of 4–11; governance
    reform 3–4; growth of 2; milk
    scandal 146; natural resources
    sector implementing CSR codes
    abroad 41–49; overseas expansion
    of 4, 11–12, 13, 28–32; ownership
    structure and regulatory environment
    for 8–10; partial privatisation of
    2; reforms 6–9; resource security
    issues 11–12; role in natural
    monopoly industries 7; urban water
    infrastructure 173–174
Syngenta 4

Trans-Pacific Partnership Agreement 30

United Nation's Sustainable
    Development Goals (SDGs) 70, 72,
    87, 166–167, 183
Unocal 12
urban water supply 168

Veolia 177–178

water law: acquisition of equity-high
    premium 177–180; BOT model
    174–177; Captain of the River
    concept 180–181; experimentation
    with public-private partnerships
    in urban sector 171–180;
    financing approaches to water
    governance 173–180; green courts
    181–182; implementation plan for
    comprehensive water law system
    173; innovative instruments for
    urban water quality/ pollution issues
    180–183; legislative and policy
    making initiatives 172–173; other
    enforcement mechanism for 182–183
water pollution 14, 112, 167, 171, 178,
    181, 183
water quality 180–183
Water Resource Bureaus (WRBs) 170
water security: agricultural water use
    168–170; concept of 165–168; issues
    168–170; mining water use 112;
    urban water supply 168
WeChat 128
World Bank 88, 174
World Business Council for Sustainable
    Development (WBCSD) 64
World Trade Organization (WTO)
    134–135, 137, 139
Worldwide Governance Indicators
    (WGI) 88

Xi'an City Tap Water Company 178

Yancoal Australia Ltd 31
Yanzhou Coal Mining Company
    Limited 31
Yihaodian (YHD) 136
Yili Dairy 145–154

ZTE Corporation 12

For Product Safety Concerns and Information please contact our EU
representative  GPSR@taylorandfrancis.com
Taylor & Francis Verlag GmbH, Kaufingerstraße 24, 80331 München, Germany